D0445718

Matthew

Charles Price

Focus on the Bible
Commentary Series

CHRISTIAN FOCUS

Charles Price has been the Senior Pastor of The Peoples Church, Toronto Canada, since September 2001. For twenty five years prior to this he was on the staff of the Capernwray Missionary Fellowship of Torchbearers in England, latterly as Principal of Capernwray Bible School. During that period he was also involved in an extensive Conference and Evangelistic ministry in many parts of the world, including Western and Eastern Europe, Africa, India, the Far East, the Middle East, the Caribbean, on numerous occasions in Australia and New Zealand and from Coast to Coast in the USA and Canada. He is the author of six books on discipleship and biblical exposition, and a contributor to several more. Some of his books have been translated into Spanish, Italian, German, French and Hindi.

Charles is married to Hilary and they have three children, Hannah, Laura and Matthew.

All scripture quotations, unless otherwise indicated, are taken from the HOLY BIBLE, NEW INTERNATIONAL VERSION®. NIV®. Copyright ©1973, 1978, 1984 by International Bible Society. Used by permission of Zondervan. All rights reserved.

© Charles Price
ISBN 1-85792-285-9

10 9 8 7 6 5 4 3 2 1

First published in 1998
Reprinted in 2005
by
Christian Focus Publications,
Geanies House, Fearn, Tain,
Ross-shire, IV20 1 TW, Great Britain.

www.christianfocus.com

Cover design by Alister MacInnes
Printed and Bound by
Bercker, Germany

All rights reserved. No part of this publication may be reproduced, stored in a retrieval system, or transmitted, in any form, by any means, electronic, mechanical, photocopying, recording or otherwise without the prior permission of the publisher or a license permitting restricted copying. In the U.K. such licenses are issued by the Copyright Licensing Agency, 90 Tottenham Court Road, London W1P 9HE.

Contents

Preface

This book is a commentary on the gospel of Matthew – but please don't let that put you off! It is designed to be picked up and read, as was Matthew's gospel. I trust the preacher, teacher, expositor and student will find it helpful and gain some insights, understanding and perhaps seed thoughts they can take and develop themselves. However my first thought is of the average Christian who wants to get a clearer view of Jesus, his teaching and the relevance of Matthew's gospel to life today.

Over several years successive generations of students at Capernwray Bible School, England, Bodenseehof Bible School, Germany and Holbsy Brunn Bible School, Sweden have listened to my attempts to explain the Gospel of Matthew. I have been immeasurably enriched by that exercise and by the feedback and conversations it has provoked. My records tell me I have given occasional series of lectures on this book, or sections of it, to additional groups of students over the years in the Torchbearer Bible Schools of the Capernwray Missionary Fellowship in Switzerland, Austria, Canada, USA, Australia and India. To all these students, now numbering several thousands, I dedicate this book.

1.

Matthew in context

Matthew's gospel is not a biography in any meaningful sense, for along with the other three gospels, Mark, Luke and John, it contains only the briefest of details of Jesus' life. It is hardly justifiable to describe any of the four gospels as books at all, they are more like tracts or pamphlets. If we put all the information together, there is a total of less than thirty days of Jesus' life accounted for in the entire New Testament record. There is only the scantiest of information about his birth in the records of Matthew and Luke (nothing in Mark or John), only one mention of an event in his boyhood, recorded in Luke, and by the third page of Matthew he is already 30 years of age. We know no details of his childhood beyond his actual birth, or of his boyhood years, apart from the visit to Jerusalem with his parents at the age of twelve. We know nothing of his teenage years, of any schooling he may or may not have had, at what age he began to work in the carpenter's shop in Nazareth, or of any details of his adult years until the age of thirty. We know nothing of his contemporaries or friends during that time, or whether any friendships survive into the three years of his ministry. Matthew's introduction of him as an adult is very matter-of-fact, 'Then Jesus came from Galilee to the Jordan to be baptised by John' (3:13). The jump from his last mention of Jesus is enormous, 'He went and lived in a town called Nazareth' (2:23) which was after his return from Egypt where, as a refugee, he had been taken by his mother and Joseph to avoid the wrath of Herod in his mass destruction of all the baby boys in Bethlehem.

The public ministry of Jesus is generally agreed to have lasted for approximately three years (Matthew does not tell us his age at any point, but Luke 3:23 states, 'Now Jesus himself was about thirty years old when he began his ministry', and John indicates his ministry covered three annual Passovers eg John 2:13; 6:4; 12:1). As the accumulated record of Jesus during this time amounts only to around one month's worth, we are left with approximately another thirty five months of activity about which we know nothing. We do know that very much took place during that time, for John writes at the end of his account, 'Jesus did many other things as well. If every one of them were written down, I suppose that even the whole world would not have room for the books that would be written' (John 21:25). On the one hand it would have been wonderful to know much more of the life of Jesus than we do, but on the other hand, we may be grateful the Scripture has been maintained in a manageable size! Had the Holy Spirit chosen to reveal for our benefit the whole story that John says he could have written down, we might have been so overwhelmed with the material available, the scriptures might have sat unopened on our bookshelves as most encyclopaedias do! We can be grateful for the brevity of the gospels!

Matthew, Mark and Luke are known as the synoptic gospels, presenting their story in a uniform pattern. If we lay them out in parallel columns we will find a very similar arrangement of material. The ministry of Jesus in the synoptics is almost exclusively in the region of Galilee, with Jesus coming to Jerusalem only in the week immediately prior to his crucifixion, where he made a dramatic entry, riding on a donkey, with a large crowd accompanying him who spread their cloaks on the road, cut palm branches to spread before him, and shouted, 'Hosanna to the Son of David'. In Matthew's record this is the first visit of Jesus to Jerusalem, but John gives other accounts letting us know there were at least three visits prior to that (see John 2:13ff; 5:1ff; followed by a period of deliberate absenteeism from Jerusalem because the Jews were wanting to take his life (see 7:1); then he visits again in 7:14 staying in Judea until the end of Chapter 11, returning in 12:12ff on the occasion recorded by all three synoptics, with the people laying palm branches in front of him and shouting 'Hosanna').

There is no conflict in this regard between the synoptic gospels and John's account, for the inclusion of material in one account does not mean it was unknown to the other writers. Matthew, Mark and Luke very likely depended on common sources for much of their material, but each writer has selected his material so as to present a particular portrait of Christ. It is important to see and to understand the individual portrait of each writer, and then in unifying the four pictures to see the full portrait of the Lord Jesus Christ intended by the Holy Spirit in his inspiration of each text.

Four Portraits
1. Matthew: Christ the King
Matthew's portrait is of Christ as King. The opening statement of his gospel, 'A record of the genealogy of Jesus Christ, the son of David...' (1:1), immediately identifies him with the royal throne of David. We shall consider the implications of this later, but his kingship as presented by Matthew is neither nationalistic or materialistic, though its roots are in Israel's royal line of David. One of the outstanding features of Matthew's gospel is the reoccurrence of the word 'kingdom' throughout the text. Thirty two times Jesus speaks of the 'Kingdom of heaven' (no other New Testament writer uses that term), four times of the 'Kingdom of God' and altogether, there are fifty four references to the word 'kingdom', together with fourteen statements or allusions identifying Christ as 'king'. The other gospel writers also record teaching of Jesus about the 'kingdom', particularly in the synoptics (Mark: nineteen occasions; Luke: forty three times, with John recording the word on only three occasions) and although the concept of the kingdom is not therefore exclusive to Matthew, it is much more the central theme of his record. Jesus Christ is king, and his business is to set up a kingdom and to exercise authority as king in that kingdom. This is Matthew's message, and the portrait he presents.

2. Mark: Christ the Servant
Mark's portrait is of Christ as servant. There is no genealogy recorded in Mark, for the ancestry of a servant is of little interest and of no consequence. If someone stood up to claim himself a king, we would want to know who his parents were. The claim to kingship is based on ancestry. If someone presents himself as a servant, the question becomes irrelevant. To be king is to be acknowledged for who you are. To be a servant is to be acknowledged for what you do. Mark's gospel records Jesus in motion, with plenty of movement and activity, but with little teaching. The theme of Mark's gospel is found in Mark 10:45 'For even the Son of Man did not come to be served, but to serve and to give his life as a ransom for many'.

3. Luke: Christ the Son of Man

Luke's portrait is of Christ as the Son of Man. The stress is on the broader humanity of Jesus, and whilst Luke records Jesus' genealogy he does not only trace it back to Abraham, the father of the Jews, (which is as far as Matthew goes), but to Adam, the father of the Human Race. Luke is the only Gentile writer of the New Testament, and he presents Jesus as more than the son of Abraham, the fulfilment of God's covenant with the Jews, but as a son of the Human Race.

4. John: Christ the Son of God

John's portrait is of Christ as the Son of God. He paints on the biggest canvas of all. There is no human genealogy in this gospel, for John's record of Christ begins outside of time and outside of space: 'In the beginning was the Word, and the Word was with God and the Word was God. He was in the beginning with God. Through him all things were made; without him nothing was made that has been made' (John 1:1-3). This is the divine incarnation, God made flesh, and living among us!

Each portrait is unique, but none is contradictory of any other. They complement, endorse, and add to one another to give us the fuller picture of the Christ we are intended to know. These four aspects are anticipated in Ezekiel's vision of four living creatures, of which he says 'Each of the four had the face of a man, and on the right side each had the face of a lion, and on the left the face of an ox, each also had the face of an eagle' (Ezek. 1:10). The face of a man may represent Luke's portrait of Christ as the son of man, the face of a lion, Matthew's portrait of Christ as king, the face of an ox, Mark's portrait of Christ as servant, and the face of an eagle, John's portrait of Christ as the Son of God. In the book of Revelation a similar vision is seen by John, this time in the order of the lion [Matthew], the ox [Mark], the man [Luke] and the eagle [John] (see Rev. 4:7)[1].

Purpose in writing

Matthew wrote his gospel for Jewish readers. The testimony of the early church fathers who commented on this gospel is unanimous about this. Irenaeus (Bishop of Lyons in the middle of the second century) wrote, 'The gospel of Matthew was written for the Jews';

---

[1] For a fuller discussion of the relationship of the four gospels see *Why Four Gospels* by Donald Bridge, Mentor, 1996.

Origen a little later wrote, 'St. Matthew wrote for the Hebrew', and Eusebius of Caesarea, the great historian of the third century to whom we owe so much of our knowledge of the early church, wrote, 'Matthew ... delivered his gospel to his own countrymen'. The content of the book confirms this view, for it is steeped in detail of concern to the Jewish people. One of the chief features of this gospel is the demonstration and confirmation that all which was expected of the Messiah was fulfilled in Jesus Christ. The Jewish people had long expected the Messiah to come, but their image of him had evolved through the years to that of a great military ruler who would throw off the shackles of Roman domination, assert their independence and dignity and make them a nation of great significance in the world.

There was good reason for this crystallisation of Messianic expectation. For over seven hundred years Israel had been the subjects of super power imperialism. They had been nothing more than a pawn on the board of international power politics, ruled, subdued, used and abused against their will to further the interests of a foreign tyrant. In the year 722 BC, Assyria had destroyed the Northern kingdom of Israel, (Israel had divided into two separate entities after the death of Solomon – Israel in the North with Samaria as its Capital, and Judah in the south with Jerusalem as its Capital), leaving Judah intact to serve as a convenient buffer state between its territory and that of its arch rival and antagonist, Egypt. During that time, Judah could hardly breathe nor move without the consent of the super power states. At the Battle of Carchemish in 605 BC, Assyria's back was broken by Egypt and a new super power, Babylon, stepped into the vacuum. In 587 BC, under Nebuchadnezzar, the architect of Babylonian supremacy, Judah was invaded and conquered, most of the inhabitants being taken into exile, and ruled with a rod of iron. In 539 BC, Persia overran Babylon and a new world order was introduced under Cyrus the Great. He was much more lenient towards his conquered peoples and allowed several mass migrations of Jews back to Judah, including Ezra and Nehemiah, well known to us for their part in Old Testament history.

After the Old Testament era closed, Greece, under young Alexander the Great, conquered the Middle Eastern world and brought some unity to the fragmentation by imposing a common language, Greek, as the language of international commerce and diplomacy. The Grecian empire lasted for over two and a half centuries until in 64 BC Rome became the super power of the Middle Eastern world, and brought

Israel under its domination. Various movements took place in Israel during this period to try to assert their national rights, freedoms, dignity and independence. Throughout this time, expectancy of a coming Messiah grew and hardened into the figure of a military leader who would once and for all throw off the shackles of imperialism and free them to fulfil God's promise to Abraham, as a nation set apart for particular blessing by God, and through whom he would bless the world. Such was their strong expectation. But the Messiah who came was not the Messiah they were anticipating nor one they could recognise. As John records in his gospel, 'He came to that which was his own, but his own did not receive him' (John 1:11). Jesus Christ did not fit the bill!

Matthew writes to his fellow Jews therefore, to show, amongst other things, that all that the Old Testament Scriptures anticipated of the Messiah was actually fulfilled in Christ. In the opening three and a half chapters, he writes seven times to the effect, 'All this took place to fulfil what was said through the prophet...' (see 1:22; 2:5; 2:15; 2:17; 2:23; 3:3; 4:14). Similar statements recur through the book, in which specific events in the life of Jesus are related to detailed prophetic utterances contained in the existing Scriptures of the Old Testament, explaining these took place, 'to fulfil what was said through the prophet...' (see 8:17; 12:17; 13:35; 21:4; 26:56 and 27:9). In addition to these statements, there are more than fifty direct quotations from the Old Testament in Matthew's gospel, and many more indirect.

Someone has counted three hundred and thirty three prophecies in the Old Testament about the person, coming and ministry of the Messiah. These prophesies were in circulation long before the birth of Christ, and concern specific details about the place and nature of his birth, his home, his work and precise details of his death by crucifixion. It has been calculated that the chances of these prophecies being fulfilled in one person are one in eighty three billion. The very remarkable thing is, that these prophecies are fulfilled in detail in the person of Jesus Christ. This is itself, a very powerful piece of evidence for the identity of Christ and the reality of Christian truth. We are grateful for all the detail of our New Testament, but the fact is, we have a better reason for believing Jesus Christ was born, lived, died and rose again than the New Testament says that he did. The better reason for believing, is that the Old Testament said that he *would*, long before the New Testament says that he *did*. If I pick up today's newspaper and read yesterday's news I am not particularly impressed by that, for I expect it to be the case. However, if I pick up today's newspaper and read next week's news, and next week events happen exactly as recorded in the paper a week before, I would probably want to meet the editor! The Old Testament contains 'next week's news' written hundreds of years in advance! It makes you want to meet the editor!

Not only does Matthew draw heavily on the Old Testament expectations of the Messiah, but he draws together some statements that might, in advance of the event, appear to be in conflict with each other. In the second chapter of his record, Matthew states three prophecies about the origin of the Messiah. He will come from Bethlehem (2:5, quoting Micah 5:2); he will come out of Egypt (2:15 quoting Hosea 11:1); and he will be called a Nazarene (2:23 an obscure quotation that is probably a play on the Hebrew quoting Isaiah 11:1 where the Hebrew word for Branch, 'nezer', becomes the basis of a play on words for Nazareth, a town not in existence in Isaiah's day). Whatever exegetical issues are raised by these quotations in this context, the understanding of Matthew was clearly that these three places, Bethlehem, Egypt and Nazareth were all anticipated as playing a key role in the origins of the Messiah. He now writes to say they did, but from a human perspective it was by sheer chance in each case. Mary did not live in Bethlehem where she gave birth to Jesus, but in Nazareth, some seventy or eighty miles to the North. It just so happened that the time she was due to give birth to her son, Caesar Augustus issued a decree that a census should be taken of the entire Roman world. Everyone had to go to his home town to register. It just so happened that Joseph, the husband of Mary, came from Bethlehem, and the very time of the census coincided with the expected birth of the baby. When they arrived, all available accommodation had been taken since many others were in Bethlehem for the same reasons, and Mary and Joseph were accommodated in the stable beneath the inn. It just happened that on that night, of all nights, Mary's baby was born. Had he been born a day or two earlier he would have been born somewhere in Samaria en route from Nazareth to Bethlehem. Had he been born a week or two later, almost certainly Joseph and Mary would have by that time returned home to Nazareth. But he was born in Bethlehem! More than seven hundred years before, the prophet Micah had written, 'But you Bethlehem, in the land of Judah, are by no means least among the rulers of Judah; for out of you will come a ruler who will be the shepherd of my people Israel' (Micah 5:2). Seven hundred years later, by what would appear to be a sheer fluke of circumstances, he was born in the right place.

The baby was then taken to Egypt, to escape the wrath of Herod who ordered the destruction of all baby boys in Bethlehem in an attempt to destroy the baby Christ. When Herod himself died, the child returned with his parents to Nazareth, at which Matthew cites the prophet Hosea, writing eight hundred years before, 'Out of Egypt I called my son.' (If you read that statement in the context in which Hosea wrote it, you will understand it as referring to Israel coming out of Egypt at the time of Moses. However, an important hermeneutic feature is identified by Matthew applying this statement to Christ, and that is that whenever God speaks of his *son*, in addition to any immediate context, it is at the same time a foreshadowing in some way of his 'one and only Son', the Lord Jesus Christ. We shall see the same principle in the next chapter, where we discuss Christ as the 'Son of David, the Son of Abraham'). For Jesus to have been born in Bethlehem, exactly as Micah had stated, to have been taken at some stage from Egypt, as Hosea's writing anticipated, is remarkable enough, but when the statement understood by Matthew, 'He will be called a Nazarene' proves equally to be true, Matthew can open his gospel with a powerful evidence for the identity and authenticity of the Christ. We will never appreciate the Old Testament fully until we know its prime value is in pointing to Christ, not only as the fulfilment of its prophecies, but more importantly, as the goal of its history. Viewed retrospectively from the standpoint of the New Testament, so much of the Old Testament is about Christ, and Matthew draws heavily on this fact.

The content of Matthew
Matthew is primarily a teaching gospel, with around sixty percent of its content being the spoken words of Jesus. Most of this is placed in five great teaching sections, which mark and punctuate the natural divisions of the book. They are as follows:

Chap. 5-7   The People of the Kingdom
(The Sermon on the Mount)

Chap. 10   The Programme of the Kingdom
(Sending out the twelve to preach, teach and heal)

Chap. 13   The Parables of the Kingdom
(Eight parables that each depict the kingdom of heaven)

Chap. 18-19   The Principles of the Kingdom
(Built around four questions: 'Who is the greatest in the kingdom?';
'How many times should I forgive my brother?'; 'Is it lawful for a
man to divorce his wife for any and every reason?'; and 'What good
thing must I do to inherit eternal life?')

Chap. 24-25   The Perfecting of the Kingdom
(Signs and parables relating to the return of Christ)

Matthew recognises a particular and unique role that Israel and
her people play in the unfolding of God's purpose. For example, Jesus
is called 'the son of David' ten times, reminding his readers of the
significance of Israel's royal house, and his mission is stated as being to
the 'lost sheep of Israel' (15:24). However, alongside this exclusiveness
is an unmistakable inclusiveness, where the appeal and effect of Jesus
Christ is unrestricted in its scope, reaching to all people. At his birth,
the Gentile wise men from the East are the first to 'worship him' (2:11).
The gospel concludes with the great commission to 'make disciples of
all nations' (28:19), and the development of teaching whilst initially
addressed to the Jews has much wider implications.

Matthew is the only gospel writer to record Jesus speaking of the
church. Twice the word 'church' comes from his lips, in 16.18 (speaking
of the universal church to which all true believers belong) and in
18.17 (speaking of the local church congregation). This inclusion is
important, and we will discuss the significance of both later on.

Authorship
Regarding the authorship of Matthew, the text itself is anonymous,
with no internal clues as to its writer, but it has been attributed to
Matthew from very early days. There is no evidence it ever circulated
without its current title, and although the title is not part of the
inspired text, there is no good reason to challenge the assumption held
since the very earliest days that Matthew, one of the twelve apostles,
was the compiler of this gospel.

All we know of Matthew is that he was a tax collector who worked
for the Romans. As such he would be a reject of Jewish society, and

branded a traitor to Israel's national interests. Whilst sitting at his tax collector's booth in Capernaum, Jesus passed by and called to him, 'Follow Me'. These are the only two words recorded as being exchanged between Jesus and Matthew. He invited Jesus to his home to eat, and they were joined by many other tax collectors and outcasts, which provoked the response of the Pharisees, 'Why does he eat with such people?' Jesus reply was, 'I have not come to call the righteous, but sinners' (Matt. 9:9-13). Matthew was the first to arrange an evangelistic meal in his home!

Mark and Luke call him 'Levi', which was probably his natural name, given by his parents. The name 'Matthew' means 'Gift of God'. It may well have been a name given to him by Jesus (as he had given Simon the name Peter). If so, I find it a very wonderful feature. As Levi the tax collector, he had sunk to the bottom of the pile as far as his fellow Israelites were concerned, he was robbed of dignity and any meaningful self esteem, he was identified with the mob of thieves and extortioners, he was despised on the street. But when he met the Lord Jesus Christ, he had his name changed to match his changed life. From now on he was a 'Gift of God'. To what greater dignity could anyone aspire?

2.

The son of Abraham and David
(1:1-17)

The first seventeen verses of Matthew's Gospel list the generations of over two thousand years from Abraham to Christ. It may be impressive that sufficient records were on hand to make this possible, but, as the opening statement of the book, it looks extremely dull! The temptation to the contemporary reader is to skip the section and begin at verse 18, 'This is how the birth of Jesus Christ came about ...' which appears much more interesting! But that would be a mistake. In these first seventeen verses, forty six names are mentioned in succession, in addition to Christ, tracing his genealogy backwards from Joseph, the husband of Mary, to Abraham and summarised in three neat groupings of fourteen generations each. Fourteen from Abraham to David, fourteen from David to the exile, and fourteen from the exile to Christ. By any measurement, the ability to trace ancestry back so far with so much detail is a remarkable achievement. Apart from royalty, few could do it today. The Old Testament from its earliest period is particular about such records. The line from Adam to Noah is given in Genesis 5, the line from Noah to Abraham in Genesis 11. The first nine chapters of 1 Chronicles devote themselves to tracing Noah's descendants through the many centuries to the time of the Babylonian exile, including each of the eighteen generations from David onwards who occupied his throne in Jerusalem until that time. So important was the keeping of family records that on return from the Babylonian exile many of the Levitical priests who had lost their family records were denied a claim to the priesthood (see Ezra 2:62). Such was the importance of family pedigree.

Why does Matthew commence his record in such a tedious way? In the light of the claims to be made in this gospel, the question of first importance concerns not, 'What did Jesus do?', but 'Who is he?'. To the first Jewish readers, if Jesus is himself insignificant, then what he says is unimportant. If he himself is significant, then what he says is important. He was dismissed by his contemporaries in Nazareth as they observed, 'Isn't this the carpenter's son? Isn't his mother's name Mary, and aren't his brothers James, Joseph, Simon and Judas? Aren't all his sisters with us? Where then did this man get this wisdom? And they took offence at him' (Matt. 13:55-57). They said in effect, We know who this man is and who he is, is insignificant – he is just the local carpenter – therefore what he says is unimportant. Don't take him seriously!

Matthew's opening statement is saying to the Jews who form his first readership, 'I want to show you first who Jesus Christ is. What he says is to be taken seriously because of who he is'. So who is he? The opening statement of the book states, 'A record of the genealogy of Jesus Christ the son of David, the son of Abraham'. Two of the key men in Israel's past are introduced in that verse: Abraham the father of the race, and David the father of the royal family. To both of these men was promised a son, who would be the means of some significant development, – but despite the promises God made, the story played out in both sons came to failure. Now says Matthew, this Jesus about whom I am to tell you, comes as **the son** of both these men.

JESUS CHRIST – the Son of Abraham
When God called Abraham from Ur of the Chaldeans, he took him to the land of the Canaanites that was to become known as 'Israel'. On getting to the great tree of Moreh at Shechem, God revealed his plan, 'To your offspring I will give this land' (Gen. 12:7). Later he promised to this childless man, 'a son coming from your own body will be your heir' (Gen. 15:4). Literally, Genesis 12:7 says, 'to your seed I will give this land', and we shall see shortly that Paul makes significant issue of the singular 'seed' in his letter to the Galatians. To understand the importance of this in relation to Jesus Christ, as inferred by Matthew, we must know a little of Israel's history.

Abraham was seventy five years of age at the time God revealed all this to him, his wife Sarah was sixty five, and she is described as 'barren' – they had no children. Nevertheless, 'Abram believed God and it was credited to him as righteousness' (Gen. 15:6). Twenty five years later their son Isaac was born. God's purpose was, of course,

greater than the expansion of Abraham's family, for he had revealed
back in Ur of the Chaldeans, 'I will make you into a great nation
and I will bless you; I will make your name great, and you will be a
blessing. I will bless those who bless you, and whoever curses you
I will curse; and all peoples on earth will be blessed through you'
(Gen. 12:2-3). Isaac makes little real contribution to the story other
than as the son of Abraham he fathered twin sons, Esau and Jacob
at the age of sixty. These two were in stark contrast to each other.
Esau, the older of the two, was 'hairy' and independent, enjoying the
outdoor life. Jacob was 'smooth' and crafty. He obtained for a bowl
of stew the birthright that belonged to his brother as Isaac's first
born son, then through a high risk act of deceit, received from his
father the blessing that accompanied and validated the birthright.
The line would now go through Jacob rather than Esau. Jacob
married and fathered twelve sons, who in turn became the fathers of
the twelve tribes by which Israel as a nation would be constituted.
Various twists and turns in the tale bring the book of Genesis to its
close with the family of Jacob having left Canaan and gone to live in
Egypt. In the four centuries between the closing of Genesis and the
opening of Exodus, the Israelites have descended from being honoured
guests in Egypt, the relatives of Joseph who had saved them from the
consequences of drought, to being slaves, used and abused at the will
of their masters.

Something appears to have gone wrong! This is not being a 'great
nation' whom those who bless are blessed and those who curse are
cursed! They are being trampled under foot and cursed with impunity!
The rest of their history follows an equally despondent path. There are
the great times, like the dramatic release from Egypt and the conquest
and reoccupation of Canaan, but for all of these good times there is
even more failure and disappointment, with very few nations around
experiencing either blessing or cursing because of their relationship
to Israel. The promise seems to have come to little or nothing! As
indicated in the previous chapter, for more than seven hundred years
until the time of Christ, Israel has been dominated and abused by
the super power of the day. It is little wonder the expectation of the
Messiah had evolved into that of a military leader who would once
and for all overthrow the tyrant of the day and give Israel her true
role in the world.

The nation of Israel were the right people, but were completely devoid of power to fulfil their destiny. This was the legacy of Abraham and the promises made to him by God so long before. 'Now', says Matthew in effect, 'against this background of the failure of Abraham's descendants to fulfil their destiny, I want to introduce you to Jesus Christ ... the son of Abraham'. Whenever God in Scripture speaks of his giving of a son, whether in the first place it applies to Israel, to Isaac or to Solomon, it ultimately speaks of Christ. The son of Abraham through whom all the promises would find their fulfilment is not Isaac, but Christ. This is part of Paul's argument in his letter to the Galatians, 'The promises were spoken to Abraham and to his seed. The Scripture does not say "and to seeds," meaning many people, but "and to your seed," meaning one person who is Christ' (Gal. 3:16). The seed of Abraham is not the nation of Israel, but Christ. Everything God promised to Abraham and which Israel has failed to experience, is going to find its fulfilment in Christ. But there is more:

JESUS CHRIST – the Son of David

Abraham was the father of the race, and David the father of royalty. David too had been promised a son (2 Sam. 7:12-13) and there were two aspects to his vocation, 'He is the one who will build a house for my Name, and I will establish the throne of his kingdom forever'. He would build the temple, and his throne would never cease. The son who followed David to his throne was Solomon, and he did build the temple in Jerusalem whereby all the rituals and regulations God had given Moses in the Sinai desert as a means of removing sin and approaching him could find their legitimate function. Solomon's temple was magnificent, but despite the fulfilment of the rituals, the whole operation became increasingly detached from the realities they were intended to depict. By the time of the written prophets of the Old Testament, the temple rituals are scorned, as corrupt and displeasing to God, and at the time of the Babylonian invasion of Jerusalem in 586 BC it was destroyed. All that God had promised seemed to have come to nothing again.

The other aspect of the promise to David's son was that his throne would be forever. For eighteen generations to the time of the Babylonian exile, a son of David sat on the throne in Jerusalem, but never again. All that God promised seem to come to nothing, yet again. When Jacob had blessed his sons in Egypt just before he died, he said to Judah, 'The sceptre will not depart from Judah, nor the ruler's staff from between his feet, until he comes to whom it belongs and the obedience of the nations is his' (Gen. 49:10). Jacob foresaw Jesus Christ, who would rule and to whom the nations would bow. This would be the fulfilment of the promise to David. The writer to the Hebrews, quotes the statement God made to David about his son, 'He is the one who will build a house for my name, and I will establish the throne of his kingdom forever. I will be his father and he will be my son' (2 Sam. 7:13-14), and says in effect, This is God speaking about Christ, 'For to which of the angels did God ever say ... I will be his father and he will be my Son' (Heb. 1:5).

The promise to Abraham of a son through whom all the nations of the world would be blessed, would never find its fulfilment until the 'seed' of Abraham came – Christ. The promise to David of a son who would restore communion with God, and whose kingdom would never end, would never find its fulfilment until the true son of David is born – Christ. Isaac and Solomon were sons of Abraham and David, but they never fulfilled the destiny promised to the sons of both men. They were only foreshadowing Christ.

This surely is the significance of Matthew's introduction. All the high expectations of a people descended from Abraham whose destiny was to bless the world, all the confidence of a people under the throne of David, whose king was to reign forever, now finds its expression and fulfilment in 'Jesus Christ the son of David, the son of Abraham'. To the Jewish reader with any discernment at all, this should excite them that all the potential of their history now narrows to one man, in whom it will truly find fulfilment. Don't confuse the promises made about Christ with the physical nation of Israel. It is in Christ that 'all the peoples of the earth will be blessed'. The physical nation of Israel provides the context in which he came, but Christ himself is the goal to which Israel's history was heading, and the pinnacle to which they must now look back.

It is interesting to note that at the conclusion of his gospel, Matthew records Jesus sending his disciples to, 'all nations', fulfilling the Abrahamic promise, and declares that 'All authority in heaven and on earth has been given to me', fulfilling the Davidic promise. His conclusion to the book, fulfils the expectancy of its introduction.

Five women in the genealogy
One of the interesting features of the genealogy of Chapter one is the place given to five women in the record. In normal circumstances

a woman would not be included in such a record. In Jewish law a woman had no legal rights and was the possession of, first her father, and then her husband. She had no rights to divorce him, though he could divorce her. An orthodox Jew daily thanked God that he was not a Gentile, a slave, or a woman!

If the inclusion of women at all is a surprise, when we examine who these women were, it is even more of a surprise. They are Tamar (1:3); Rahab (1:5); Ruth (1:5); Uriah's wife – whom we know to be Bathsheba (1:6); and Mary (1:16).

Tamar

Tamar's story is found in Genesis 38. She was married to Judah's eldest son, Er, who died leaving no children. As custom required, Tamar was married to Er's younger brother Onan, who also died leaving no children. Judah told Tamar she must live as a widow until his third son, Shelah, was of age to marry her. He intended however that Shelah should not marry Tamar. Perhaps he was suspicious of the cause of death in his first two sons. Tamar realised this in due course, and one day when Judah went to the Enaim, where Tamar lived, to shear his sheep, she dressed in disguise and offered herself as a prostitute to Judah for the price of a young goat which he would send from his flock. In the meantime she accepted his seal and its cord as a pledge, and when Judah returned home he sent the goat by his friend only to have him return to say there was no known prostitute at Enaim. Judah was no doubt embarrassed by the whole episode and decided to let her keep the seal and its cord. Some time later he heard his daughter-in-law was pregnant, as a result of prostitution. Judah was so angry he called for her to be burned to death. As she was being brought out she held up Judah's seal and cord and announced herself to be pregnant by the man who owned them. Judah's response was to declare her to be more righteous than he, because he wouldn't give his third son to her as a husband. In due course she gave birth to twin boys, Perez and Zerah. Perez is listed in the genealogy of Christ.

Most of us if announcing our family tree would rather hide this kind of detail. Matthew pulls it right out into the open. Why?

Rahab

Rahab also has a rather unsavoury history. She was a Canaanite and appears on the scene as a professional prostitute in the city of Jericho before its conquest by Israel. She hid the two spies sent by Joshua to report on the city, and in exchange for her protection of them, her life and that of her family was preserved, then she lowered a scarlet cord from the window of her house on the city wall, thus identifying herself as singled out for preservation by the invading Israelite army. After the conquest of Jericho, she was incorporated into Israel by marrying Salmon and became the mother of Boaz who features in the Old Testament story in his own right when he married Ruth. Why is this alien Canaanite prostitute specifically mentioned in the line of Christ?

Ruth
The story of Ruth is a well known love story, but her inclusion in the genealogy of Jesus is even more surprising when we consider her identity. She was not a Jewess but a Moabitess. God had cursed the Moabites for their hiring of Balaam to curse the Israelites whilst in the wilderness, and declared of them, 'No ... Moabite or any of his descendants may enter the assembly of the Lord, even down to the tenth generation' (Deut. 23:3). Ruth came well within the scope of that rejection, yet is included in the line of the Messiah. Why is this woman from a cursed tribe mentioned as in the line of Christ?

Bathsheba
Bathsheba is the fourth woman and is not mentioned by her own name, but rather described as the one who 'had been Uriah's wife'. King David had seduced her whilst her husband was fighting David's battles in David's army. He had made her pregnant, then arranged for the death in battle of her husband Uriah to cover his own infidelity, and leave the assumption the baby was Uriah's. When Uriah was dead he took Bathsheba as his own wife, and although the baby conceived through their adulterous association died at birth, she later conceived another son to David, and named him Solomon. Why mention her, and at the same time heighten David's sin by describing her pointedly as, 'Uriah's wife'?

Mary
The last women mentioned is Mary, the only obvious and inevitable woman to be named. It is Joseph's line that gives the legal line of descent to Jesus, and as Joseph's wife, and the mother of Jesus, she is named in the list.

Why are these specific women mentioned in this list. Matthew doesn't tell us, but I would like to suggest a possibility. In introducing us to the King, he is also giving us some indication of the kingdom he comes to establish. In Christ certain barriers are to be broken down. Firstly *social barriers* are broken in Christ. Gentiles (Rahab and Ruth) are united together with Jews. The sense of racial superiority that caused Jews to look at Gentiles as 'dogs', in whatever form that racism may appear, is to be broken and levelled in Christ.

Secondly, *sexist barriers* are broken in Christ. Sexism is that distinction made between male and female for the discrimination and exploitation of one by the other – usually the female by the male. Here male and female are on common ground.

Thirdly, *sin barriers* are broken in Christ. There is sin that makes people outcasts of society and there is sin that has been sanitised, tolerated and excused. Sin differs in its consequences of course, but in Christ the outcasts and the respectable are brought together in their common relationship to him. The pagan prostitute is in line with the respectable Jew. To the first readers of this gospel, this is revolutionary stuff! Paul affirms this levelling of the artificial barriers of human society when he affirms, 'There is neither Jew nor Greek, slave nor free, male nor female, for you are all one in Christ Jesus' (Gal. 3:28).

I suggest that in giving us this genealogy of Christ, Matthew is not only establishing the pedigree of the King, but he is giving insight into the nature of the Kingdom he comes to establish.

3.

The birth of Jesus
(1:18–2:23)

Matthew devotes thirty one verses in all to recording events surrounding the birth of Christ. He does not give any details of the miraculous conception, or of the visit of the angel Gabriel to Mary in which he announced that she would bear the child (see Luke 1:26-38 for that detail), but simply states the basic facts, 'Mary was pledged to be married to Joseph, but before they came together, she was found to be with child through the Holy Spirit'. The ensuing events need some explanation to Western thinking. Mary is stated to be 'pledged to be married to Joseph' (1:18) yet because of her pregnancy, Joseph 'had in mind to divorce her quietly' (1:19). We would ask why a divorce was necessary if their relationship at this stage was only in terms of a pledge to be married.

There were three stages to a Jewish marriage. First there was the *engagement*, made often when the couple concerned were very young, and usually without any meaningful consent on their part. Two sets of parents might agree with each other that their very young children should in due course marry each other. Occasionally a professional match-maker might be employed to establish the right contacts on behalf of the parents. The arrangement might be made without the couple concerned having ever met each other, much less having consented. Marriage was of a higher order in society than simply the cementing of human passion, and parents took this responsibility seriously.

Following this, there would one day come the *betrothal*. This was a confirmation of the engagement that involved the consent of both parties. This was a formal arrangement, with witnesses on both sides and an agreement about the bride's dowry. If for some reason, on meeting each other, one or both of the engaged couple decided they did not wish to go on with the arrangement, it could be broken prior to the betrothal. They would of course need some good reason for this, for in all likelihood most other eligible youngsters would have been accounted for by similar arrangements made on their behalf, so to break the engagement may potentially be to forfeit the opportunity of marriage at all. The betrothal, once entered, had the legal force of marriage and could only be broken by divorce. It was sealed by the bridegroom paying all or part of the dowry. The couple would be known as husband and wife, but would not live together and sexual relations would not be expected or permitted.

The third stage was of course the *marriage* proper. This would normally take place at the home of the bride's father and be followed by seven days of festivity and the moving of the bride to her husband's home.

It was during the second stage, the betrothal, that the conception of Jesus took place. Joseph and Mary were legally committed to each other, but were not yet living together as man and wife. Hence Joseph's understandable response was to assume Mary to have been unfaithful to him, so he planned to divorce her quietly. We have no record of the conversation that took place between Mary and Joseph about her pregnancy, though it is most likely she informed him, and no doubt tried to explain the circumstances. Like most other normal people, Joseph found the story incredulous, and it took the visit of an angel to assure him, 'what is conceived in her is from the Holy Spirit' (1:20).

The angel then appeared in a dream to Joseph and spoke about two aspects of the expected baby: his nature, 'from the Holy Spirit', and his name, 'you are to give him the name Jesus'.

His nature

The conception of this baby is declared to be 'from the Holy Spirit' and therefore without human father. The genealogy of Jesus concludes with a reference to, 'Joseph the husband of Mary, of whom was born Jesus who is called Christ' (1:16), thus detaching Joseph from any direct biological relationship to the baby.

The virgin birth generally carries little theological weight in our thinking, but is in fact crucial to everything else that is true of Christ. If the deity and work of Christ is being undermined by a theologian or church leader, they usually begin with an attack on the historicity of the virgin birth. We who believe otherwise often fail to respond adequately at this point, because we consider it to be not as essential as other details in the life of Christ. The reality is, to destroy the virgin birth of Christ, is to destroy his ability to accomplish what he came to do. It is argued that the gospels of Mark and John make no reference to the virgin birth and that Paul never alludes to it in his writings, and therefore it is not a serious issue. The exclusion of any fact from some of the New Testament writings does not in any way invalidate its positive inclusion in other writings, and what must be recognised are the unambiguous statements of Matthew and Luke, confirmed by Matthew in his quotation of Isaiah 7:14, 'The virgin will be with child and will give birth to a son' (1:23).

Why is the virgin birth of Christ essential to his function? To say, 'Jesus Christ was born to die,' is not just to state the obvious! The nature of the death he was born to die was not physical alone, but spiritual. The death he was born to die was the same death Adam experienced in the Garden of Eden, when he was forbidden to eat of the tree of the knowledge of good and evil on the grounds that, '... in the day you eat thereof, you shall die' (Gen. 2:17). Together with Eve, Adam ate of the tree, but did they die that day, as God had forewarned? The answer is that he did, for God does not threaten in vain. But the death he died was spiritual and not physical. Physically he lived for many more years, but the day he acted in independence of God he became, 'separated from the life of God' (Eph. 4:18), which is the nature of spiritual death. Physical death was not the immediate consequence of sin, though it is an inevitable result due to the decay and perishing process instigated by the entry of sin into the world, but the 'wages of sin' (Rom. 6:23) paid in the Garden of Eden is spiritual death. This sentence was not only imposed on Adam and Eve but became the state of all their descendants, for the Apostle Paul states, 'In Adam all die' (1 Cor. 15:22). This is the condition into which we are already born. The Scripture never declares that any person will die *for* their sin, for the reality is, it is too late – they are already dead. The 'wages of sin' were paid in the Garden of Eden, and every human being since then is born in the state of death (see Eph. 2:1). Paul's statement is in the present tense, 'The wages of sin *is* death'. It is already part of our experience. The option open to us is not to die *for* our sin, since we are already dead, but to die *in* our sin. We may continue in our state

27

of alienation from God and live beyond the grave with its eternal consequences. The issue the gospel presents to us involves the choice of either remaining for ever in the state of death into which we were born, or of coming alive, by receiving the life Adam forfeited in the Garden of Eden – the life of God.

There is only one prerequisite for death – and that is life. This is true spiritually as it is physically. To die one has first to be alive! If Jesus Christ was born to die the death Adam died in the Garden of Eden, then the one prerequisite to qualify him to die was life! Only two men have been qualified to die for sin – Adam and Christ – for only two men have themselves been fully alive – Adam and Christ. Hence Christ is described by Paul as the 'second man', when he writes, 'The first man was of the dust of the earth, the second man from heaven' (1 Cor. 15:47). Christ is 'the second man' in contrast to Adam, 'the first man'. Earlier Paul made the same contrast when stating, 'So it is written: "The first man Adam became a living being"; the last Adam, a life-giving spirit' (1 Cor. 15:45). As the 'second man' and the 'last Adam', Christ was not born as a result of procreation, but of creation – he was the second human being in the sense of being the second original. It is this that enabled him to accomplish as our substitute for our sin, what Adam did in his own right for his own sin – to die.[1] Take away the virgin birth and regard the conception of Christ as normal procreation, and we have robbed Christ of his ability to deal with our sin, for we have robbed him of the ability to die the death required as penalty for sin. Paul has in mind more than the *physical* death of Christ as atonement for sin, when he wrote, 'God made him who had no sin to *be sin* for us....' (2 Cor. 5:21). He was made to be sin! He would cry from the cross, 'My God, My God, why have you forsaken me' (Matt. 27:46), experiencing for our sin the separation Adam endured for his own sin the day he ate of the tree – and died.

---

[1] Some are very unhappy with the concept of Christ enduring spiritual death, but that in fact is the penalty for sin. By definition, spiritual death is alienation from the life of God, for it is the presence of the life of God in human experience that is the nature of spiritual life. It was as a man that Jesus Christ endured this, and his cry, 'My God, My God, why have you forsaken me?' is consistent with spiritual death – alienation from God. It was not just the willingness of Christ to die for our sin that made his sacrifice acceptable, but his ability to do so – an ability shared by no other.

His name

Two names are given Jesus prior to his birth, '... they will call him Immanuel...' (1:23), and '... you are to give him the name Jesus...' (1:21). The name Immanuel tells us who he is, 'God with us', and the name Jesus tells us what he will do, 'he will save his people from their sins'. We must never detach who he is from what he does. His ability to do what he does derives only from who he is. It is only as God incarnate in human form that he could accomplish the saving of his people. Drive a wedge of any kind between who he is and what he does and we destroy the validity of what he does.

The visit of the wise men (2:1-23)

The second chapter of this gospel is devoted to Matthew's account of the visit of the Magi and the subsequent fleeing of Joseph, Mary and Jesus to Egypt to ensure his safety. Matthew alone records this incident, and describes the quest of these men from the East as being to find the '... one born king of the Jews' (2:2).

Who are these men? There are a number of myths that have grown around this story. They were not kings, and there is no indication of how many of them there were (their gifts of gold, frankincense and myrrh has given rise to the idea of their being three), and they were not following a star that moved ahead of them like a UFO (as Christmas cards often portray). They reported 'We saw his star in the east' (2:2). This was a past tense statement, but had they been following the star it would have been in the west. These men are described as Magi, a Persian word difficult to translate accurately, but more popularly known in some translations of the Bible as 'wise men'. This is not to be confused with necessarily being men of great wisdom, but as those who almost certainly practised magical arts and astrology. There have been various attempts to identify the 'star of Bethlehem'. In the seventeenth century the suggestion was made by a triple conjunction of the planets Saturn, Jupiter and Mars which took place in 7 BC. In those days Jupiter was understood as a star of kings and Saturn was associated with the Jews. Another suggestion is that the wise men saw an exploding nova or supernova which would produce an unusual amount of light, increasing the light of a distant star up to millions and even billions of times, and continuing for several weeks. It has been suggested the star might be Halley's comet, visible in 12/11 BC[2]. William Barclay in his comments on this passage in The Daily Study Bible says this: 'In the years 5 to 2 BC there was an unusual astronomical phenomenon. In those years on the first day of the Egyptian month, Mesori, Sirius the dog star, rose at sunrise and shone with extraordinary brilliance. Now the name *Mesori* means *the birth of a prince*, and to those ancient astrologers such a star would undoubtedly mean the birth of a great king. We cannot tell what star the Magi saw; but it was their profession to watch the heavens, and their observation of some heavenly brilliance spoke to them of the entry of a king into the world.'[3] It is possible this was something entirely unique and miraculous which cannot be explained naturally (like the visit of the angels to the shepherds), but it is more likely there was a natural phenomena that had caused these men to ponder its meaning and set out to follow its message.

Foretelling the future from the stars was a common belief in those days, and any interruption of the normal orderly routine of the heavens was given particular interpretation. We cannot know for sure, but it is interesting, if not extraordinary, that reading the stars should bring these men to Christ. The Bible has little to say about astrology, but where it is mentioned it is always with scorn and with rebuke for any dependency placed on it. For instance, Isaiah writes, 'Let your astrologers come forward, those stargazers who make predictions month by month, let them save you from what is coming upon you. Surely they are like stubble; the fire will burn them up. They cannot even save themselves from the power of the flame' (Isa. 47:13-14). There may be knowledge obtainable through astrology – but it is forbidden knowledge, and is unrelated to divine revelation. It is very interesting therefore that these Magi should be brought to Christ.

There is an important principle stated by Jesus in Matthew 7:7-8 when he said, 'Ask and it will be given to you; seek and you will find; knock and the door shall be opened to you. For everyone who asks receives; he who seeks finds; and to him who knocks the door will be opened'. Jesus is affirming that the people who do not receive are the people who do not ask; the ones who do not find are the ones who do not seek; and those to whom the doors stay closed are those who never knock. But what happens if someone genuinely asking is asking for the wrong thing? God will give them the right thing.

---

[2] See *Jesus The Messiah* by Robert Stein pp. 55-56.
[3] The Daily Study Bible, The Gospel of Matthew Vol 1, by William Barclay, p.17. The Saint Andrew Press, Edinburgh, 1975.

What happens if the person genuinely seeking is seeking in the wrong direction? God will take them in the right direction. What happens if a person is genuinely knocking but knocking on the wrong door? God will open the right door. This is not to say sincerity is enough, but to say that no one can claim they genuinely want to find God but can't! Jesus affirmed '... everyone who asks receives'. Here, a search in the wrong direction and a knocking on the wrong door brought them in the right direction and opened the right door – and the Magi came to Christ!

In similar fashion, Saul of Tarsus knocked on the wrong door of his Pharisaic Judaism, but God who knew his heart, brought him in touch with Christ on the Damascus Road. The conversion of Saul of Tarsus in such dramatic circumstances on the Damascus Road may seem to us as unfair when others don't have an equal opportunity of a blinding vision of Christ and the hearing of his audible voice. But God knew Saul's heart, and as he later explained to the Philippians, it was out of sincere desire to please God that he persecuted the church, believing it to be contrary to the Jewish revelation of the Old Testament scriptures. Jesus had promised 'If you seek you will find'. Although Saul was seeking in the wrong direction, God took him in the right direction and he met the Living Christ unexpectedly on his way to Damascus.

Cornelius was a Roman centurion and a good man, but he did not know Christ. None of his goodness, his generous giving or his fervent prayers in themselves made him a Christian, but God knew the genuineness of his seeking heart and said to him, 'Your prayers and gifts to the poor have come up as a memorial offering before God' (Acts 10:4). He too met with Christ as Peter was directed to his door. It is the disposition of our heart to which God responds. Every one of us knows as much of God as we genuinely want to know!

The trail the Magi followed came to an end when they got to Jerusalem. They unwisely enquired of King Herod where the new king was to be born, and he consulted the Scribes whose reading of the Scriptures enabled them to give the answer that it was in Bethlehem the child was to be born. En route, a star did mysteriously appear and it led them to the place where the baby Jesus was (thus the UFO idea depicted on Christmas cards!).

We do not know the timing of this visit. Anything from a few days after the birth of Jesus up to two years has been suggested. It is unlikely to have been long after the birth, for Joseph and Mary were in Bethlehem to take part in the Roman census, and presumably would return home to Nazareth within a fairly short space of time.[4]

There are three responses to Christ in this passage which become the three main responses throughout the rest of Matthew's gospel. There was antagonism and rejection; shallow indifference and humble worship.

Antagonism and rejection: This was the response of Herod (2:8, 16). To have heard any story of a new 'king of the Jews' was a threat. This may be a baby, but babies grow up, and should the idea grow with him, Herod's throne was under threat. To eliminate such a threat he planned to visit the baby too and have him killed. When the Magi failed to return and tell him of his location, he ordered the slaughter of every baby in Bethlehem under the age of two years. Never is such intense antagonism aroused as when an unyielding person is faced with the kingship of Christ.

Shallow indifference: It is most remarkable that the priests and scribes in Jerusalem should be so casual and uncaring about the news of the birth of this king. When consulted, they could quote chapter and verse, and reply the Messiah was to be born, 'In Bethlehem in Judea' quoting the relevant passage from the book of Micah. But there is no evidence they made it their business to seek him out in Bethlehem for themselves! They knew the facts and could quote accurately the Scriptures, but they couldn't care less about the implications to them, nor the response demanded from them. It was sheer indifference.

Humble worship: The third response was that of the Magi themselves, and it was one of reverence and worship. I like the combination of thoughts where Matthew writes, '... they bowed down and worshipped him. Then they opened their treasures...' (2:11). To worship is to open our treasures to God! True worship is always extravagant.

These three responses to Jesus Christ remain the options to any person today. We may *reject* him, like Herod. We may *neglect* him, like the scribes and priests. We may *accept* him, like the wise men.

---

[4] For further discussion of the timing of the visit of the Wise Men, see *Jesus The Messiah* by Robert Stein p. 53.

The immediate consequence for Joseph, Mary and the baby Jesus was that an angel appeared in a dream to Joseph and warned him to take the child and his mother to Egypt to escape the wrath of Herod. They left during the night, and remained in Egypt until the death of Herod. Then the angel appeared to Joseph in a dream and told him it was safe to return to Israel, but not to Jerusalem where Herod's son Archelaus was reigning, but to Galilee in the north. Thus they returned to live in the town of Nazareth.

4.

John the Baptist
(3:1-17)

Between Chapters two and three of Matthew there is a missing thirty year period in the life of Jesus about which Matthew makes no comment at all.[1] Our only insight into this period comes from Luke's account of Jesus' visit to the temple in Jerusalem at the age of twelve, and the general comment that 'Jesus grew in wisdom and stature and in favour with God and men' (Luke 2:52), that is, he grew intellectually, physically, spiritually and socially. More than ninety percent of his life was spent in obscurity in Nazareth, fulfilling the duties of the eldest son, added to by the likely death of Joseph before the family had grown up. There he learned to be faithful in the little things, the prerequisite for being entrusted with greater things.[2] But as to details, we know no more.

The new era opens, 'In those days John the Baptist came preaching in the Desert of Judea'. There is no introduction to John the Baptist or any explanation of his relationship to Christ. To Matthew's initial Jewish readers no introduction was necessary. John was one of the most famous men of his day. In the biblical scheme of things, John's role was that of forerunner of the Messiah, and beyond that he has little significance. That however was not the contemporary view of John. Before Christ began his ministry, John was stirring up the crowds and demanding a radical response to his message of the coming kingdom of heaven. There is more historical record of John the Baptist outside of the biblical writings than there is of Christ.[3] Then who was John the Baptist?

---

[1] Luke 3:23 tells us 'Jesus himself was about thirty years old when he began his ministry'.

[2] See Hebrews 5.8. Jesus 'learned obedience...'.

1. The ministry of John the Baptist

It is Luke who fills out John's background, and from his record we know him to be the son of Elizabeth, a first cousin of Mary the mother of Jesus, and Zechariah, her husband. His conception was the result of divine promise at a time when, 'Elizabeth was barren; and they were both well along in years' (Luke 1:7). Elizabeth joined a succession of 'barren' women in Scripture who conceived children destined to become significant in the unfolding story of redemption. The pregnancies of Elizabeth and Mary overlapped, and therefore Jesus and John were born within months of each other. We do not know when John began his work, but he was creating a stir in Judea long before Christ began his ministry at the age of thirty, calling for repentance and baptising people in the river Jordan on confession of their sin.

Matthew quotes Isaiah's statement, 'A voice of one calling in the desert, "Prepare the way for the Lord, make straight paths for him"' (Isa. 40:3) as foreshadowing John. Certainly John was anticipating a completely new order, declaring, 'And do not think you can say to yourselves, "We have Abraham as our father". I tell you that out of these stones God can raise up children for Abraham. The axe is already at the root of the trees, and every tree that does not produce good fruit will be cut down and thrown into the fire' (3:9-10). To proclaim, 'the axe is already at the root of the trees' was a radical declaration that the old order was no longer sufficient. To be a child of Abraham was no longer in itself the source of security – there is to be a new relationship, a new order, a new dimension. We are given no statistics of the response to his ministry, but he undoubtedly provoked the wrath of the religious hierarchy, and certainly provoked the wrath of those whose sin he publicly identified, as evidenced by his imprisonment and subsequent beheading by Herod.

The Old Testament concludes with the promise, 'See I will send you the prophet Elijah before that great and dreadful day of the Lord come' (Mal. 4:5) When asked by his disciples when Elijah would come, Jesus replied he had come already, and they knew him to be speaking of John the Baptist (Matt. 17:10-13). This does not mean John was a reincarnation of Elijah, or that Elijah having been taken up to heaven

---

[3] See *Jesus and Christian Origins Outside The New Testament* by F. F. Bruce, Hodder & Stoughton, 1974.

in a chariot of fire (see 2 Kgs. 2:11-12) had been orbiting for some eight hundred years, before returning in a different guise, but that John the Baptist came in the spirit and image of Elijah. Elijah was the first of the era of itinerant preaching prophets, who stood against the status quo, preached righteousness and provoked the wrath of the political hierarchy of the day. There are superficial similarities between Elijah and John the Baptist: both wore garments made of hair, both wore a leather belt around the waist (cf 2 Kgs. 1:8 with Matt. 3:4), and both went through periods of doubt (see 1 Kgs. 19 and Matt. 11). But the significant similarities are found in their bold proclamation of the demands of God on his people.

2. The message of John the Baptist

Historically, John's key role was in preparing the way for Christ, but the abiding value of John the Baptist is found in the conciseness of his message. There were two aspects to it. He had a message for the Jews (3:2, 7-10), and he had a message about Christ (3:11-12).

a). His message to the Jews

His message to his Jewish audience sums up as, 'Repent, for the kingdom of heaven is near' (3:2). He calls for a *response* (repent) and he gives them a *reason* (the kingdom of heaven is near). This introduces two key aspects of the New Testament gospel. If the word *repent* is the first recorded word of John, it is also the first recorded public word of Jesus (4:17 cf Mark 1:15), and the first word of response instructed on the Day of Pentecost when the church was born (Acts 2:38). It is a neglected and sometimes forgotten word in contemporary evangelism.

I have sometimes asked the question of a congregation of people whether repentance is correctly defined as something we *feel*, something we *think* or something we *do*. The majority always respond that it is something we do. The truth is that repentance is essentially something we *think*. The Greek word 'repent' is the word 'metanoeo' being a combination of two words, 'meta' to change, and 'noia' to perceive, or 'nous' the mind. In the preaching of John the Baptist true repentance involves the three ingredients of thought, word and deed.

Thought: Repentance is essentially a change of mind. Paul wrote, '... be transformed by the renewal of your mind' (Rom. 12:2). A person may *feel* bad about their sin yet not change their mind about it. I have sat with enough people who have wept over their failure and sin, but who have evidently not changed their mind about it. There is an emotional, (but perhaps sentimental) rejection of sin, but their minds remain hooked. The book of Proverbs states, 'As a man thinketh in his heart so is he' (Prov. 23:7 AV). Changing the mind is the first step in true repentance.

Word: 'Confessing their sins they were baptised by him in the Jordan River' (3.6). The only way sin leaves the body is through the mouth! We must not disguise it, nor make excuses for it, but in honest recognition of the true diagnosis of our sin we are to confess it to God. (see also 1 John 1:9).

Deed: 'Produce fruit in keeping with repentance' (3:8). The evidence of true repentance, says John the Baptist, is fruit in keeping with it. Luke's record of John's ministry records his expectations that the fruit of repentance is generosity, integrity and contentment. To the crowd he said, 'The man with two tunics should share with him who has none, and the one who has food should do the same...', to tax collectors he said, 'Don't collect any more than you are required to', and to soldiers he said, 'Don't extort money and don't accuse people falsely – be content with your pay' (Luke 3.10-14). These are the very practical expressions of repentance.

If the **response** of the people is 'Repent', the **reason** for this is 'the kingdom of heaven is near'. This introduces one of the key themes of Matthew's gospel. No other writer uses the term 'kingdom of heaven', whereas Matthew uses it over thirty times. It is an interchangeable term with 'kingdom of God' which is also used four times by Matthew, 14 times in Mark, 31 times in Luke and twice in John. In addition, Jesus speaks of 'my kingdom', 'his kingdom' and 'your kingdom' (referring to God), making the word 'kingdom' the second most frequent word on the lips of Jesus (the most frequent being 'Father'). The use of the word by Jesus covers such wide aspects that '... it is practically impossible to frame a definition within which all the sayings of Jesus concerning the kingdom can be included'.[4] However, on its most simple level, to speak of a kingdom is to speak of a king. A 'kingdom' is by definition the sphere in which a king reigns. The idea was not new to John's listeners, for the Jews expected the Messiah to establish a visible,

---

[4] Quote from Graham Scroggie, *A Guide To The Gospels*, Pickering and Inglis, 1973, who is quoting G. Jackson, *The Teaching of Jesus*.

earthly theocratic kingdom, of which Jerusalem would be the capital, and that by its establishment foreign domination would be thrown off and Israel's enemies would be humiliated. However the kingdom of which Jesus spoke was not to be earthly or physical, but inward and spiritual. As Luke records, 'Once, having been asked by the Pharisees when the kingdom of God would come, Jesus replied, "The kingdom does not come with your careful observation, nor will people say, 'Here it is' or 'There it is' because the kingdom of God is within you"' (Luke 17:20-21). The kingdom is the sphere of the kingship of Christ which is essentially within his people.

The reason John called people to repentance was not primarily a subjective one (something within the people demanded it), but an objective one (something about Christ demanded it) – 'the kingdom of heaven is near'. In other words, the King is about to set up his kingdom and the implications are such that you need to repent and become aligned with him. In the gospels the kingdom is preached as future, 'the kingdom of heaven is near', but in the book of Acts it is preached in the present tense (e.g. 'Philip ... preached the good news of the kingdom of God,' Acts 8:12) i.e. 'the kingdom is here'. Something happened to bring into the present what had previously been declared as future. It was after the death and resurrection of Jesus that he declared, 'All authority in heaven and on earth has been given to me ...' (Matt. 28:18). Peter declared on the Day of Pentecost, 'Therefore let all Israel be assured of this: God has made this Jesus whom you crucified both Lord and Christ' (Acts 2:36). He, of course, was already Lord, but something happened through his death and resurrection that 'made this Jesus ... Lord ...'. Paul writing about the Lord Jesus Christ becoming obedient to death goes on to say, 'Therefore God exalted him to the highest place and gave him the name that is above every name, that at the name of Jesus every knee should bow in heaven and on earth and under the earth..' (Phil. 2:9-10). The kingdom, in terms of our personal experience of the kingship of Christ, was established at Pentecost on the basis of his death for us, and his resurrection from the dead to impart his life to us who repent and believe. If we need further evidence, Jesus said to his disciples, 'I tell you the truth, some who are standing here will not taste death before they see the Son of Man coming in his kingdom' (Matt. 16:28). This is obviously not a reference to his second coming, for that did not take place in the lifetime of his disciples. Some see it as referring to their witnessing his resurrection, but I think it is more probably a reference to Pentecost, when he came to establish his kingdom within his people.

The reason John calls the people to repentance is the kingship of Christ. We do not *make* him King or Lord! God has made him Lord (Acts 2:36). Our response must be to recognise who he is and submit to him in repentance, so that the agenda of his kingdom becomes our agenda, the interests of his kingdom become our interests and the destiny of his kingdom becomes our destiny.

b) His message about Jesus

John says about Jesus, 'I baptise you with water for repentance.... He will baptise you with the Holy Spirit and with fire' (3.11). John says in effect, 'I have a baptism but I can only take you so far. There is something I cannot do for you. There is something only Jesus Christ can do for you – He will baptise you with the Holy Spirit and with fire'. The term 'baptism with (or in, or by) the Holy Spirit' occurs seven times in the New Testament, four of them by John (Matt. 3:11; Mark 1:8; Luke 3:16; John 1:33), one by Jesus quoting John (Acts 1.5); one by Peter quoting Jesus quoting John (Acts 11:15-17) and one other by Paul (1 Cor. 12:13).

In the statements of John the Baptist, Jesus and Peter there is no explanation given as to what was exactly meant by the baptism with the Holy Spirit. The word 'baptise' signifies to 'drench', 'dip' or 'plunge'. The activity of the Holy Spirit is going to be indispensable to the work and purpose of Jesus Christ. This book does not have scope for a full explanation of the term, but the contrast made with John's baptism would suggest that John's baptism was designed to bring the people *out* of their old life, whereas Jesus' baptism was designed to bring the people *into* a new life. To be brought out of sin, represented by John's baptism, does not represent the work Jesus Christ is going to accomplish, that is a means to the real end, which is a baptism with the Holy Spirit. It is one thing to come out of the old life, another to come in to the new life. The preacher can explain what the people must do to come out of their old life, but only the Lord Jesus Christ is capable of bringing them into the new purpose for which they have been brought out – union with Christ, and all entailed in that. Paul, in his reference to baptism by the Spirit, gives it a doctrinal context, 'For we were all baptised by one Spirit into one body ... and were all given the one Spirit to drink' (1 Cor. 12:13). This baptism brings us *into* Christ, and makes us sharers together of his life. It also, says John, is a baptism of fire, which cleanses and destroys in order to make possible renewing and rebuilding. We can point people to Christ, but then we must leave them with him who alone baptises with the Holy Spirit and brings them into that union with himself where he lives in them and they are in him. True Christian experience goes beyond believing facts and making appropriate response, but to actually experiencing God.[5]

3. The meeting of Jesus and John

What was the significance of Jesus being baptised by John? John's baptism was for repentance, and Jesus was not in need of repentance. He was not one of the crowd who needed to change his mind, to confess his sins or to produce fruit in evidence of that. Recognising this, John tried to deter him and queried, 'I need to be baptised by you, and do you come to me?'. Jesus' reply was, 'Let it be so now; it is proper for us to do this to fulfil all righteousness' (3:15). In what sense did this fulfil all righteousness?

Baptism does not in itself actually accomplish anything. It is an external symbol of an internal response, an outward ritual demonstrating an inner reality. The baptism of Jesus would seem to be the outward symbol of several important things.

a) His identification with human beings in their need
His identification with us in our need comes to its climax in the cross, but existed throughout his incarnation in the subjecting of himself to the limitations of a real human body. Paul describes him as, '... being in very nature God ... made himself nothing ... being made in human likeness' (Phil. 2:6-7). Elsewhere he writes, 'For you know the grace of our Lord Jesus Christ, that though he was rich, yet for your sakes he became poor...' (2 Cor. 8:9). Speaking prophetically of Christ, Isaiah writes, he '... was numbered with the transgressors' (Isa. 53:12). His baptism demonstrated in the first instance, his identification with our need for cleansing.

b) His anticipation of the cross
Jesus spoke of '... the baptism I am baptised with' (Mark 10:38) in a clear reference to his crucifixion. The baptism of a Christian believer

---

[5] For a fuller treatment, see *Baptism and Fulness* by John R. W. Stott, IVP.

looks back on the death, burial and resurrection of Christ, and identifies that person with the completed work of Christ on their behalf. For the Lord Jesus Christ, his baptism looked forward to his death, burial and resurrection, and is a symbolic demonstration in advance of what will be his experience.

c) His separation to the ministry he is about to fulfil
It was at his baptism that the Holy Spirit descended like a dove upon Jesus, and the voice of the Father was heard from heaven saying, 'This is my Son whom I love; with him I am well pleased' (3:16-17). Many recognise this statement of the Father as the combination of two Messianic statements of the Old Testament. 'This is my Son...' (Ps. 2:7), which was recognised as a description of the coming Messiah, and 'My chosen one in whom I delight' (Isa. 42:1), one of the suffering servant passages of Isaiah that the Jews largely saw as descriptions of Israel, not of the Messiah. The idea of a suffering Messiah had no place in Jewish thinking, which is why the cross of Christ is a stumbling block to Jews (see 1 Cor. 1:23). This statement of the Father brings together the two themes of Messianic prophecy: Who he is (the Son), and What he does (the suffering servant).

Jesus' baptism is one of the few occasions in Scripture when the Trinity function together in independent roles, in tangible ways and at the same time. The Father spoke from heaven, the Son was standing in the River Jordan, and the Spirit descended in the form of a dove. It is interesting the Father said of the Son, '... with him I am well pleased,' for as yet he had not done anything that appears significant. He had never preached a sermon, never performed a miracle and never disclosed his identity, not even to his own family. It is not our activity that pleases God, it is our disposition towards him – and if that involves remaining silent for thirty years, then so be it! He is pleased.

This event marked a new era in the earthly life of Jesus. Until now he had been a carpenter in Nazareth. He would not return to his carpenter's shop, for from this moment he began the business for which he had become a man. From a human perspective this must have been an exciting moment in his life, but on first reading his first assignment comes to us as something of a shock! It was an assignment that would be fulfilled alone in the wilderness, with an empty stomach, under attack from the devil.

5.

Temptation and testing in the wilderness
(4:1-11)

The first assignment of Jesus following his baptism and setting aside for his ministry in Jordan is a very interesting one. 'Then Jesus was led by the Spirit into the desert to be tempted by the devil' (4:1). To be subject to attack by the devil whilst alone in the wilderness was deliberate strategy. The first assignment given him was not to preach the Sermon on the Mount, or to perform some great miracle, but forty days of solitude in the hostile environment of the desert, with the devil on his back, all guns blazing! This is the consequence of his being 'led by the Spirit'. There is an insupportable idea around that our comfort and God's interests coincide. This is simply not the case. The Holy Spirit's presence does not set us free from difficulties but equips us for them, and so often the rough, tough situations in life are his tools for accomplishing his will within us.

This time in the desert needs to be understood from two points of view. From the point of view of the antagonist, the devil, and from the point of view of the instigator, God. From the devil's point of view, these were forty days of temptation, designed to weaken and disqualify Jesus from his ministry. From God's point of view they were forty days of testing, designed to strengthen and qualify Jesus for his ministry. The exact same events had the potential of the exact opposite effects. Every attack of Satan is a potential springboard to growth, as we respond to God within it, and every experience of the Holy Spirit carries with it a potential opportunity of shipwreck if we allow the devil to intrude! It was Satan who attacked Jesus in the wilderness, but it was the Spirit who led him into the sphere of conflict. The very thing the devil would use to destroy us is the very thing God uses to build us. That is why it is true to say that sometimes the devil does you good! It is never his intention of course, but in the appropriate response such as we shall see in Jesus, his attack becomes the springboard to greater blessing and deeper enrichment.

The source of this account must be Jesus himself, for he was alone with the devil. Matthew and Luke differ in the order in which the second and third temptations come, but there need not be any great significance in that.

1. Temptation from the devil's point of view

The temptations of the devil came along three familiar and vulnerable areas. John writes in his epistle, 'For all that is in the world, the *lust of the flesh* and the *lust of the eyes* and the *pride of life*, is not of the Father but of the world' (1 John 2:16 RSV).

Lust of the flesh: The first temptation was an appeal to satisfy legitimate human appetite. 'After forty days and forty nights he was hungry. The tempter came to him and said, "If you are the Son of God, tell these stones to become bread"' (4:2-3). There is nothing wrong with eating bread. It is not a violation of God's law! The devil attacked when Jesus was humanly at his most vulnerable for it was, 'After forty days and forty nights ...'. Six weeks is about the limit a healthy man can go without food before the possibility of doing permanent damage to himself. At this point, the devil invited him to satisfy the legitimate appetite of his body, but to do so outside the will of God.

Lust of the eyes: 'The devil took him to a very high mountain and showed him all the kingdoms of the world and their splendour. "All this I will give you" he said, "if you will bow down and worship me"' (4:8-9). (Matthew gives this as the third temptation but Luke gives it as the second.) Satan's strategy was to appeal to his senses and 'show him all the kingdoms of the world', to try to awaken a covetousness that would steer him from his course.

Pride of life: 'Then the devil took him to the holy city and had him stand on the highest point of the temple. "If you are the Son of God" he said, "throw yourself down. For it is written: 'He will command his angels concerning you and they will lift you up in their hands, so that you will not strike your foot against a stone'"' (4:5-6). In other words he was saying, 'If you are the Son of God, let everyone know! Jump off the highest point of the temple, and rather than die as your body hits the ground, your Father will send angels to catch you, and word will spread like wildfire. If you are the Son of God, get yourself on the map'.

It was an unashamed appeal to pride. The devil even uses Scripture at this point, quoting from Psalm 91:11-12, though conveniently ending at the point he does, for the next sentence says, 'You will tread upon the lion and the cobra, you will trample the great lion and the serpent'. To have quoted that would have been suicidal for the devil, for he is described both as a lion (e.g. 1 Pet. 5:8) and as a serpent (e.g. Gen. 3:1 and Rev. 20:2). The selective use of Scripture taken from its context may distort and twist its meaning, and become, as in this case, a reason for disobedience rather than obedience, misinformation rather then information, confusion rather than enlightenment! Be very careful of random proof texts!

These tactics are not new. When the devil tempted Eve in the Garden of Eden to eat of the tree of the knowledge of good and evil, it was along the same channels he came. 'When the woman saw that the fruit of the tree was good for food' (an appeal to the lust of the flesh) 'and pleasing to the eye' (lust of the eye) 'and desirable for gaining wisdom' (pride of life) 'she took some and ate it' (Gen. 3:6). Look at almost any example of temptation to sin in Scripture and you will find a similar pattern, appealing to one, two or all three of these three appetites.

The 'lust of the flesh' is an appeal to the fulfilment of legitimate physical appetite in the wrong way at the wrong time. There is nothing wrong with food in itself, – it is necessary – but gluttony is sin. There is nothing wrong with sexual relationship in itself, – it is good – but premarital, extramarital and homosexual activity is sin. There is nothing wrong with rest in itself, – it is important – but laziness is sin. It is all too much at the wrong time and in the wrong context!

The 'lust of the eyes' is the attraction to our senses that awakens a desire for something out of reach. In our day of mass communication and visual stimulation we are probably more vulnerable to this than people have ever been. Advertising is designed to create a dissatisfaction with what we are and have, so that we go after the product presented as the solution to our need. The visual stimulates the sensual and our eyes need severe discipline.

The 'pride of life' is the appeal to that which boosts my ego and promotes my interests exclusively. Centuries ago when church leaders identified 'the seven deadly sins', pride was first in the list. It is the sin through which Lucifer (the 'morning star') fell and was cast out of heaven,[1] and it lies at the root of most other expressions of sin.

Temptation to do what is wrong, and temptation to do what is right

In comparing the temptations of Jesus in the wilderness with Eve in the Garden of Eden, it is important to note two very important differences between them. Firstly, Eve was tempted to do what was wrong in violation of the direct command of God, whereas Jesus was tempted to do what was right – but at the wrong time. There was nothing wrong with Jesus eating bread, for him ruling the kingdoms of the world, or being recognised as the Son of God. All of these things would be legitimately his in due course, given to him by his Father. Once the basic issue is settled that we are going to live on the side of right instead of wrong, we will still not have check-mated the devil in his attempts to destroy us. He will instead dangle before us legitimate things which are intrinsically good, but because of our particular circumstances may take us away from the will of God. What is good may become the enemy of what is right.

Temptation to weakness and temptation to strength

The second important difference is that Eve was tempted to give in to weakness, whereas Jesus was tempted to give in to strength. Jesus was tempted along lines no one else could be tempted along. I have never been tempted to turn stones into bread – it is beyond my ability. I have never been tempted to rule the world – it is outside my capacity. I have never been tempted to jump off a high building to be caught by angels! The biggest danger to the effectiveness of a Christian is not found in the exploitation of his weaknesses, but in the exploitation of his strength. If we can be persuaded of our own sufficiency, of our own inherent ability and then act in independence of God we are beaten. By all means we must guard our weaknesses, but as Christians intent on business with God, we need to watch our strengths. They may become a foothold for the devil.

---

[1] See Isaiah 14:12-15 and Ezekiel 28:12-19. These accounts begin as descriptions of the king of Babylon (Isaiah) and the king of Tyre (Ezekiel), but evidently begin to speak of someone other than either. The general consensus is that this can only be a description of how the most beautiful of all God's angels became corrupt and was cast out of heaven on account of his pride, to become the arch enemy of God and of all that is good.

2. Testing from God's point of view

If it was the devil who attacked Jesus, it was God who set up the appointment, 'led by the Spirit into the desert *to be tempted* by the devil' (4:1). From the point of view of God, this was the object of the exercise. What was God's vested interest in an attack on his Son by Satan? From God's perspective it was to test the Son in three significant areas – areas in which it is likely he will test you and me too. He tested his attitude to resources; his attitude to his reputation and his attitude to responsibility.

a) His attitude to resources

The first testing came to Jesus at his weakest point 'after fasting forty days', when the devil suggested he, 'tell these stones to become bread'. This faced Jesus with an alternative. Either he would trust the Spirit who had led him into the desert, to provide him with the resources he needed at the right time, or he would take the situation into his own hands and manipulate his circumstances to turn stones to bread. God does not always meet our perceived sense of need. Paul who stated, 'My God will meet all your needs according to his glorious riches in Christ Jesus' (Phil. 4:19), also testified, 'I have known hunger and thirst and have often gone without food. I have been cold and naked' (2 Cor. 11:27). There may be many 'needs' we are conscious of, which God has not met. At that point we may take things into our own hand and produce the desired result in independence of God, or we may trust God for his timing.

Abraham had been promised a son, but when after ten years there was still no son he 'turned stones to bread'. He took the situation into his own hands and fathered his son Ishmael by the maid Hagar. Fifteen years later God gave him Isaac. God then tested him again. He told him to take his son Isaac to the region of Moriah and 'Sacrifice him there as a burnt offering on one of the mountains I will tell you about'. This time Abraham went right through to the '40th day', ready to do exactly as he had been told until the last moment when God intervened and said, 'Now I know that you fear God'.[2] To be of any significant use to God there comes a time when we are taken out of our safety zone, and left with nothing and no one on which we may

---

[2] See Genesis 16 for the birth of Ishmael, and Genesis 22 for Abraham's willingness to offer Isaac.

safely depend, but God alone. This was the first testing of the Son by the Father.

b) His attitude to reputation

When the devil had him stand on the highest point of the temple and said, 'If you are the Son of God, throw yourself down' and quoted from Psalm 91 that 'he will command his angels concerning you, and they will lift you up in their hands so that you will not strike your foot against a stone', his appeal was that Jesus do something dramatic to get himself on the map. For thirty years he has been the Son of God but has lived in anonymity! 'Get out there and be someone' is the thrust of the temptation. 'Give yourself a reputation!' The devil discovered in this appeal that Jesus wasn't interested in his reputation.

Paul writes of Jesus, 'He made himself of no reputation' (Phil. 2:7 AV). In other words, he was not interested in what people thought of him, he was only interested in what his Father thought of him, 'I always do what pleases him' (John 8:29). We cannot help but have a reputation, but it is wise to keep a distance from it, and not be interested in it. Once we become interested in establishing a reputation for ourselves, we then have to work at maintaining that reputation, and in that very interest lie the seeds of hypocrisy. When Jesus rebuked the hypocrites in the Sermon on the Mount, they were those who loved to be, 'honoured by men' (Matt. 6:2), and 'seen by men' (Matt. 6:5) and he says of them, 'they have received their reward in full'. Their reward was a reputation before people they worked hard to establish, but which left them bankrupt where it really counted: before God.

The Father tested his Son's attitude to his reputation. In the events of the next three years his reputation would be torn to shreds, he would be maligned, abused and eventually crucified, but his Father knew he had no personal agenda. He would not care what people thought about him, only that he might say to his Father, 'I have brought you glory on earth by completing the work you have given me to do' (John 17:4).

c) His attitude to responsibility

The third testing from the Father came with the temptation to Jesus to take for himself the kingdoms of the world. 'Again the devil took him to a very high mountain and showed him all the kingdoms of the world and their splendour. "All this I will give you," he said, "If you will bow down and worship me'" (vv. 8-9). Whether this was a literal mountain or a vision is not clear in the text. To view the kingdoms of the world would not be possible from any one mountain, so it may well be a vision (as could be his standing on the highest point of the temple in the previous temptation). However, the thrust of the devil's approach is to offer him the means of taking charge and being a leader for his own ends to fulfil his own interests. Again, he wasn't interested, and responded, 'Worship the Lord your God and serve him only' (4:10).

It is good to be willing to take responsibility, but responsibility should be *given, not taken.* Jesus would later say, 'All authority in heaven and on earth has been *given* to me' (Matt. 28:18). His position was not something he had obtained through his own ambitious manipulation, and pacts with the devil, but received from his Father, it was 'given'. If we scheme, and manipulate people and circumstances to gain position, someone else is as likely to come behind to manipulate circumstances to get us out, and we will be insecure. But when God puts us into position and gives us our responsibilities, we are secure until God moves us on.

Many characters in the Bible resisted the temptation to manoeuvre themselves into position, trusting God to fulfil their destiny in his timing. Moses at the age of forty knew God was using him to rescue Israel from their slavery in Egypt (see Acts 7:25) but it was not until he was eighty that God commissioned him at the burning bush. Moses did not go back into Egypt on a personal crusade to free Israel, but with an agenda he had received from God to further God's interests, and to that extent he was secure! David was called by God to replace Saul as king of Israel many years before he came to the throne. In the meantime he had opportunity on more than one occasion to end Saul's life and thus get the throne, but he waited for God's timing. His reasoning was: 'God put Saul on the throne and he, in his own time, will take him off. God has given me the throne, and he in his own time, will put me on. I don't need to manipulate events, I simply rest confident in God' (for example see 1 Sam. 26:9-11). Jesus as a boy of twelve was, 'about my Father's business' (Luke 2:49), but he waited his Father's timing to begin his ministry. Until set apart at his baptism, Jesus never preached a sermon, never performed a miracle and never made any claim as to his identity. He waited and trusted his Father's timing.

These three areas of testing were crucial in the life of Jesus. Luke records after this event that, 'Jesus returned to Galilee in the power of the Spirit' (Luke 4:14). He had been described as 'full of the Spirit' and had been 'led by the Spirit' (Luke 4:1), but it was the consequence of this testing that brought him back to Galilee in the 'power of the Spirit'. In human terms, now the Father could trust the Son with power. The day would come when he would hang on a Roman cross, his resources drained. He could take himself down from the cross, but he wouldn't. He would wait for his Father to raise him from the dead. His reputation would be in tatters as people mocked and despised him, but one day his Father would 'exalt him to the highest place and give him the name that is above every name' (see Phil. 2:9). His responsibilities would one day seem to be taken from him as he became a victim of corrupt Roman justice. But the Father knew he would not react, but trust him completely for the accomplishment of his will.

The issue at stake is not so much whether we can trust God, but whether God can trust us, and whether God can trust us to trust him!

6.

The beginning of his ministry
(4:12-25)

After Jesus returned from his fast of forty days and forty nights in the desert, a remarkable period covering as much as twelve months of time is passed over without comment. Between the conclusion of his time of temptation in the desert, 'Then the devil left him and angels came and attended him' (4:11) and the next paragraph which begins, 'When Jesus heard that John had been put in prison he returned to Galilee' (4:12) a considerable period is omitted. All three synoptic gospels make this same omission, and only John gives us some record of it.

1. His movements (4:12-16)

It may be of background interest to attempt to fill in the little we know of this gap. Following his experience in the wilderness, Jesus seems to have rejoined John the Baptist for a few days, initially standing unrecognised amongst the crowd but known to John. On that first day John said to the crowd, '... among you stands one you do not know. He is the one who comes after me, the thongs of whose sandals I am not worthy to untie' (John 1:26-27). On the second day, John saw Jesus coming towards him in the crowd and announced, 'Look the Lamb of God who takes away the sin of the world' (John 1:29). It was then John gave testimony to an earlier event when he had seen the Spirit of God come down from heaven as a dove and remain on him. This had taken place at his baptism prior to his forty days in the wilderness (see Matt. 3:16-17). He then affirms, 'I have seen and I testify that this is the Son of God' (John 1:34). On the third day, John was at the Jordan again with two of his disciples when Jesus passed by. He exclaimed for the second time, 'Look the Lamb of God' (John 1:36), and his two disciples left John and followed Jesus. One was Andrew, who ran to tell his brother Simon and brought him to Jesus. On the fourth day,

Jesus decided to leave for Galilee, inviting Philip to follow him, who in turn found Nathanial and told him they had found the Christ (John 1:43ff.). These four, Andrew, Simon (whom Jesus called Peter), Philip and Nathanial formed the first nucleus of Jesus' disciples.

The following sequence of events, all omitted by Matthew, would appear to be that he first went to Cana in Galilee as a wedding guest, where he performed his first miracle of turning water into wine (John 2:1-11). After this he spent a few days with his family in Capernaum (John 2:12), before going up to Jerusalem in time for the Jewish Passover. There he entered the temple, found it had been turned into a market and drove the people and animals out with a whip he made himself out of cords (John 2:13-22). Whilst in Jerusalem for the Passover Feast he performed miracles and as a result many people believed in him (John 2:23-25). One night in Jerusalem he was visited by Nicodemus, the Pharisee and member of the Sanhedrin, the Jewish ruling council, to whom he explained the necessity of being born again (John 3:1-21). After this he travelled to the Judean countryside with his disciples and people came to them to be baptised. At the same time John the Baptist was still baptising at Aenon on the other side of the Jordan (John 3:22-26). His reputation amongst the people was that, 'Jesus was gaining and baptising more disciples than John' (John 4:1), although in fact it was not Jesus who baptised, but his disciples. When Jesus heard this, he left Judea and went back once more to Galilee. On his way he passed through Samaria and met the woman at the well, whose life was transformed by the encounter and whose testimony led to many other Samaritans believing in him (John 4:1-42). After two days in Samaria he went on to Galilee, where he was warmly welcomed, many of them having been in Jerusalem for the Passover Feast and witnessed many of his miracles there (John 4:43-44).

At what precise time following this period of Jesus' activity John the Baptist was arrested by Herod we do not know. Perhaps it was during this return to Galilee, or more likely during a second visit Jesus made to Jerusalem to attend another of the Jewish feasts (John 5:1). When John is next mentioned, Jesus speaks of him in the past tense, 'John was a lamp that burned and gave light' (John 5:35) suggesting John himself was now removed from the scene. It may well have been of this second visit to Jerusalem that Matthew writes when he says, 'When Jesus heard that John had been put in prison he returned to Galilee' (4:12).

Matthew then tells us that Jesus left Nazareth, his home since boyhood, and went and lived in Capernaum, a distance of some twenty five to thirty miles away, but does not tell us why. It is Luke who tells us why. Jesus at some point had stood up in the synagogue in Nazareth and had read the Messianic statement from Isaiah 61, 'The Spirit of the Lord is on me, because he has anointed me to preach good news to the poor. He has sent me to proclaim freedom for the prisoners and recovery of sight for the blind, to release the oppressed, to proclaim the year of the Lord's favour'. He then rolled up the scroll and announced, 'Today this scripture is fulfilled in your hearing' (Luke 4:18-21). Although they were initially impressed and amazed by his statements, asking him to say more, the final outcome of this event was the people in the synagogue carried him out of the town and tried to kill him by throwing him from a cliff. At this point he left Nazareth and made his home in Capernaum.

Only on one other occasion is it recorded Jesus returned to Nazareth and he received a frosty reaction. The narrative of that visit concludes, 'And he did not do many miracles there because of their lack of faith' (13:54-58). In his home town Jesus carried the baggage of a reputation that did not give room for him to be recognised as the Messiah. He was the carpenter. They did not consider him to have attended the right schools to give the kind of teaching he was giving. They knew his brothers and sisters. They were offended by what they perceived as his arrogance. And so he left them.

Capernaum became his base of operation for the rest of his ministry. It was strategically situated on the northern side of the lake of Galilee. Consequently, most of his ministry takes place around the lake of Galilee, and most of his disciples were Galilean.

2. His message (4:17)

From that time on, Matthew tells us, Jesus began to preach, 'Repent, for the kingdom of heaven is near'. This is the identical message to John the Baptist (see 3:2), and we have already considered its meaning and implications. Throughout the book, the kingdom of heaven is the major theme of Jesus' teaching, and it may be helpful at this point to put together the major statements of Jesus in Matthew about entry and participation in the kingdom.

- Blessed are the poor in spirit, for theirs is the kingdom of heaven (5:3)

- Unless your righteousness surpasses that of the Pharisees and the teachers of the law, you will certainly not enter the kingdom of heaven (5:20)
- Not everyone who says to me, 'Lord, Lord', will enter the kingdom of heaven, but only he who does the will of my Father who is in heaven (7:21)
- Unless you change and become like little children, you will never enter the kingdom of heaven. Therefore whoever humbles himself like this child is the greatest in the kingdom of heaven (18:3-4)
- It is hard for a rich man to enter the kingdom of heaven. I tell you, it is easier for a camel to go through the eye of a needle than for a rich man to enter the kingdom of God (19:23-24)

Participation in the kingdom of heaven, beginning with repentance (a change of mind about sin, self and God) involves a humble assessment of ourselves (poor in spirit), an internal rather than an external righteousness (surpassing that of the Pharisees), obedience to the will of God, a child-like spirit of dependency on God, and a rejection of any sense of dependency on other sources (it is hard for a rich man, dependent on other things, to enter the kingdom). There is much other teaching regarding the kingdom in this gospel, but these are the initial conditions upon which a person may enter and enjoy the kingdom.

3. His methods (4:18-22)

The calling of two sets of brothers to leave all and follow him is recorded at this point. Simon Peter and Andrew were casting a fishing net into the lake, and James and John were preparing their nets in a boat with their father Zebedee. The brief blunt record of Matthew sounds very dramatic. To Simon and Andrew he said, 'Come follow me, and I will make you fishers of men' (4:19) and 'At once they left their nets and followed him'. Similarly, he called James and John and, 'immediately they left the boat and their father and followed him' (4:22). The brevity of the record almost gives the impression Jesus did not even slow his pace as he called from the shore, but kept moving as these four young men fell into line behind him!

The reality is this was not the first meeting of Jesus with these men. Andrew had been a disciple of John the Baptist, and after John had pointed Jesus out as the Lamb of God, Andrew had left John to follow Jesus (John 1:40). The first thing he did was go and find his brother Simon and bring him to Jesus. On that first meeting, Jesus had given Simon the new name, 'Peter', meaning 'rock' (John 1:41-42). The relationship Andrew and Peter enjoyed with Jesus at this stage had not involved any call to leave their occupation as fishermen, that was to come as a separate invitation.

There is no record of James and John prior to this call of Jesus but as business partners of Andrew and Peter (see Luke 5:10), they would certainly have been aware of Jesus and the interest Andrew and Peter had in him. This was not the only time Jesus called this foursome, for there is another record in Luke's gospel which contains interesting detail of Jesus calling these same four men, though on a different occasion.

Jesus was teaching a crowd of people on the water's edge, when he got into the boat of Simon and spoke to the people a little from the shore. When he had finished speaking he asked Simon to put out into deeper water and let down the nets. Simon responded, 'Master, we've worked hard all night and haven't caught anything. But because you say so, I will let down the nets'. The consequence was that they caught such a large number of fish, their nets began to break! They called James and John in another boat to come and help them and filled both boats so full they began to sink. When they landed the catch, Jesus said, 'Don't be afraid; from now on you will catch men'. It was then, 'they pulled their boats up on shore, left everything and followed him' (Luke 5:1-11). Jesus gave them the best catch of fish they ever had, then presented them with a choice. Either take advantage of this enormous catch, take it to the local market and make good money, or leave everything behind to follow me. They chose the latter. I sometimes fear that we think the best motivation for following Christ is when everything else goes so wrong in people's lives that in desperation they will turn to him. Some may well come that route, but it is not the best route. These disciples were given the best day of fishing they had ever had, and they recognised that to follow Jesus was not the best choice in a set of bad alternatives, but to be his disciple was better than the best alternatives. Often when we have to make a significant choice of obedience to the will of God, we are presented with very attractive alternatives, and the role of the will of God amongst attractive alternatives is a good test of discipleship.

Ultimately Jesus called twelve disciples whom he set apart from the rest of his followers to be with him as apostles (see comments on

10:2-4). The concentration of his ministry was with these twelve men. Most of what is recorded of Jesus' teaching was not addressed to the crowds, but to these twelve. He taught them, trained them, disciplined them and ultimately made his impact through them. They were a mixed group of very ordinary men. They lacked formal education, they were young, most disgraced themselves in some way, not least when they all forsook him and fled after his arrest, and one of them, Judas Iscariot, committed suicide in the early hours of the same day Jesus was crucified. Yet, he turned their weakness to strength. His invitation was, 'Come, follow me, and I will make you fishers of men' (4:19). He did not challenge them to become fishers of men by a series of techniques they could learn, or methods they could follow, but took upon himself the responsibility to *make you fishers of men*. This was to be his business, as it is today in your life and mine.

4. His ministry (4:23-25)
Matthew highlights three aspects of Jesus' ensuing ministry. He '... went throughout Galilee, *teaching* in their synagogues, *preaching* the good news of the kingdom, and *healing* every disease and sickness among the people' (4:23). These three functions of teaching, preaching and healing are highlighted.

Teaching: Jesus taught in the synagogues. The synagogue was the most significant institution in Judaism, and was essentially a place of teaching. There was only one Temple, the temple in Jerusalem, which existed for the offering of sacrifice and the practice of the many associated rituals in the law of Moses. However, every Jewish community had its synagogue. In fact wherever the Jews dispersed, they built a synagogue. It was the popular place of learning. Synagogue services began with prayers, then readings from the Scriptures, then an address. There was no professional elite to whom the ministry was restricted. Anyone could speak if the ruler of the synagogue considered it appropriate. If anyone had some teaching or ideas related to the Jewish scriptures that he wanted to spread, the synagogue was the place to start. In most of Paul's missionary journeys he began his ministry in a new place by seeking out a synagogue in which to commence. Jesus, before him, began his teaching ministry in the synagogues, though like Paul, in due course he soon became an unwelcome guest.

Teaching is primarily addressing the mind. The end result of good teaching is that people *know* something. This is the basis on which any significant response to God is made. To be swept along by the emotions of a moment, without adequate roots in an understanding of God and his truth, will prove itself to be superficial in time.

Preaching: If teaching is primarily addressing the mind, preaching is primarily addressing the will. If the end result of teaching is that people *know* something, the end result of preaching is that people *do* something. The subject of Jesus' preaching was, 'the good news of the kingdom'. The good news only ever becomes good news when the will is made to respond. Minds may be stretched, stimulated and dazzled by impressive teaching, but lives are only changed when the teaching becomes preaching and hearers are caused to cry out as those who listened to Peter preach on the Day of Pentecost, 'What shall we do?' (see Acts 2:37). Teaching is the foundation to preaching, and the two should not be divorced. To teach and not preach may produce full minds but will leave barren lives. To preach and not teach may be to evoke a response that is in danger of being little more than seed that springs to life with no root, only to wither and die.

The necessity of both teaching and preaching is kept in balance throughout the New Testament. Later in his ministry, Matthew records of Jesus, '... he went on from there to *teach* and *preach* in the towns of Galilee' (11:1). On return from the meeting of the Council in Jerusalem, between the first and second missionary journeys, 'Paul and Barnabas remained in Antioch, where they and many others *taught* and *preached* the word of the Lord' (Acts 15:35). The book of Acts concludes with the statement about Paul in Rome, 'Boldly and without hindrance he *preached* the kingdom of God and *taught* about the Lord Jesus Christ' (Acts 28:31). Paul exhorted Timothy, 'Until I come, devote yourself to the public reading of Scripture, to *preaching* and to *teaching*' (1 Tim. 4:13). These two should never be separated.

Healing: Jesus healed every disease and sickness amongst the people. It was this aspect which provoked the interest of large crowds from Syria, Galilee, the Decapolis, Jerusalem, Judea and the region across the Jordan (see 4:24-25). Matthew tells us they brought to him those who were sick, diseased, paralysed, having seizures and demon possessed, 'and he healed them'. He ministered to the body and the soul. He dealt with pain (healing), he dealt with ignorance (teaching), and he dealt with disobedience (preaching). It may well be right to acknowledge the greater importance of the soul than the body, but people are usually more conscious of the needs of the body than they are of the needs of the soul, and the truth is that Jesus Christ is interested in the whole person.

7.

The ingredients of true happiness
(5:1-12)

Part 1

The Sermon on the Mount, occupying chapters five to seven of Matthew, is the most concentrated of Jesus' teaching recorded anywhere in the New Testament. It is not presented as a collection of thoughts and ideas given by Jesus at different times, but as one address given at a particular time, in a particular place to a particular people. The record begins, 'Now when he saw the crowds he went up on a mountainside and sat down. His disciples came to him and he began to teach them saying ...' (5:1-2), and concludes, 'When Jesus had finished saying these things the crowds were amazed at his teaching ...' (7:28). The fact that similar material to that found in the Sermon on the Mount occurs at different times and different places in other gospels, presents no real difficulty. Why should Jesus not say the same things many times and tell similar stories again and again? There is no doubt that he did.

It is important in the first instance to understand to whom the Sermon on the Mount is addressed. Although a crowd was present, Matthew records, 'His disciples came to him and he began to teach them saying ...' (5:2). The crowd was present and went away amazed at the end, having heard what Jesus had to say, but he was not addressing them. He spoke to his disciples. This therefore is not primarily an evangelistic sermon, addressed to unbelievers with a view to bringing them to discipleship. There are certain things Jesus said that do not apply to those not yet his disciples. For example, 'You are the salt of the earth ... You are the light of the world' (5:13, 14).

The three chapters may be divided into two main sections. In 5:1-16 he talks of *The Character of a Christian*, (the beatitudes and being salt and light) and then 5:17-7:27 he talks of *The Conduct of a Christian* (in relation to the law [Ch. 5], in relation to reputation and treasure [Ch. 6] and in relation to priorities [Ch. 7]). The first part concerns what we are intended to BE (5:1-16), and the second part, what we are intended to DO (5:17-7:27).

It is important to understand the relationship between these two. The teaching on *conduct* only makes sense in the light of the teaching on *character*. We do not evolve from conduct to character, by doing the right things we do not become the right person. Rather it is the reverse. By becoming the right person we do the right things. Jesus is always saviour before teacher. He changes what we are before changing what to do. Fail to understand this and his teaching on conduct becomes legalism, an external imposition, rather than an internal transformation. Overlook this central truth and his teaching on conduct will produce despair in the mind of the conscientious reader! It is this central principle which lifts Christianity above every other religious or philosophical system. Jesus did not come to preach ethics or to refine a moral code, but to invade the life of ordinary human beings with the life of God and consequently transform their behaviour from within.

The Beatitudes

The Sermon on the Mount begins with nine statements, all commencing with the word 'Blessed' (5:1-12). The word 'blessed' has become a rather vague word, ranging from a warm sense of God doing something, somewhere, somehow, sometime, to an almost blank, nondescript word to be used if we don't know what else to pray! We say to God of someone, 'Bless them', and hope he will fill in the blank himself! The Greek word however has meaning! It is the word 'makarios', and literally means 'to be happy'.

Although most translators at some stage translate that word as 'happy' in other parts of the New Testament, they generally steer clear of 'happy' in this passage. Our use of the word 'happy' tends to have superficial connotations to do with nice feelings based on good circumstances. If it is a nice hot day and we are sitting on the beach with an ice cream in one hand and a good book in the other, we are happy. But if a dark cloud comes along and hides the sun, drops cold raindrops on us and the ice cream falls into the sand, we are not happy! It is a rather superficial feeling based on good circumstances.

But this is not the meaning of *makarios* style happiness! This speaks of a deep sense of contentment and well being that is real, irrespective of the circumstances. God has never promised good circumstances to his people, but he has promised a sense of well being and deep contentment that may override the most horrendous circumstances.

Most people are interested in being happy! The pursuit of happiness is the driving force of our affluent western culture. However, when you look at the list of ingredients Jesus gives for happiness, there is a big shock in store! This is a strange list to say the least, and many of these qualities appear the very antithesis of what most of us are looking for. He says for instance, 'Blessed (happy) are the poor ...'. Whoever heard of poverty making for happiness? Most people in their dreams of happiness imagine themselves rich! Millions play the lottery each week to gain happiness in instant riches. Jesus says, 'Blessed (happy) are those who mourn ...'. How strange it would be to hear someone say, 'I am feeling so miserable today, I wish someone would die so that I could have a good cry and mourn – and that would cheer me up'! He said, 'Blessed (happy) are the meek ...'. Meekness has connotations of being spineless, spiritless and weak. Not the macho, self sufficient, assertive self most would want to be, carving our own niche in life and finding happiness on our terms! He adds, 'Blessed (happy) are those who hunger and thirst ...'. Hunger and thirst don't sound very happy, they sound like a frustrated longing for what is out of reach. And so the list goes on. It concludes, 'Blessed (happy) are those who are persecuted ...'. Since when has persecution been a source of happiness? Can you imagine meeting someone who said, 'I am so miserable, I wish someone would attack me, beat me up, leave me dizzy and bleeding on the side of the road, then I would be really happy'. Jesus' list seems so strange and unusual that on first reading it whets no appetite, and instils no confidence. Rather, it is a list of things most of us spend our lives running away from!

However, on second glance you pick up things that may have been missed the first time! He does not speak of the 'poor in pocket' but the 'poor in spirit' – whatever that may mean. He does not speak of 'hunger and thirst for gourmet food', but 'for righteousness' – whatever that may mean. He does not speak of being persecuted as an unfortunate consequence of being in the wrong place at the wrong time, but 'persecuted because of righteousness' and '... because of me' – whatever that may mean. The major difference in this list is that Jesus is not talking of qualities in the physical realm (the area in which most people look for happiness), but in the realm of the spirit.

The Bible teaches we are made up of three parts – body, soul and spirit (see 1 Thess. 5:23 and Heb. 4:12 for a clear distinction between each). Some prefer to think of human beings as bipartite, merging the spirit and soul into the division of the tangible (body) and non-tangible (soul and spirit), rather than tripartite. However, the Scripture does seem to distinguish between soul and spirit, and with the risk of some oversimplification we may understand it this way. The body is the obvious physical part of us. It is what we see every morning in the mirror! We feed it, clothe it, exercise it, rest it, paint it and hang jewellery on it! It comes in various shapes and sizes and each one is distinct. The soul is the physical life which indwells the body and which consists of mind (the ability to think), emotion (the ability to feel) and will (the ability to decide). We are at least subconsciously, if not consciously, aware of the distinction between body and soul, which is why it is a priority for most of us to make sure we do not do anything that may cause the soul and body to separate. If they do the body is of little value any more, and is usually laid to rest in the ground! The spirit however is an additional dimension, unique to human beings, in which we are designed to know and experience God. It is the part of us that causes the soul to ask questions like: 'Where did I come from?', 'Where am I going?', 'What is the meaning of my life?', looking up into the night sky we ask, 'What is up there?' The spirit in human beings is that capacity which causes us to reach out of ourselves, and is designed that we might know and enjoy God.

The myth of our day is that happiness is found in satisfying our physical desires, comforts and appetites. Those desires may be entirely legitimate, but the engine room of each human being is the spirit which is designed to be inhabited and governed by God. It is for this reason Jesus said, 'Seek his kingdom and his righteousness, and all these things will be given to you as well' (6:33), the 'these things' being the physical necessities of food and clothes.

Satisfying the body is never the source of true happiness for it is not the seat of our true appetites! Our true appetite is expressed in the famous prayer of Augustine, 'You have made us for yourself, and our hearts are restless until they find their rest in you'. The teaching of the Sermon on the Mount works from the spirit to the soul and out to the body. The norm of our day reverses that process, and tries to satisfy the deep needs of the human spirit by focusing on physical satisfaction. In this regard, either Jesus Christ has got it all wrong, or the world at large has it all wrong. You choose!

There are nine beatitudes in this passage (statements beginning with 'Blessed are ...'), but as the last is repeated twice, eight different ingredients in Jesus' description of happiness. These are not descriptions of eight different people, one is poor in spirit, another is mourning, another is meek etc, but the description of eight ingredients that will be true of each one person who is happy, '*makarios*' style. The list of these eight is progressive. Beginning with the first, the second grows out of it, the third out of the second until the eighth gives the completed picture of the person to whom Jesus then says, 'You are the salt of the earth.... You are the light of the world...'. We will look at them one by one and compile the profile of true happiness.

1. Blessed are the poor in spirit, for theirs is the kingdom of heaven

The first step to real happiness is an acknowledgement of spiritual poverty, the recognition of the fact I do not have in myself what it takes to be the person I was created to be. This is deeper than recognising I fail, it is realising I do not have the capacity within myself to do anything else! As Paul wrote, 'I know that nothing good lives in me, that is, in my sinful nature' (Rom. 7:18), more literally, 'in my natural self'.[1] Human beings have been so created that the Spirit of God within them is indispensable in their ability to function as intended. David wrote, 'I said to the LORD, "You are my LORD; apart from you I have no good thing"' (Ps. 16:2).

This does not mean there is nothing good in any of us, for it is self evident there are lots of good things. The ability to love, to do a good day's work, to paint a picture, to play music, are all in themselves good and may be accomplished in independence of God. Then what does Paul mean when he states, 'nothing good lives in me'?

---

[1] The NIV expression 'sinful nature' is from the Greek word *sarx*, literally 'flesh'. This word has a wide range of meaning in the New Testament, but in this context speaks of the 'natural' human state. That is, all that a person is in the totality of themselves, apart from God.

Just imagine I had a brand new Rolls Royce parked outside my home. It is fully equipped with leather upholstery, quadraphonic sound, telephone, television in the back seat and even a bar! If you were to visit my home and look over my car you would be very impressed. But suppose my car had no engine! You would remain impressed until you asked me for a ride. Then you would discover that although there is nothing wrong with the leather upholstery, the telephone, television or sound system (all of which is fine in itself), but as far as being a car is concerned, it is incapable of functioning as a car is supposed to function. All it would be good for would be keeping chickens in – but I couldn't go anywhere! When Paul says, 'nothing good lives in me', it is not that everything about him is bad! Elsewhere he lists some things about which he says he could boast (Phil. 3:4-6), but he is saying that apart from the indwelling presence of Jesus Christ, everything else which may be good about me is ultimately good for nothing. I am like a car without an engine.

It is to face this fact and acknowledge our own poverty of spirit which is the first step to real happiness. It is to this person Jesus says, 'the kingdom of heaven is theirs'. All the riches of the kingdom of heaven are available to the person who recognises their own bankruptcy without God.

2. Blessed are those who mourn, for they will be comforted

The second ingredient in Jesus' list of happiness follows logically from the first. To recognise my poverty in spirit is to mourn that poverty. This is not a verse about bereavement and funerals, but the logical response to the discovery of my own poverty stricken nature. When God in his kindness reveals to us the true nature of ourselves, we may respond in various ways. We can try to hide our poverty, to cover it up, to pretend it is really not so, or we can face it honestly and mourn our condition. This is called repentance. Repentance is a change of mind,[2] not just concerning *what I do*, but more fundamentally, concerning *who I am*. True repentance must go much deeper than changing our minds about what we do. We are normally made first aware of the failure of our behaviour, but that discovery must go deeper to an awareness of the fact it is what we *are* that is the cause of what we *do*, and this is our major area of need.

---

[2] See comments in Chapter 3 on the Greek word *metanoeo* as used by John the Baptist in 4:2.

Later in the chapter, Jesus goes on to teach that murder is not the real issue (what we do), but anger (what we are), adultery is not the real issue (what we do) but lust (what we are). The external manifestations of our sin, which are visible and therefore conspicuous, are only a symptom of the real problem, our poverty of spirit. We do what we do because we are what we are, and if the measure in which we seek God's help is to *change what we do*, rather than attending to *what we are*, we will find ourselves continually doing the same things again and again, despite the sincerity of our repentance. It is when we honestly mourn our condition we begin to discover some solution!

To those who mourn, Jesus said 'they will be comforted'. They will not be condemned, not written off as a dead loss, but 'comforted'. Comforted by whom? By the Comforter. Who is the Comforter? It is a title given by Jesus to the Holy Spirit on several occasions. The word Jesus used here, translated comforter is *parakaleo*. The title Jesus gave to the Holy Spirit in John 14:26; 15:26 and 16:7 is *Parakletos*. Parakaleo is the verb of the noun Parakletos. It is not an easy word to translate into English, sometimes rendered Counsellor or Advocate, and its meaning is to 'draw alongside', to act as one who pleads as a substitute for another (as in a court of law). It is in response to the disposition of repentance (mourning) that the Comforter, the Holy Spirit, does his work in our lives. And what is his work? It is to *replace all that I am, with all that he is.*

The Holy Spirit's role in the life of a Christian is not one of *repairing* what he is but of *replacing* what he is. He replaces our poverty with his riches. He replaces our defeat with his victory. He replaces our weakness with his strength. He replaces our sin with his righteousness. That is very comforting! The Christian life does not depend on our ability to change, but on the ability of the Holy Spirit, whose life fills our lives in response to repentance, and lives the life of Jesus within us.

3. Blessed are the meek, for they will inherit the earth

The logical and inevitable consequence of being aware of our poverty of spirit and mourning that poverty, is to become meek. To be meek is not to be weak or spineless, but to be submissive and humble. Recognising our poverty and mourning that poverty we have no grounds for anything but genuine humility, and glad, free submission to Christ as Lord. As the mourning of our poverty corresponds to the fulness of the Holy Spirit, so our meekness corresponds to the Lordship of Christ.

The Lordship of Jesus Christ in the life of his people is not an optional-extra to the Christian life, but an indispensable ingredient. Paul writes, 'For this very reason, Christ died and returned to life so that he might be the Lord of both the dead and the living' (Rom. 14:9). Jesus Christ is spoken of as 'Saviour', twenty five times in the New Testament, but he is described as 'Lord' over six hundred times. It is wonderfully true he saves, but his saving activity cannot be detached from his Lordship, and the disposition of a healthy wholesome Christian life is one of meek, humble submission to him as Lord.

Of the meek, Jesus said, 'they will inherit the earth'. He does not say 'they will inherit heaven', though they will, but 'they will inherit the earth'. It is the person who has faced their poverty of spirit, who mourns that poverty, who submits themselves meekly to Jesus Christ on earth who discovers what life on earth is all about. Every human being living on earth, has a blueprint for their lives compiled in heaven. David wrote, 'My frame was not hidden from you when I was made in the secret place. When I was woven together in the depths of the earth, your eyes saw my unformed body. All the days ordained for me were written in your book before one of them came to be' (Ps. 139:15-16). Before I was ever born, David says, God had a plan compiled before my conception. This does not mean its implementation is automatic, for it is not. We may live in complete disregard of God, his ways and his will, but to become a Christian involves, amongst other things, coming back under his authority and being taken up again with his interests and his purposes. It is at that point, life on earth makes sense, and every new day is filled with possibilities and potential.

But what if we know nothing of 'inheriting the earth' in this way? What if our life is not lived with confidence in his purpose? Let me suggest why. We are not meek. It is the meek who inherit the earth. If we are not meek, it is because we are not mourning our condition. If we are not mourning, it is because we are not aware of our poverty of spirit. We still think we have what it takes to be what we are supposed to be, and if we do not know our poverty of spirit, we will not be happy! These are the first three ingredients of true happiness – makarios style – according to Jesus and he knew exactly what he was talking about.

8.

The ingredients of true happiness (5:1-12)

Part 2

We began to look in the last chapter at the eight ingredients of true happiness, according to Jesus. Facing our poverty of spirit, we mourn our poverty and discover at that point the Comforter, the Holy Spirit, replaces our weakness with his strength, our poverty with his riches, and our sin with his righteousness. Our logical response is meekness, where in humility we submit ourselves in obedience to Christ as Lord, and discover life on earth has meaning and purpose – we 'inherit the earth'.

So far all of this addresses the fundamental issues we must come to terms with in order to become and be a Christian. Then what kind of evidence should we expect? The next three beatitudes give us three essential evidences.

4. Blessed are those who hunger and thirst for righteousness for they will be filled

The first evidence of wholesome life is healthy appetite. Hunger and thirst are the strongest physical cravings a person can have, and Jesus applies them to our attitude to righteousness. Righteousness is not some pious stance, a large Bible held at a correct angle across the chest with the head at the corresponding angle adorned with a permanent smile, the body somehow giving the impression of gliding along six inches above the ground! Righteousness is behaviour. It is doing what is right. The only valid evidence of the fulness of Jesus Christ in a person's life is their behaviour. This is not the cause of his fulness, it is the expression of it. It is a desire for likeness to Christ in moral character and conduct that gives evidence of his presence.

Jesus did not say, 'Blessed are those who are righteous ...', but those who 'hunger and thirst for righteousness'. To hunger and thirst is to long for something that as yet I don't have. At five in the afternoon I may be hungry. At seven I am not. What is the difference? At five my appetite is awake and I want to eat. By seven I have finished a meal and am no longer hungry. The evidence of Jesus Christ in a person's life is not that they are righteous, but that they have an appetite for it. In this life we will always be characterised by failure, and if we look inside ourselves with any degree of honesty we will be more conscious of that than anyone else. Sometimes I talk to people who say, 'I am sick of my sin and my failure', and it is precisely that which is the evidence God is at work in them.

Appetite is not self produced. You cannot will yourself to be hungry. You can create the environment for hunger, but hunger and thirst are symptoms. To face up to our poverty of spirit, not to hide or cover it, but to mourn and meekly submit to Christ as Lord, is the source of an appetite for righteousness. From that appetite comes a deep sense of fulness and satisfaction, for Jesus said, 'they will be filled'. The satisfaction is not with oneself, but with Christ who 'has become for us ... our righteousness....' (1 Cor. 1:30). Our satisfaction is not in our own performance but in the righteousness of Jesus Christ which he now shares with us.

But how is that righteousness to be expressed? The next ingredient tells us.

5. Blessed are the merciful for they will be shown mercy

One of the expressions of a hunger for righteousness is mercy. This is an interesting statement of Jesus for he does not say, 'Blessed are those who are shown mercy for they will be merciful', which we may have expected. Rather it is, 'Blessed are the merciful ...' those who show mercy, 'for they will be shown mercy'. There is an important spiritual principle here. God is not pouring his blessing, his mercy and his grace willy-nilly. The condition to receiving from God is giving. We pointed out earlier that the Sermon on the Mount was not addressed to the crowd who listened – it was not an evangelistic sermon – but to the disciples. 'His disciples came to him and he began to teach *them* saying ...' (5:2). This principle does not apply to those outside of Christ, teaching that to receive from God they must first give, but it does apply to living the Christian life.

This principle is repeated elsewhere. In the 'Lord's prayer' Jesus says, 'Forgive us our debts as we have forgiven our debtors ...' (6:12). In other words he is teaching us to pray as a Christian, 'Forgive me my sins in exactly the same way I forgive other people their sins'. The principle is the same – the condition to receiving from God is giving. In that context Jesus went on to say, 'If you do not forgive men their sins, your Father will not forgive your sins' (6:15). This is not a condition to becoming a Christian, but it is a condition for maintaining a wholesome growing relationship with the Lord Jesus Christ, and is in fact a result of our receiving the mercy and forgiveness of the Lord Jesus Christ in the first place. Paul wrote to the Colossians, 'Bear with each other, and forgive whatever grievances you may have against one another. Forgive as the Lord forgave you' (Col. 3:13). We forgive as he forgave us, but it is as we forgive he goes on forgiving.

Later still Jesus said, 'Whoever wants to save his life must lose it, but whoever loses his life for me will save it' (16:25). This criteria for receiving life is losing it. For now we are concerned only with the principle: the condition to receiving is giving. The extent to which we know the enrichment of God in our lives is the extent to which we allow ourselves to be an enrichment to others.

I remember an elderly man praying to God in a meeting, 'Thank you we are not called to be like cups but pipes'. He didn't explain himself, and was perhaps referring to something said earlier which I had missed, but the image struck me forcibly. A cup is something which, when it is full, is full. We like that idea. However a pipe is different. Everything poured in at one end will flow out through the other.

This is the idea Jesus spoke about when he said, ' "If anyone is thirsty, let him come to me and drink. Whoever believes in me as the Scripture has said, streams of living water will flow from within him". By this he meant the Spirit ...' (John 7:37-39). If you are thirsty, said Jesus in effect, do not remain thirsty, come to me and drink. But that is not the end result, 'streams of living water will flow from within him'. There will be an overflow from your life of that which God has put in you. John adds, 'By this he meant the Spirit'. This is the work of the Holy Spirit.

Looking after ourselves first has little to do with the Christian life, but we will be looked after when our interests become the interests of other people. If you really want to know the blessing of God in your life, don't just pray, 'Lord bless me' but pray, 'Lord make me a blessing', and you will be blessed. If you really want God to teach you something, don't just pray, 'Lord teach me something new', but 'Lord help me to teach somebody something useful today', and you will learn. The condition to receiving is giving.

That in turn will lead to the next ingredient in happiness:

6. Blessed are the pure in heart, for they will see God

There are three words for 'pure' in the New Testament. The word used here is the word 'katharos'. It may be used to speak of something pure in the sense of being clean, but its more general usage is of being unmixed with other things. For an example, if wine has not been diluted with water it may be described as 'katharos', that is pure wine. It may not be good wine and may even taste like vinegar, but it is pure wine in the sense it is not mixed and diluted. This is the thrust of this statement. It is not a purity of heart in the sense of being perfect in heart, but in the sense of being unmixed with other things.

The word 'single-minded' is probably a good description. It is the kind of thing Paul spoke of when he wrote, 'this one thing I do ...' (Phil. 3:13). He did not say, 'these twenty five things I dabble with. One of them is my Christianity, but I have many other interests too'. He says, 'this one thing I do'. That does not mean he had no other interests, but that everything else in his life derived its place and its significance from this central spinal cord to which everything else was attached, '... one thing I do ... I press on toward the goal ... for which God has called me heavenward in Christ Jesus' (Phil. 3:13-14). He is saying that God has a goal to which Paul has been called, and that goal is 'to reveal his Son in me' (Gal. 1:16). Anything which hinders or obstructs that goal is to be jettisoned. The Psalmist prays, '... give me an undivided heart ...' (Ps. 86:11). You may be sure that the secular will always swallow the sacred in a divided heart.

Those who are pure in heart, 'will see God'. This is not referring to a physical seeing of God for one day '... every eye will see him, even those who pierced him' (Rev. 1:7). But when single-minded in our disposition towards God, we shall see him all around us. We will see him in creation. 'The heavens declare the glory of God, the skies proclaim the work of his hands' (Ps. 19:1), and all of creation reveals something of the Creator. When an artist paints a picture he normally does two things. He copies something, and he expresses himself. If you look at a work of Picasso you may quickly recognise it was a woman he was painting, but you will probably conclude Picasso saw things differently from the way you do! His art may tell us something about the woman he painted, but it tells us more about Picasso himself. When God, the supreme artist, created the universe, he did only one of those two things. He did not copy anything for there was nothing to copy, he only expressed himself. George Wade Robinson wrote these words:

> Heaven above is softer blue,
> earth around is sweeter green,
> Something lives in every hue,
> *Christless eyes have never seen,*
> Birds with gladder songs o'erflow,
> flowers with deeper beauties shine,
> Since I know as now I know,
> I am his and he is mine.

He says there are beauties that, 'Christless eyes have never seen'. When Jesus lives in our lives there is a new appreciation of beauty, for behind the creation is the mind and heart of the Creator.

We will also see God in circumstances. We need no longer fear the events we did not anticipate or which seem bigger than ourselves, for 'we see God' in his sovereignty working out purposes that are good. Paul assured the Romans, 'God works for the good of those who love him and who have been called according to his purpose' (Rom. 8:28). Any event which may frighten us will not frighten him, and the pure in heart, whose minds are set on his interests, will see God.

If the first three beatitudes speak of the foundation of Christian experience, and the next three speak of the features of characteristics of Christian experience, the last two speak of the fruit, or impact, of Christian experience. What kind of impact is this person going to make on the world?

7. Blessed are the peacemakers for they will be called sons of God

The first impact is that of a peacemaker. If there is something our world desperately needs it is peacemakers, but what does this mean? Is this referring to those who sit in the United Nations discussing the trouble spots of the world with a view to putting them right? We may be grateful for the U.N. but I don't think this, or its equivalent, is what Jesus is referring to. There is no doubt the world is filled with strife, but what is its cause? We are well aware of the symptoms, vividly portrayed on our news bulletins each day, but what is their cause?

Some time ago I was speaking to a High School class of fourteen year olds, and we talked about what they thought was wrong with the world. It did not take long for them to identify the most fundamental problem as being people! I then asked them to suggest what they thought was wrong with people. Various ones gave some instance or other from the news or from personal experience, that they thought typified some of what was wrong. We then tried to reduce each problem to a one word description which I wrote on the blackboard in the front of the room. We ended up with an interesting list that included words like greed, selfishness, pride, jealousy etc. Everyone agreed these words probably described the basic problem with the world.

I then asked them if they thought they had anyone in that class who was greedy, or selfish, or proud or jealous. They were a little taken aback, but quickly began to point to each other and give me some names of who was greedy, who was selfish, etc. etc. I asked them to recognise they had a serious problem here. We had earlier discussed trouble spots in far off distant lands, crime and debauchery reported in the national newspapers and we had all been agreed about those people 'out there'. I pointed out the problems they had identified in the world were actually right there in the classroom. So I asked them what kind of family they came from, and was there anyone in their family who was proud, greedy, selfish and occasionally jealous. The boys tended to agree their big sisters were like that and the girls tended to agree their little brothers were like that, and most thought their parents could get that way too! I pointed out this was serious – the problem was not just in the world outside, it was not just in their classroom, it was in their own homes. I then singled out one boy, pointed to him and said, 'Are you ever greedy? Do you ever get jealous? Have you sometimes been a bit selfish?' He replied incongruously, 'Me?' I said, 'Yes. You'. He said, 'I don't know'. The rest of the class joined in unison, 'Yes, you have'. I thought that might happen, so quickly pointed to another who seemed the most vocal and said, 'What about you?'. He answered, 'Well I suppose so'. I said, 'Don't say, "I suppose so". Is it Yes or No?!' He then said 'Yes'. I pointed to another, then another, then another and went to almost everyone in the room, asked them the same question and despite some smart answers to begin with they eventually said, 'Yes'. I said to them, 'Now we are getting somewhere. What is wrong with the world? You are. I am.'

This is the whole point. James writes, 'What causes fights and quarrels among you? Don't they come from your desires that battle within you' (Jas. 4:1). All the problems we recognise in our world are symptoms of what is going on within us. To be a true peacemaker is not to impose some structure on the symptoms (that has its important place, but the same causes will express themselves in other symptoms again) but to go to the source. The greatest need of every human being cannot be met because of their alienation from God. It is reconciliation with God that brings *peace with God* (see Rom. 5:1), which in turn leads to experiencing the *peace of God* (see Phil. 4:7). One of the great privileges of the Christian life is that having come to peace with God ourselves we share the means of peace with those whose deepest need is to know Christ. We become a peacemaker! This concern is an inevitable and unavoidable consequence of the previous six ingredients in the list of beatitudes being in place.

The peacemakers, said Jesus, will be 'called sons of God'. In bringing others to peace with God we share the ministry of the Son of God. God's business in his Son is, '... to reconcile to himself all things ... by making peace through his blood, shed on the cross' (Col. 1:20). Paul writes of the ministry of Christ, 'For he himself is our peace ... thus making peace ... He came and preached peace ...' (Eph. 2:14-17).

When we share the message of, 'peace through his blood, shed on the cross', one of two things may happen. There will be those who respond and come to peace, there will be those who react and persecute.

8. Blessed are those who are persecuted because of righteousness, for theirs is the kingdom of heaven

To be an active witness to the Lord Jesus Christ will lead to persecution. Paul promised his young colleague Timothy, 'Everyone who wants to live a godly life in Christ Jesus will be persecuted' (2 Tim. 3:12). That is a promise! It is not the kind of promise we would wish to memorise or pin on the wall, but we should remember it and not be taken by surprise. Persecution may come in various ways. 'Blessed are you when people insult you' (i.e. to your face), 'persecute you' (i e. perhaps involving physical violence), 'and falsely say all kinds of evil against you because of me' (i.e. behind your back). 'Rejoice and be glad, because great is your reward in heaven, for in the same way they persecuted the prophets who were before you' (5:11-12). The response is not to 'react and get mad', but to 'rejoice and be glad', for two reasons: one, because we are in good company 'they persecuted the prophets before you' and we stand in an unbroken line from Abel, who stood his ground and paid the price, to our own day; and two, because 'great is your reward in heaven'.

Persecution has so often in history had a positive effect on the church. The saying, 'the blood of the martyrs is the seed of the church' has proved itself time and time again. Peter wrote his first epistle to suffering and persecuted Christians whom he described as, 'strangers in the world' (1 Pet 1:1). He said to them, 'In this you greatly rejoice, though now for a little while you may have to suffer grief in all kinds of trials. These have come so that your faith – of greater worth than gold ... may be proved genuine' (1 Pet. 1:6-7). Persecution is never God's choice as it is the result of evil intent, but he is never out manoeuvred by it. We learn more from the hard times than we do from the good times. We grow faster under pressure than we do in the calm.

But what if no one persecutes me? Don't go looking for it, but if no one is ever troubled by you it may be because you are not a *peacemaker*. People neither react against you, nor do they respond to you. It is the peacemaker who is persecuted! If you are not a peacemaker, it will be because you are not *pure in heart*, that is, single minded with a 'this one thing I do' sense of direction. If you are not pure in heart, it may be because you are not *merciful*, more concerned to give than to receive. If you are not merciful, it may be because you are not *hungering and thirsting after righteousness*, concerned with what is right. If you are not hungering for righteousness, it may be because you are not *meek*, humbly submitting yourself to Christ as Lord. If you are not meek it may be because you are not *mourning* the condition of your own bankruptcy. If you are not mourning, it may be because you do not really know you are *poor in Spirit*, but still think you have what it takes to be what you are supposed to be. If you do not recognise your poverty of spirit, you are not happy – *makarios* style!

This list of beatitudes is not a disjointed list of unrelated qualities, they are inextricably linked together, each building on the next to present a portrait of the ingredients of true happiness.

9.

Salt and light
(5:13-16)

The most important thing about any of us is not what we do, but what we are. To the person described in the eight beatitudes covered in the previous two chapters, Jesus said, 'You are the salt of the earth' (5:13) and 'You are the light of the world' (5:14). The true influence we exercise in the world derives more from what we are than from anything we might do. What we do is of course important, but it never speaks as loudly as what we are. The effectiveness of what we say to others (what they *hear*), depends largely on the nature of our relationship with them (how they *feel* about us), which in turn derives from what we *are* (what they see in us). What they *see* determines how they *feel*; how they feel determines how they *hear*. Paul wrote boldly to the Philippians, 'Whatever you have learned or received or heard from me, or seen in me – put into practice' (Phil. 4:9). He invites the Philippians to not only listen but to watch! The credibility of what they hear will be determined by the integrity in what they see. To quote an old dictum, 'The most important things in life are *caught*, not *taught*'.

Both salt and light affect their environment. In the last beatitude Jesus speaks of the impact of the world on the Christian when he says, 'Blessed are you when people insult you, persecute you and falsely say all kinds of evil against you because of me' (5:11). Now he describes the impact of the Christian on the world, 'You are the salt of the earth ... You are the light of the world ...'. In saying this, Jesus warns it is possible the, 'salt may lose its saltiness', and people may put their light, 'under a bowl' with the inevitable result that we are 'thrown out and trampled by men' and the light is to no one's benefit. There is no guarantee of perpetual 'saltiness', or that of perpetual 'light'. Both must be maintained through disciplined dependency on God.

Salt

1. It is used as a preservative

There are several main functions to salt. In primitive societies it was, and still is, used primarily as a preservative. I have seen meat and fish caked in it to halt the process of perishing.

When the Bible speaks of perishing it is not primarily speaking of a future state but a current condition. Paul writes in the present tense, '... the message of the cross is foolishness to those who *are* perishing' (1 Cor. 1:18); 'For we are to God the aroma of Christ among those who are being saved and those who *are* perishing' (2 Cor. 2:15); '... if our gospel is veiled, it is veiled to those who *are* perishing' (2 Cor. 4:3). There is of course a future aspect to the process, as when Jesus said, 'Unless you repent you too will all perish' (Luke 13:3), but that is the ultimate consequence of the present condition. Perishing is a process. There is only one ultimate alternative to the state of perishing, and that is replace that process with another process, 'eternal life'. In his gospel John sets the contrast, 'For God so loved the world that he gave his one and only Son that whoever believes in him shall not perish but have eternal life' (John 3:16), and 'I give them eternal life, and they shall never perish' (John 10:28). It is the reception of eternal life that halts and replaces the process of perishing. As the salt of the earth, God's strategy is that the presence of his people in the world is his means of activating that new process, by introducing people to Christ, the source of eternal life. 'How can they hear without someone preaching to them?' (Rom. 10:14).

2. It is associated with purity

The Old Testament depicts this in the story of Elisha cleansing a well in Jericho (see 2 Kgs. 2:19-22). The people complained to Elisha of the water being, 'bad and unproductive'. He asked for a bowl of salt, and threw the salt into the spring that served the well saying, 'This is what the Lord says, "I have healed this water. Never again will it cause death or make the land unproductive"'.

Salt could also indicate the very opposite of purity, and render land unproductive, as shown in God's judgement on Israel in the wilderness, 'the whole land will be a burning waste of salt and sulphur – nothing planted, nothing sprouting, no vegetation growing on it. It will be like the destruction of Sodom and Gomorrah....' (Deut. 29:23), and again when Abimelech captured the city of Shechem, 'he destroyed the city and scattered salt over it' (Judg. 9:45), as a sign of its desolation. Although the distribution of salt in these instances was as a judgement, that judgement was a declaration of the moral character of God, and a symbol therefore of the purity which had been violated.

It is as 'salt of the earth' God portrays his purity through his people. The purity of Jesus did not condemn the sinner, it made him attractive to them. It is one of the remarkable features of Jesus' life that although no one was as pure as he, yet those in the gutters of society, the tax collectors, the prostitutes and the outcasts felt attracted by his company. Genuine purity does not so much expose the impurities of those around, as raise their sights and stimulate them to seek something better. This is the difference between true righteousness, that comes from God, and self righteousness that comes from our own self discipline, so often motivated by an ego which has a vested interest in an image of righteousness. Self righteousness always condemns the unrighteous and makes them unwelcome. God's righteousness attracts the unrighteous. It is to display God's righteousness, with its source in the Holy Spirit, that we are called to be salt!

These first two effects of salt in Scripture are the more significant, but there are one or two aspects, perhaps more superficial, but nevertheless worth commenting upon.

3. It gives flavour
This is probably the most common idea associated with salt in our western world. Salt draws out the distinctive flavour of food, and without it some foods seem insipid and unattractive. It is the Christian that should bring flavour to life. There is a radiance, a fulness of life, a security, a sense of joy, an appreciation of beauty and an atmosphere of vitality that ought to characterise the Christian and set them apart as alert and alive in a drab, dysfunctional world. So often the reverse is true! William Barclay quotes the Roman Emperor Julian (who succeeded Constantine after he made Christianity the religion of the empire following his own conversion to Christ), who wanted to withdraw the recognition given to Christianity on these grounds, 'Have you looked at these Christians closely? Hollow-eyed, pale cheeked, flat breasted all; they brood their lives away, unspurred by ambition: the sun shines for them, but they do not see it: the earth offers them its fulness, but they desire it not; all their desire is to

renounce and to suffer that they may come to die'.[1] What a sad, dismal
and pathetic picture, but it has been a feature of some Christians in
every age to withdraw from the world rather than be characterised
by a true sense of mission in the world, to be defensive rather than
vibrant, to be in the wings rather than centre stage, to be re-active
rather than pro-active! The attractiveness of the Living Christ in the
Christian speaks of life and health and vitality.

4. It creates thirst
At the end of an address I gave on this passage of Scripture, a young
man suggested to me that an important feature of salt is that it creates
thirst. He was right. It is not only what we say about the gospel that
points people to Christ, it is the quality of life we ourselves have found
and enjoy in him which creates a thirst in others for God. Certainly the
reverse is true. There is little that adversely affects people's attitude
to Jesus Christ more than the absence of spiritual reality in those who
claim to know God.

It is for this reason there is a warning in Jesus' statement too. 'If
salt loses its saltiness, how can it be made salty again? It is no longer
good for anything, except to be thrown out and trampled by men'
(5:13). The essential quality of salt is the difference it brings to the
environment in which it is placed. It resists the perishing process, it
brings purity into decay and it brings taste to what may otherwise
be bland. But Jesus warns it may lose its saltiness. It may no longer
be distinctive, its essential difference may be lost. In such cases it is
trampled underfoot by others who see nothing of its value, and tread
it into the ground. This is the sad possibility for every Christian who
is not content with the distinctives that set them apart. The world
won't persecute him (5:12), but neither will it respect him (5:13).

There are no grounds for opting out of the world. Conversely we are
mandated by Jesus to go into the world. In his prayer for the disciples
in the Upper Room immediately prior to his arrest and crucifixion,
Jesus prayed to his Father, 'My prayer is not that you take them out
of the world, but that you will protect them from the evil one. They
are not of the world, even as I am not of it ... As you have sent me into
the world, I have sent them into the world' (John 17:15-18). Separation

---

[1] William Barclay, 'The Daily Study Bible, Gospel of Matthew Vol. I'. St.
Andrew Press, Edinburgh 1975.

from worldliness is not isolation from the world. Worldliness is an attitude to be resisted at all costs. John described the essential nature of worldliness when he wrote, 'Do not love the world nor anything in the world ... For everything that is in the world – the cravings of sinful man, the lust of his eyes, and the boasting of what he has and does – comes not from the Father but from the world' (1 John 2:15-16). The more poetic language of some other translations, 'the lust of the flesh, the lust of the eyes and the pride of life', describes the disposition that is in conflict with Christ.

Worldliness is an attitude of life that seeks the fulfilment of my own desires, the satisfaction of my own agenda and the feeding of my own ego. This has very little to do with the environment in which we live and work, it has everything to do with the attitudes that govern us within them. It is a mistake to see our main battle grounds as external, for they are internal. We may so engineer our circumstances to live in isolation from the world at large, yet be completely 'worldly' in the sense in which John speaks. Our motivation for a detachment from the world may even be the 'pride of life' – proud to be holy! Worldliness is to be resisted, but the world itself is our workshop. It is there our lives, our relationships and our behaviour become an exhibition of Jesus Christ to those around us. It is his indwelling presence that equips us to function as salt.

Light

Jesus' statement, 'You are the light of the world' is particularly interesting in the light of the fact he said elsewhere, 'I am the light of the world' (John 9:5). However on the latter occasion he qualified it, 'While I am in the world, I am the light of the world'. The implication is clear, 'What I am whilst here, in terms of bringing illumination to the world, you will be when I am not here'. What I am, you are to be.

How are we to be what Christ was? It is not so much by *imitation* as it is by *derivation*. If it is by *imitation*, then I am to be the source of the reproduced light. I may be congratulated or criticised on the quality of light, but the source is within myself. The buck stops with me! If this light is by *derivation* the source is outside of myself. To derive is to draw from an objective source. We bear clear responsibility for the extent to which the light is visible, but it is not self produced, for it derives from a source. It is probably unwise to impose an example of modern day electricity onto the ancient context of Scripture, but there is an obvious illustration of this. A light bulb is never to be congratulated on its ability to shine! It bears some responsibility of course, for it may fail to give expression to the electricity to which it is connected, but the visible light that emanates from the bulb has its origin in the electrical source. Take the same bulb and detach it from the electrical supply and there may be nothing wrong with the bulb in itself, but it is completely incapable of shining. Trying to shine by *imitating* other light bulbs will not help. It will only shine by *deriving* its light from another source. Whether it is the light that comes from the wick in an oil lamp, or a wick in a candle, the consistency of light does not come from the wick itself. Left to its own resources the wick would burn itself out very quickly. Its constancy comes from the oil or the wax from which it derives its energy.

There is only one possibility of being 'the light of the world', and that is through a relationship with Jesus Christ which allows him to be in us, what he was himself, here on earth. He does not teach us how to shine as a technique, for he is himself, the light. Jesus said of John the Baptist, 'John was a lamp that burned and gave light, and you chose for a time to enjoy his light' (John 5:35). John was the lamp. He was the vehicle through which the light was expressed. This is the sense in which we, in our dark, confused world, are the light of the world.

When Simeon took the baby Jesus in his arms, he declared him, '... a light for revelation to the Gentiles' (Luke 2:32). John describes Jesus as, 'The true light that gives light to every man ...' (John 1:9). The whole thrust of 'light' is that it exists for the benefit of others. Putting our own interests first, finding personal fulfilment in shining, has little to do with our function as light. Its function is to bring benefit to others, that ultimately this light, as Jesus said, might be to people, 'the light of life' (John 8:12). Paul tells the Philippian Christians to be, 'blameless and pure, children of God without fault in a crooked and depraved generation, in which you shine like stars in the universe' (Phil. 2:15). Like pinpricks of light in the dark night sky, by which lost and lonely travellers have always been able to find their way home. This is our function!

A lamp is of no value tucked away under a bowl, says Jesus, it is intended to give light to everyone in the house. The life of a person indwelt by Jesus Christ is intended itself to be a message that people can read. As Jesus Christ, the incarnate God was the 'light of the world', so we now are, in the words of Paul, '... a letter from Christ, ... written not with ink but with the Spirit of the living God, not on tablets of stone but on tablets of human hearts' (2 Cor. 3:3). God reveals himself in us, and our lives become part of the message God has for the world. Francis of Assisi, it is said, when sending his men out to evangelise would say something to the effect, 'By every possible means preach Christ as you go. If necessary use words'. It is the evidence of Jesus Christ living within us that gives credibility to anything we might say.

It is because the origin of the light is in God, not ourselves, that Jesus says, 'Let your light shine before men, that they may see your good deeds and praise your Father in heaven' (5:16). What they see is 'your good deeds', what they recognise is 'your Father in heaven'. Our behaviour ceases to be explained in human terms, and is instead the consequence of the invasion of deity into our weak, failing humanity, so that God is recognised and God is praised. This is the light that shines and has impact!

10.

Understanding the law
(5:17-48)

If in the first section of the Sermon on the Mount, Jesus talks about the *Character of a Christian* (5:1-16, the beatitudes and being salt and light), then in the larger and remaining part (5:17–7:27) he talks of the *Conduct of a Christian*. This can be divided into teaching on the law (5:17-48), on reputation (6:1-18), treasure (6:19-34) and priorities (7:1-27). I pointed out earlier that the first part concerns what we are intended to *BE*, and the second part, what we are intended to *DO*. The relationship between these two aspects is crucial to understand. The teaching on *conduct* is only possible having understood and embraced Jesus' teaching on *character*. We do not evolve from conduct to character, rather we evolve from character to conduct. By becoming right in our disposition towards God we do what is right as an outworking consequence. Jesus is saviour before teacher. Fail to understand this and his teaching on behaviour becomes not only legalism, (an external imposition), but unreasonable to the point of being impossible. To the conscientious reader his teaching will produce despair!

For this reason, when Jesus begins to speak about the law, its demands and obligations, he does so in a way that is completely new. He does not speak in terms of what we must do for him (the terms of the Old Covenant), but in terms of what he will do for us (the terms of the New Covenant), 'I have not come to abolish the law ... but to fulfil them' (5:17).

It is important to distinguish between the various aspects of law given by God to Moses on Mount Sinai, so as to avoid any confusion. There are three categories of law in the Old Testament. There is the *ceremonial law*, the rituals and regulations by which a person could approach God. It centred on a representative priesthood, on blood sacrifices and a tabernacle, and later a temple. Much of the second half of Exodus and the book of Leviticus deal with the terms and details of this. The demands of this law however, were fulfilled and abolished by the work of Jesus Christ as a full and final sacrifice for sin. Speaking of this the book of Hebrews states, 'The law is only a shadow of the good things that are coming – not the realities themselves' (Heb. 10:1). At the moment Jesus cried from the cross, 'It is finished', the curtain of the temple in Jerusalem which divided the Holy Place from the Most Holy Place (entered only once a year by the High Priest on the Day of Atonement) was torn in two from top to bottom (27:51). Now God was not approached through a curtain, by a priest, with animal blood in his hands, he is approachable by any person, anywhere, at any time, on the basis of the blood of Jesus. Since that moment every priest has been out of a job, and every altar redundant. The ceremonial law was abolished, and is not the aspect referred to in the Sermon on the Mount.

Secondly, there is the *civil law*, which God gave as the constitutional law for ordering the national life of Israel as a theocracy. It concerns itself with obligations and responsibilities, marriage and family, crime and punishment, and the myriad of detail enabling a society to function in a civilised and wholesome way. There is no suggestion this was intended for universal application outside the domestic affairs of Israel itself, and is not the aspect referred to in the Sermon on the Mount.

The third category of law is the *moral law*, the ten commandments given by God as the standard of behaviour for all people, in all places and at all times. It is this aspect of the law Jesus speaks about in this passage.

The basis of conduct is enshrined in the moral law of God. This section begins with three general statements about the law of God which we may summarise as follows.

The law is realistic (v. 17)
'Do not think I have come to abolish the Law or the Prophets; I have not come to abolish them but to fulfil them' (5:17). We will look later at the full implications of this, but for the moment point out that the thrust of this statement is that their demand is realistic, what they call for is accessible. It may not appear to be so from a human perspective, but as we shall later see, from the divine perspective, the law is utterly realistic.

The law is relevant (v. 18)

Jesus said, '... until heaven and earth disappear, not the smallest letter, not the least stroke of a pen, will by any means disappear from the law until everything is accomplished' (5:18). In other words he states that the law is more secure than the earth on which we stand, and even more secure than the heavens above us. These may disappear, but the law remains intact! It is as timeless as eternity, as relevant in every century as it was when first given. We will discuss later why this is so.

The law is right (v. 19)

'Anyone who breaks one of the least of these commandments and teaches others to do the same will be called least in the kingdom of heaven, but whoever practices and teaches these commands will be called great in the kingdom of heaven' (5:19). Greatness in the kingdom of heaven has a direct relationship with conformity to the law, and the violation of the law has a direct relationship to being, 'least in the kingdom of heaven'.

If the anxiety level of the listeners to this Sermon on the Mount was not already rising as they heard the demands of the old law so underlined, reinforced and insisted on, they would have been stunned by the following statement, 'For I tell you that unless your righteousness surpasses that of the Pharisees and the teachers of the law, you will certainly not enter the kingdom of heaven' (5:20). The Pharisees and the Scribes (the teachers of the law) were those who instructed others in the demands and details of the law, so it is reasonable to suppose they at least made some attempt to keep them! The Pharisees were renowned for their discipline and strict observance of the law in all its facets. They tithed their money, were careful about the company they kept, the clothes they wore, and the food they ate, in order to conform fully to the law. To avoid breaking the law God gave Moses, they made hundreds of secondary laws to surround the real law to prevent them getting anywhere close to breaking God's law. Now Jesus said, 'unless your righteousness surpasses that ... you will not enter the kingdom of heaven'. What was he talking about? What is this righteousness?

We will try to understand this under three headings. We will look first at, *The demand of righteousness*, and ask what was Jesus actually demanding of the people in a righteousness that surpasses the Pharisees and Scribes. Then we will talk about, *The dynamics of righteousness*, and ask what the resources are to fulfil these demands. Thirdly, we will look at, *The disciplines of righteousness*, and see what Jesus says in this chapter about the role of discipline in the whole exercise.

The demand of righteousness
Jesus explains this with six statements that follow a similar formula: 'You have heard that it was said.... But I tell you....'. When he says, 'You have heard that it was said...', he quotes a statement that represents the righteousness of the Pharisees and Scribes. But, when he adds, 'But I tell you...' he speaks of the righteousness demanded by him. The righteousness of the Scribes and Pharisees may have been entirely legitimate, and in most cases involved a direct quotation from the Old Testament scriptures, but which nevertheless carried a subtle flaw. Their righteousness was external, and dealt with activity. The righteousness of Jesus was internal and dealt with the attitudes from which the activities sprang.

'You have heard that it was said, ... "Do not murder"' (5:21). That is one of the ten commandments, and the Scribes and Pharisees enthusiastically observed that law. It had to do with activity and external behaviour. 'But I tell you, "Anyone who is angry with his brother will be subject to judgement"' (5:22). If murder is an effect, anger is a cause. If murder has to do with external activity, anger has to do with internal attitude. It is not the righteous effect, Jesus speaks about, but the righteous cause. It is more than growing righteous fruit, it is having righteous roots! You may be angry with someone without the opportunity or courage to murder them, but the opportunity to murder is irrelevant to the attitude of mind.

'You have heard that it was said, "Do not commit adultery"' (5:27). That is also a direct statement from the ten commandments, and the Scribes and Pharisees enthusiastically kept that law. It has to do with activity and external behaviour. 'But I tell you that anyone who looks at a woman lustfully has already committed adultery with her in his heart' (5:28). If adultery is an effect, lust is a cause. If adultery has to do with external activity, lust has to do with internal attitude. Again it is not a righteous effect Jesus talks about, but a righteous cause. It has more to do with root than fruit. A man may lust after a woman without the opportunity or courage to invite her to bed with him, but the opportunity of adultery is only a development of the attitude of mind.

'It has been said, "Anyone who divorces his wife must give her a certificate of divorce". But I tell you that anyone who divorces his wife except for marital unfaithfulness, causes her to commit adultery' (5:31-32). The righteousness of the Pharisees and Scribes said that if you are going to divorce your wife, do so legally and tidily. Make it respectable! Don't just walk out, give her a certificate. The righteousness of Jesus says in effect, 'Do not do it at all'. True righteousness is not found in a means to legitimise your divorce legally, but in the attitude towards your wife that does not allow for divorce at all. (Under Jewish law women could not divorce their husbands, only husbands their wives. Roman law permitted woman to divorce too, as was possible in Corinth. cf. 1 Corinthians 7.10-11). Jesus does speak here of the exception, 'except for marital unfaithfulness', but it is the unfaithfulness of the partner that has already broken the bond, not the initiative of the person who has 'given a certificate' to legally dispose of his wife. In a later chapter (Matt. 19) Jesus talks in more detail about marriage and divorce and we will examine them more fully then, but the point here is that it is the attitude of a man to his wife that makes his marriage unbreakable.

'Again you have heard that it was said to the people long ago, "Do not break your oath, but keep the oaths you have made to the Lord". But I tell you, Do not swear at all ... Simply let your "Yes" be "Yes" and your "No" be "No"; anything beyond this comes from the evil one' (5:33-37). We are not obligated to be truthful because we swore to be truthful, we are obligated to be truthful because we spoke! It is not the external demand of an oath, but the internal demand of integrity and honesty that is the righteousness required by Jesus, 'anything beyond this comes from the evil one'. The very issue designed to establish truth (swearing) has its root in evil (the assumption of our lack of honesty)!

There is a logical sequence and progression in these last three issues. Jesus speaks of adultery (5:27-28), then of divorce (5:31-32), leading to remarriage, which, he bluntly describes as legalised adultery ('anyone who divorces his wife ... causes her to become an adulteress'), then of breaking oaths. The roots of adultery and divorce lie in broken oaths. It is not the attractiveness of a flirtatious woman that leads a man into adultery, it is the lack of integrity in his own heart that makes him available to the opportunity. Temptation may be strong and relentless, but victory or defeat in the situation is not primarily related to an individual response to the individual temptation, it is related to the integrity of heart that says, 'I love my wife and am committed exclusively to her! I love God and am committed exclusively to him! Adultery therefore is not an option'. Violate that inner integrity and you have to fight every temptation one by one. Establish the integrity of heart and you have settled the issue before it ever arises in individual temptations. We may never legitimately blame our environment for adultery, we may only blame our lack of integrity. Our 'Yes' to our wives and husbands is not really 'Yes', and our 'No' to alternatives is not 'No', and, says Jesus, 'this comes from the evil one'.

'You have heard that it was said, "Eye for eye and tooth for tooth". But I tell you, Do not resist an evil person. If someone strikes you on the right cheek, turn to him the other also....' (5:38-42). The main difficulty in this statement of Jesus is that 'Eye for eye and tooth for tooth' is a direct quotation from the Old Testament civil law (Exod. 21:23-24; Lev. 24:19-21; Deut. 19:21). However, the original context is not speaking about personal response or revenge, but the workings of the law court. The reference in Exodus applies to punishment inflicted by the court on men who hit a pregnant woman whilst fighting amongst themselves. If there is serious injury they are to take, 'life for life, eye for eye, tooth for tooth, hand for hand, foot for foot, burn for burn, wound for wound, bruise for bruise'. Similarly, in Leviticus it applies to someone who injures his neighbour, and Deuteronomy refers generally to the principles of justice to be exercised in a court of law when a man stands guilty of a crime. The punishment is to fit the crime, and is to be equal to the crime.

However, in personal life and behaviour we are not to take the law into our own hands and give, 'eye for eye, tooth for tooth', but rather to refuse to resist the evil person ourselves. This however does not mean the evil person can do as he pleases with no response. It is the function of the law courts to administer justice and punishment on the criminal, and this is God's order. It may be wrong of me to resist the imposition of an evil man upon myself, but it would be equally wrong if I tried to prevent the law administering appropriate punishment on him for his wrong. Paul speaks similarly of this. He writes, 'Do not repay anyone evil for evil' (Rom. 12:17), but do not take that verse in isolation. Seven verses later he writes, '... rulers hold no terror for those who do right, but for those who do wrong ... He is God's servant to do you good. But if you do wrong, be afraid, for he does not bear the sword for nothing. He is God's servant, an agent of wrath to bring punishment on the wrong doer' (Rom. 13:3-4). We are not to repay evil for evil personally, but we are to stand firmly on the right and responsibility of rulers to do exactly that, in the exercise of authority entrusted to them by God (cf. Rom. 13:1).

The main instruction of Jesus regarding this in the Sermon on the Mount is that as we are not to be concerned in the first instance with our activity, but with the attitude from which that activity derives, so in our personal dealings with others who may take advantage of us, we are to go beyond the external behaviour to the inner person. If someone wants your tunic, perhaps they have need, give your cloak too. If someone forces you to go one mile (a Roman citizen may have had the right to demand that of a non-Roman if he wished help in carrying a burden), then go beyond the legal requirement and go two miles. Again, it is a righteousness not related to external legal requirements, but to the internal attitude of heart.

'You have heard that it was said, "Love your neighbour and hate your enemy", but I tell you: Love your enemies and pray for those who persecute you, that you may be sons of your Father in heaven' (5:43-45). The first clause has no origin in the Old Testament scriptures, but had evidently evolved as a misconstruction of the command to 'love your neighbour'. If the command is specified as, 'love your neighbour', then by deduction we are not instructed to love anyone else, so logically it developed that hating your enemy was legitimate! If the righteousness of the Pharisees and Scribes fulfilled the legal specification of 'neighbour', the righteousness demanded by Jesus goes beyond categorising people into the 'loved' from the 'unloved' and the attitude of true righteousness is an all embracing love that includes 'enemies and those that persecute you'.

Loving people who love us does not require the grace and enabling of God! In fact, Jesus said, 'If you love those who love you, what reward will you get? Are not even the tax collectors doing that? And if you greet only your brothers what are you doing more than others? Do not even pagans do that?' (5:46-47). To love those who love us qualifies us to be tax collectors, not Christians! To greet only our brothers makes us good pagans! Christians who love only Christians are no different from Freemasons who love Freemasons, or Mormons who love Mormons. The love of God is undiscriminating, and love that expresses the righteousness required by the Lord Jesus Christ is equally undiscriminating. It is in this context Jesus said, 'Be perfect, therefore, as your heavenly Father is perfect' (5:48). We will refer to this statement again later, but for the moment it is worth noting that the criteria for love and behaviour is not determined by circumstances or conditions, it is determined by who God is, for righteousness is ultimately the expression of the character of God.

The fundamental flaw in the righteousness of the Pharisees and teachers of the law lay not in their external behaviour. Some had mastered that superbly. Paul could testify of his own past, '... in regard to the law, a Pharisee, ... as for legalistic righteousness, faultless' (Phil. 3:5, 6). To claim to be 'faultless' is some claim, and Paul could make it in good conscience. However, it was as true of him as Jesus stated it to be true of other Pharisees when he denounced them saying, 'Woe to you teachers of the law and Pharisees, you hypocrites! You clean the outside of the cup and dish, but inside they are full of greed and self-indulgence ... You are like whitewashed tombs, which look beautiful on the outside but on the inside are full of dead men's bones and everything unclean ... on the outside you appear to people as righteous, but on the inside you are full of hypocrisy and wickedness' (Matt. 23:25-28). The outward activity was impressive, but the inward attitude was as corrupt as any pagan in the street.

True righteousness never works from the outside in, but from the inside out. Doing the right things does not make us the right person. The reverse is true. It is in becoming the right person inwardly, that we are able to do the right things with moral integrity and inner harmony. The only question is: How?

11.

Fulfilling the law
(5:17-48)

In the last chapter we tried to clarify and understand exactly what Jesus required of his disciples, when he demanded their righteousness must 'surpass that of the Pharisees and teachers of the law' (5:20). It was not the external activity (murder, adultery etc.) but the internal attitude (anger, lust etc.) that is the area in which true righteousness is established. The Pharisees and scribes had learned well to discipline their activity and conform to the requirements of the law in their external behaviour, but they had never been able to deal with the source of their activity. Jesus said of them, 'On the outside you appear to people as righteous but on the inside you are full of hypocrisy and wickedness' (23:28). They had mastered the outside well, but the inner person remained corrupt. It is this which is the concern of Jesus Christ in establishing true righteousness.

It is one thing to applaud this principle as true, even logical and fairly obvious, but another to understand how it works out. There may be some obvious disciplinary steps we may take to deal with our actions (at which the Pharisees were superb), but how do we deal with the attitudes that lie at their root? If the demand of righteousness made by the Lord Jesus Christ is understood, we must ask the question: How is this possible?

The dynamics of righteousness
What is it that makes this quality of life possible? Tucked away in the beginning of this section is a statement that might easily be overlooked, but which is the key to everything else. Jesus said of the law, 'I have not come to abolish them, but to fulfil them' (5:17).

To understand what it means for Jesus to fulfil the law, we need to address two related issues, the purpose of the law, and the effect of the law. To examine this properly involves what may appear to be a deviation from the text of Matthew 5, but is essential if we are to understand what is taught here.

The purpose of the law

Why did God give ten commandments, and why these particular ten? Were they randomly chosen or is there a particular reason? What criteria, if any, determined the content of the law? To answer this question we need to compare two verses in Scripture that define all sin.

Firstly, the apostle John writes, 'Everyone who sins breaks the law; in fact sin is lawlessness' (1 John 3:4). John defines sin as breaking the law. The word sin literally means 'to miss the mark'. It was used of archery. To shoot an arrow and miss the target was 'sin'. By how far one missed was irrelevant to it being sin – whether by a millimetre, a centimetre, a metre or kilometre! Sin is not primarily a measurement of how bad a person is, it is primarily a measurement of how good a person is not! Sin does not comment on how far we miss, only on the fact we have missed. To miss a bus by one minute, or one hour is irrelevant to the fact we have missed. If sin is to 'miss the mark', sin is a relative word, relative to the mark that has been missed. The apostle John in this passage says the mark we miss is the law.

Paul however, gives a different criterion when he writes, 'for all have sinned and fall short of the glory of God' (Rom. 3:23). The standard against which we are measured is the 'glory of God'. Compare these two statements. John says the target we miss is *the law of God*, Paul says the target we miss is *the glory of God*. That indicates to us that the law of God and the glory of God represent the same thing. Therefore to discover why the law of God is what it is, we need to discover what the glory of God is.

The word 'glory' occurs in Scripture with slight variation of meaning, depending on its context. Vine's expository dictionary describes the glory of God as, 'the character of God ... What he essentially is and does'.[1] It is what John had in mind when writing of Jesus, 'The Word became flesh and lived for a while among us. We

---

[1] W. E. Vine, *Expository Dictionary Of New Testament Words*, p. 153, Oliphants, London 1969.

have seen his glory, the glory of the one and only Son who came from the Father full of grace and truth' (John 1:14). When he writes, 'We have seen his glory', he is not writing of some physical manifestation, like a bright light encircling his head, but he is saying in effect, 'In the behaviour of Jesus was seen the character of God'. In looking at Jesus, whether as a boy in Nazareth, as a carpenter in his shop or in the years of his public ministry, people saw in his behaviour, in his actions and reactions, an exact portrayal of the moral character of God. The book of Hebrews states, 'The Son is the radiance of God's glory and the exact representation of his being' (Heb. 1:3). In other words, if you want to know what God is like, look at Jesus! There is a particular sense in which, when Jesus commenced his ministry John writes, 'He thus revealed his glory' (John 2:11), for the only legitimate explanation of the work he did and the miracles he performed was the presence and activity of his Father. He was expressing himself through his Son.

However, if this was true of Jesus, it was not intended only to be true of Jesus, but of every human being. Humankind has been created in God's 'image' (see Gen. 1:26). This is not a physical, but a moral image. If we had been able to observe the way Adam and Eve behaved in the Garden of Eden, we would have seen in them an exact portrayal of God's character. To be in his 'image' can have no other meaning than that human beings were designed to portray God – not in his unique attributes of deity of course, but in his moral character. But our first parents 'sinned and came short of the glory of God'! They ceased to show what God is like. If the law of God and the glory of God equal the same thing, then the purpose of the law is supremely to reveal the character of God, in order that human beings might understand what it means practically to have been created in his image.

When God said in the law, 'You shall not steal', it was for one primary reason. God is not a thief! As human beings we were created to be in his image, therefore stealing is inadmissible, for to steal would be to misrepresent God and distort the character of the One in whose image we are designed to function. When God said, 'You shall not give false testimony', it is because God does not lie, and we are created to be his image. When he said, 'You shall not commit adultery' it is because God is totally faithful, and we are created to be in his image. When God said, 'You shall not covet ...', it is because God is not greedy. When he said, 'You shall not murder' it is because

God does not murder and gives dignity to every human being. When he says, 'Six days shall you labour and do all your work, but the seventh day is a Sabbath to the Lord ...', he explains it is because, 'God rested on the seventh day'. He did not rest because he was tired, but because the work was finished! The Sabbath is not designed to enable us to get over six days of hard work, but that we might rest in the complete sufficiency of God. That is why for Adam the first day was a day of rest. Having been created on the sixth day, he rested on the seventh not because he was tired but in acknowledgement of his utter dependency on God. As the writer of the book of Hebrews later wrote, 'There remains a Sabbath-rest for the people of God; for anyone who enters God's rest also rests from his own work, just as God did from his' (Heb. 4:9-10). When the law states, 'Honour your father and mother ...' it is because within the Trinity, the Son says, 'I always do what pleases him (the Father)' (John 8:29), and having been created in the image of God, children are to honour their parents, as the Son seeks to please his Father.

The law is not designed as an arbitrary set of rules or as a series of guidelines to help us to behave. The law is more profound than that, it is a revelation of the character of God. This is why Jesus concludes this section in the Sermon on the Mount by saying, 'Be perfect, therefore, as your heavenly Father is perfect' (5:48). That may seem totally unreasonable, and from the human perspective it is! But from the divine perspective it is the whole purpose for which we have been created, that the image of his character may be visible in us. To state we are to be as, 'perfect as your heavenly Father is perfect', is only to repeat what God said in the Garden of Eden when he stated, 'Let us make man in our image, in our likeness ...', and what he said on Mount Sinai when he wrote the ten commandments as a revelation of his own character.

The effect of the law

If the purpose of the law is to reveal the character of God, then we must be honest about the effect of the law, for the effect of the law is to reveal the failure of human beings. When Moses came down Mount Sinai with the Ten Commandments in his hands, he discovered that in his forty day absence the Israelites, under Aaron's supervision, had built a golden calf to substitute the true God. The first command God had given Moses was, 'You shall have no other gods before me', and the second was, 'You shall not make for yourself any idol in the form of anything in heaven above or on the earth beneath ... You shall not bow down and worship them.' (Exod. 20:3-5). When Moses saw them worshipping the golden calf in direct violation of the first two commandments, he was shocked! So shocked in fact, he took the tablets of stone and in anger smashed them on the ground! Moses was shocked, but God wasn't! God did not learn anything new about human beings, but human beings learned something new about themselves! They discovered their own inability and failure.

Paul writes, 'I would not have known what sin was except through the law' (Rom. 7:7), and '... through the law we become conscious of sin' (Rom. 3:20). We might be up to our necks in sin, enjoying every minute of it with a clear conscience, until the law comes. The law does not make us sinners, it only reveals our sin. The effect of the law on us is to make us conscious of our own inability and failure. One of the things God has to do in our lives is make us conscious of our inherent failure. This is an unavoidable necessity if we are to discover what it means for Jesus to 'fulfil the law'. It is one thing to acknowledge that what we *do* is wrong, but we must go beyond that to discover what we *are* is incapable of what is right. That is why Jesus took the disciples back beyond their behaviour as the problem, to themselves! It is not just 'murder' that is the problem, but 'anger' (5:21-22). It is not just 'adultery' that is to be corrected, but 'lust' (5:27-28). It is not just, 'an eye for an eye' but loving your neighbour and 'praying for those who persecute you' (5:38-44). I imagine the people listening to the Sermon on the Mount must have squirmed. The law was hard enough when they weren't allowed to do any of these things, now they weren't allowed to even think about them!

What was Jesus doing in speaking this way? He was driving his listeners into a corner where they could only come to one honest conclusion – This life is impossible! Until a person arrives at the honest conclusion, 'I cannot be the person I am designed to be', they will never discover the full force of the gospel. They will only think of him in terms of dealing with symptoms, like forgiving their past sins, but not of him dealing with the cause. If we have a gospel which only deals with outward activities like 'murder' and 'adultery', but not with their cause, 'anger' and 'lust', then we have a gospel not significantly different from that already available under the Old Covenant! The prime difference becomes essentially that the cross of

Christ was permanent in its effect, rather than the necessary repetition of sacrifices in the old covenant. But such a message still only attends to the symptoms!

The fulfilment of the law

This now leads to the most crucial aspect. What did Jesus mean when he said of the law, 'I have not come to abolish them but to fulfil them' (5:17). How are the demands of the law fulfilled in human experience? We might equally ask, how is the 'glory of God' to be restored to us? If the 'law of God' and the 'glory of God' equal the same thing as we earlier suggested, then to fulfil the law of God and to restore the glory of God represents the same thing.

Paul, writing his letter to the Colossians, explains he is presenting the 'word of God in its fulness', something he describes as a 'mystery that has been kept hidden for ages and generations, but is now disclosed to the saints'. Previously there has been a missing element in the revelation God has given – a 'mystery'. Now, he states, it is no longer a mystery for it has been fully revealed as, 'the glorious riches of this mystery, which is *Christ in you, the hope of glory*' (Col. 1:25-27). In Christian slang, 'glory' has come to mean heaven. But that is not its meaning in Scripture. 'Glory' is the moral character of God, seen in Jesus (John 1:14) and of which we have fallen short (Rom. 3:23). The mystery, says Paul, which is now revealed is that Jesus Christ not only did something *for* us, in which he fulfilled all the rituals of the Old Covenant, but he does something *in* us. Living his life in us, he is our hope of glory, that is, our hope of hitting the target we have come short of. Jesus does not fulfil the law as an example to us, he fulfils it within us as our life and as our strength.

Speaking to Jeremiah of the New Covenant he would establish, God said, 'I will put my law in their minds and write it on their hearts' (Jer. 31:33). The New Covenant will not involve a re-writing of the law, but a re-locating of the law. Instead of being on tablets of stone it will be written 'in their minds' and 'on their hearts'. It will be internalised! God said to Ezekiel, 'I will put my Spirit in you and move you to follow my decrees and be careful to keep my laws' (Ezek. 36:27). Placing his Spirit in people would be the terms of the New Covenant brought into effect on the Day of Pentecost, but the consequence will be that we follow his decrees and keep his laws.

We may summarise it by saying that for Jesus to fulfil the law, for him to be in us our hope of hitting the target we have missed – 'your hope of glory' – for him to put the law in our hearts and on our minds, to place his Spirit in us and move us to follow his law, means that what is a command under the Old Covenant becomes a promise under the New Covenant.

A man serving sentence for theft had been led to Christ by a prison visitor. On his release from prison he visited a church and saw the ten commandments written on the front wall. His initial reaction was to feel condemned, knowing he had broken almost every one of the ten. As he began to read them however, he found he was reading it very differently. Previously he had read them only as commands, but now he read them as promises: 'You shall not steal', and he could say, 'Thank you, Lord, I shall not steal'; 'You shall not commit adultery' – Thank you, Lord, I shall not commit adultery – 'You shall not covet' – Thank you, Lord, I shall not covet – 'You shall not bear false witness' – Thank you, Lord. What had been commands which only exposed his failure were now promises that liberated!

Under the New Covenant our righteousness does not depend on what we do for God (that was the law under the Old Covenant, and only produced failure), but it depends on what God does for us (the New Covenant), by the indwelling of his Spirit to live the life of Jesus in us and produce the character of Jesus in us.

The gospel involves, at its bottom line, the restoration of the character of God which was lost in the Garden of Eden. The consequence of the fall then was death, 'separation from the life of God' (Eph. 4:18); the cause of the restoration of godliness now is life, 'He who has the Son has life' (1 John 5:12). It is the life of God indwelling the human life, lived in union together, that is the source of true righteousness.

This does not mean perfection is available to us in this life. The Bible holds out no prospect of this. Rather there is a process of growth in godliness. Paul writes, 'We, who with unveiled faces all reflect the Lord's glory, are being transformed into his likeness with ever-increasing glory, which comes from the Lord, who is the Spirit' (2 Cor. 3:18). The tense of that verse is neither past nor future, not speaking of either, 'having been transformed into his likeness', nor that one day we 'will be transformed into his likeness'. It is in the present continuous tense of, 'are being transformed into his likeness with ever-increasing glory'. The nature of true spiritual growth is that there is more evidence of the character of God in our behaviour now, than there used to be in the past. One day the process will be complete when we are, 'glorified' (see Rom. 8:30), when we will be morally indistinguishable from Christ himself. That is what awaits us in heaven. In the meantime, the work of Jesus Christ is to fulfil all the demands of the law in us and increasingly restore the image of God in which we were originally created.

This however does not mean we go into a passive stance, where the righteousness of God becomes automatically evident in us. We are full participants in our growth in godliness, and Jesus speaks of that in the Sermon on the Mount. If we have sought to understand 1) The demand of righteousness, and 2) The dynamics of righteousness, then we must look at an equally important third aspect.

The disciplines of righteousness

Jesus speaks specifically about discipline in two areas.

Discipline in relationship with others (5:23-26)

Having spoken of anger as a cause of murder, Jesus says, 'Therefore, if you are offering your gift at the altar and there remember that your brother has something against you, leave your gift there in front of the altar. First go and be reconciled to your brother; then come and offer your gift' (5:23-24). When he says, 'your brother has something against you', it may be that he has legitimate reason for this and you are in the wrong, or it may be that he is in the wrong and his attitude to you is part of the wrong. Either way, his instruction is to put it right. This is not to just 'pray about it', but to actively pursue the means of restoring a broken relationship.

Jesus gave some particular details about this elsewhere, when he said, 'If your brother sins, rebuke him, and if he repents forgive him' (Luke 17.3). In most cases this may suffice. An appropriate rebuke may bring the proper response and the issue is dealt with and past. However, should he not respond, Jesus also spoke of a chain of events that take this to a conclusion. 'If your brother sins against you, go and show him his fault ... But if he will not listen, take one or two others along ... If he refuses to listen to them, tell it to the church; and if he refuses to listen even to the church, treat him as you would a pagan or a tax collector' (18:15-17). We will look at this passage more fully in its context later, but Jesus gives a clear four step process to resolving personal conflict amongst Christians. At any point in the process there is the possibility of reconciliation and restoration of the relationship, but if that point is resisted, the process moves along to the point of alienation and the offending brother being treated as 'a pagan or a tax collector', meaning he is in need of repentance towards God before there can be restoration. It is the principle not the details which are the primary concern at this point. The discipline of wholesome relationships is a vital ingredient in the process of growth in godliness.

Discipline in relationship to ourselves (5:29-30)

'If your right eye causes you to sin, gouge it out and throw it away ... If your right hand causes you to sin, cut it off and throw it away....' (5:29-30). The context of this abrupt statement is Jesus speaking about adultery and lust. To interpret this within its context we need to recognise the main agents of sexual arousal are sight and touch. In this area of sexual temptation he speaks about drastic discipline of the eye and hand. This is not a literal mutilation of the body, for that would violate the dignity of the human body, and there is no evidence it was ever understood or practised as literal from the time Jesus said it. This must refer to a discipline of the body that treats the eye and hand as though they were not there, and denies them the opportunity of sinful expression. Lust is not the same as sexual arousal, which is a natural God-created human function. Lust is entirely selfish in its motivation, and self-centred in its gratification.

When Amnon, the son of David, raped his half sister Tamar having deceived himself into thinking he loved her, it reports that when the deed was over, 'Amnon hated her with intense hatred. In fact he hated her more than he had loved her' (2 Sam. 13:15). Of course he did! He had never loved her in the first place, he had only loved himself, and lust is destructive. The expression of sexual love in the context of marriage, designed by God as good, is satisfying in the measure to which it brings pleasure to the partner – the wife or husband. Its motivation is other-centred, whereas lust is self-centred. Artificial sexual stimulation of any kind is by definition lust, for its prime function is selfish gratification. It is in this area Jesus speaks of discipline.

In a later passage Jesus extends this command to include the foot, 'If your hand or your foot causes you to sin, cut it off and throw it away' (18:8).

Discipline of the body is an essential component of true godliness. The function of discipline is not to create something within us, (working from the outside in) but to release the life of Jesus that is in us (working from the inside out). Paul instructed, 'Continue to work out your salvation with fear and trembling, for it is God who works in you to will and to act according to his own purpose' (Phil. 2:12-13). Our responsibility is not to work *in* holiness, but to work *out* the consequence of God working in us. It is like the discipline of driving a car. The driver's responsibility is to release the resources under the bonnet of the car to take it down the road in the right direction, at the right speed in accordance with the rules of the road. Nothing is worked *in* to the car, it is the potential of the engine that is worked *out*. That is the function of discipline in the Christian life. It is not to make up for any deficiency in God who now indwells us, but to enable him to function in a person who obeys orders.

The Pharisees, with whom Jesus contrasts true righteousness, worked hard on producing righteousness by giving attention to their external behaviour, in the hope that it would work its way *in* from externals to the heart. True righteousness works in reverse to this. 'God works in you', so 'work out your salvation' into practical realistic living. Paul testifies of himself, 'I beat my body and make it my slave....' (1 Cor. 9:27). A slave to what? To an external law? He spends much of his time repudiating that. He disciplines his body to make himself a slave to the life of Christ within him. We will never meet a lazy, undisciplined but effective Christian, for the two are contradictory. Discipline is not the cause of godliness, but it is the means by which it is expressed.

The role of Christ in the Christian involves his fulfilling the demands the law makes upon us. He is indispensable to our godliness. But his role in us is given expression through disciplined, humble dependence upon him and obedience to him. Remove any ingredient from that process and we are left with either the empty shell of pragmatic Pharisaism, or equally empty pious mysticism.

12.

Reality with God
(6:1-18)

True righteousness is not expressed in the ability to avoid what is wrong, but in the ability to do what is right. In Chapter 5 Jesus spoke of righteousness from a negative perspective and talked primarily about what we are not to do. In Chapter 6 he speaks of righteousness from a positive perspective, and talks primarily about what we are to do. In both chapters the external actions take second place to the internal attitude from which those actions originate. He specifies four practical 'acts of righteousness' (6:1) as: Giving (6:2-4); Praying (6:5-15); Fasting (6:16-18) and Possessing (6:19-34).

Acts of righteousness (6:1)
The opening statement of the section sums up its message: Acts of righteousness may be done 'before men to be seen by them', but if so, 'you will have no reward from your Father in heaven' (6:1). This theme of external actions seen by men in contrast with internal attitudes seen by God runs on through the chapter. Regarding giving to the needy, he speaks of those who, 'announce it with trumpets ... to be honoured by men' rather than, 'when you give to the needy, do not let your left hand know what your right hand is doing, so that your giving may be in secret. Then your Father, who sees what is done in secret, will reward you' (6:2-4). With regard to praying he speaks of the hypocrites who, 'love to pray ... to be seen by men' rather than praying 'in secret' (6:5-6). Regarding fasting, again the hypocrites, 'disfigure their faces to show men they are fasting' rather than fasting in such a way, 'that it will not be obvious to men that you are fasting, but only to your Father who is unseen' (6:16-18).

The whole theme of these first three instances is that of doing these acts of righteousness either for the applause of men, in which case the reward is received in full (that of being approved by other people), or to satisfy heaven by being concerned with the interests of our 'Father who is unseen'. This theme continues by Jesus saying, 'Do not store up for yourselves treasures on earth ... But store up for yourselves treasures in heaven' (6:19-20). Our treasures are either earth-oriented, immediate and tangible or they are heaven-oriented, eternal and intangible. Material possessions and a concern for reputation pay their dividends immediately, 'they have received their reward in full'. But whatever those rewards may be in the short term, they leave us with empty hands where it really counts in the long term, before God 'who sees what is done in secret and will reward you' (6:6). The issue is not the things we do (giving, praying, fasting) but the reason for which we do them. It is not the activities in themselves, but the attitudes that lie behind the activities that count.

Giving (6:2-4)

When Jesus talks about 'giving to the needy', he primarily addresses the motivation with which we give. There are however some assumptions we may make about giving from this passage. He says, 'When you give ...' (6:2, 3) not 'if you give'. The assumption is that giving is to be a normal activity. Under the Old Covenant the tithe of ten percent was levied on the Israelites, almost like a tax, and included a tenth of their grain, fruit, herds, flocks, garden plants and cash. If a man retained his tithe, he added to it a standard 20% of the value of the tithe (see Lev. 27:30-33). In addition to his tithe, which was mandatory, he may add offerings which were voluntary. Thus the Old Testament speaks of 'tithes and offerings' (e.g. Mal. 3:8).

Tithing is not taught in the New Testament, and is only mentioned by Jesus in connection with the Pharisees' obsession with the outward manifestations of the law (e.g. Matt. 23:23 and Luke 11:42). An altogether different principle applies in the New Testament, where one hundred percent belongs to God. (cf. Luke 14:33). That is a good principle but impractical as a guideline for specific giving. Paul wrote, 'Each man should give what he has decided in his heart to give, not reluctantly or under compulsion, for God loves a cheerful giver' (2 Cor. 9:7). Specific giving is to be freely and cheerfully! There are benefits in giving for Paul stated in the same passage, 'Whoever sows sparingly will also reap sparingly, and whoever sows generously will also reap generously' (2 Cor. 9:6) but that is not in itself the motive! It is simply a fact. No one is ever poverty stricken because they gave away too much. The wisdom of Proverbs states, 'One man gives freely, yet gains even more. Another withholds unduly, but comes to poverty. A generous man will prosper' (Prov. 11:24-25). Certainly our attitude to God will be reflected in our attitude to money and our generosity or lack of it. I once saw engraved on a wooden offering plate being passed around a church in Harlem, New York, 'Despite all we say and do, This is what we really think of you'. I am not sure this is the kind of bullying tactic we should encourage, but there is some truth in the statement!

Praying (6:5-15)

In addition to what Jesus has to say about prayer in regard to hypocrisy, there is some general teaching in this section, including the giving of what we often call 'the Lord's prayer'.

1) How to pray (6:5-8)

I want to suggest four key words that sum up Jesus' teaching on this from this section.

a. Pray Regularly: Again he says 'when you pray' (6:5, 6, 7), not 'if you pray'. He assumes prayer to be a normal discipline of life. This raises the question: What is prayer? There are at least two answers to that question. One is subjective (it has its effects on the prayer), the other is objective (it has its effects elsewhere). We will look at the objective reasons for prayer in Matthew 16, but comment here on subjective reasons.

By definition the Christian life is not primarily an experience, nor is it primarily feelings, though these have their place. It is primarily a relationship. Jesus defined it this way, 'Now this is eternal life: that they may know you, the only true God, and Jesus Christ whom you have sent' (John 17:3). Eternal life is defined as 'knowing God' and 'knowing Christ'. Prayer on its simplest level is the talking part of the relationship. All relationships grow or wither in proportion to the depth of communication that takes place. When governments get into trouble they have to make room to listen to the people. When industrial relationships break down, the invitation goes out to 'get around the table' and negotiate. When marriages hit hard times there has invariably been a breakdown of communication and understanding. When the Christian life runs dry there has too often been a breakdown in prayer. We have stopped talking and stopped listening. If God did not answer one prayer, and if no prayer ever made a difference to what happened in the world, praying would still be necessary! Prayer is the talking part of the relationship.

b. Pray secretly: When Jesus said, 'When you pray, go into your room, close the door and pray to your Father who is unseen' (6:6) he did not mean that the only valid praying is that which is in secret. Elsewhere Jesus said, 'If two of you on earth agree about anything you ask for, it will be done for you by my Father in heaven' (18:19), and there are examples of one hundred and twenty praying together in the book of Acts (e.g. Acts 1:14-15). The context of this statement is warning about hypocrisy. The real test of our prayer life is not the praying that goes on in public but the praying that goes on in secret. In one sense anyone can pray in public, particularly when motivated by an audience. It is the time alone with God behind a closed door that gives evidence of the reality of our prayer lives.

c. Pray naturally: 'When you pray, do not keep on babbling like pagans, for they think they will be heard because of their many words' (6:7). To pray with a special vocabulary or to put on a special voice is often a symptom of unreality with God. We approach God reverently and humbly, but nevertheless confidently and naturally. We are children speaking to our heavenly Father.

d. Pray believingly: He says here, 'Your Father knows what you need before you ask him' (6:8). Notice he does not say, 'Your Father knows what you need *so you do not need to ask him*', but you ask, knowing your Father knows your need much better than you do, and long before you did. The sovereignty and wisdom of God does not preclude the necessity, nor the effectiveness, of prayer. The nature of our believing in prayer is not that God is going to give what we ask, but that he is going to give what is right. If what we ask coincides with what is right, so much the better, but it is the will of God that is paramount. This conviction must permeate our sense of dependency on God as we pray. We do not hold a pistol to God's head when we pray, insisting he do things our way, but acknowledging his way as supreme and sufficient, and inviting him in to our circumstances to fulfil his agenda.

2) What to pray (6:9-15)

It is here Jesus gives what we commonly call 'the Lord's prayer'. There is no indication this was intended to be repeated word for word, almost parrot fashion, particularly as Jesus has just said, 'Do not keep babbling like pagans ... This then is how you should pray, Our Father....'

The prayer may be divided into two sections. The first part being concerned with God (6:9-10) and the second part concerned with need (6:11-13).

Concern with God

a. The worship of God: The prayer begins, 'Our Father in heaven, hallowed be your name'. We must never forget who God is. This description of God as 'Father' implies a relationship with him. In a general sense God is, 'the Father from whom all things came' (1 Cor. 8:6), but in a particular sense in the New Testament we are by new birth brought into that special relationship with him as Father, the source of our life. Paul wrote, 'For you ... received the Spirit of sonship. And by him we cry, "Abba, Father"' (Rom. 8:15). It is as our Father, his name is hallowed. Our interest in God must be much more than what he may do for us, or what we may get from him, and true prayer begins with a recognition of who he is. Worship is different from praise. Praise is a response of gratitude for all that he does. Worship is a recognition of all that he is. When the wise men came to Jesus as a baby in Bethlehem, they stated their intention by saying, 'We saw his star in the east and have come to worship him' (2:2). When they arrived at the place where he was staying, 'they bowed down and worshipped him' (2:11). What was the nature of their worship? It did not consist of thanking him for what he had done, for as yet he had done nothing. They worshipped him in recognition of who he was, and that he was worthy of their submission.

b. The work of God: 'Your kingdom come'. Whatever else may be involved in this, to pray 'Your kingdom come' is to pray, 'My kingdom go'. Basic to effective praying is the recognition of the sovereignty of God and the Lordship of Christ and the consequent jettisoning of my own agenda to the extent to which it differs from his. Whatever we are praying for, it has to do with the expansion of his kingdom.

c. The will of God: 'Your will be done' follows logically, however different it may be from my own will. I feel very concerned when I hear people command God in their prayers. I remember some time ago going to a hospital to visit a lady I knew who was very ill, and perhaps not going to survive. Several of us visited her that evening and prayed for her. On leaving the hospital and walking to our car, one of our group said to me, 'Your prayer was not a prayer of faith tonight'. I asked her to explain what she meant. She told me I had prayed that God would heal this lady *if it was his will,* which was evident of my lack of faith that he would heal her, and a convenient let out for my unbelief if she did not get well. I reject that understanding totally. To pray, 'if it is your will' is evidence of the existence of faith, not the lack of it, for it is the expression of confidence that God knows exactly what he is doing and is capable of doing it.

There is a great danger in insisting on our own way with God, and the danger is very simply that he may give it to us! There are various instances in Scripture of God giving what was asked for, but with disastrous effect. When the Israelites grumbled in the wilderness and insisted God give them meat in addition to the diet of dull manna he sent them each day, he answered their prayers and sent them quail. However, most of the people died from a severe plague as they ate the meat, and in the place they had asked for the meat, 'they buried the people who had asked for other food' (see Num. 11:4-34).

Commenting later on this, the Psalmist writes, 'In the desert they gave in to their craving; in the wasteland they put God to the test. So he gave them what they asked for and sent a wasting disease upon them', or as the Authorised Version puts it, 'he gave them their request; but sent leanness into their soul' (Ps. 106:14-15). God gave them what they insisted upon, but at what cost – 'leanness to their souls'.

King Hezekiah is another example. He was a good king who followed a succession of bad kings in Judah. At one time Hezekiah became ill and was at the point of death when the prophet Isaiah came to say God wanted him to put his house in order, because he was going to die and not recover! On hearing this Hezekiah turned his face to the wall, cried, and pleaded with God to heal him and extend his life. As Isaiah was leaving Hezekiah's palace after delivering his sorry message, God told him to go back and tell Hezekiah that God had heard his prayer, he had seen his tears, and in three days he would be fully healed and live for another fifteen years. Hezekiah was thrilled, and lived for another fifteen years as God had said. During this time he continued his reign as a good king. After fifteen years he died and his son Manasseh succeeded him to the throne. If you know anything of Old Testament history you may know Manasseh became the most evil king to reign in Judah. For fifty five years he occupied the throne, turning the nation from God and erecting altars to pagan gods in the temple of Jehovah. He became an occultist, getting his direction from astrology and spiritist mediums, and gave his own son in sacrifice to a pagan god. All the good work of his father Hezekiah was undone and reversed by Manasseh.

Do you know how old Manasseh was when he came to the throne? 'Manasseh was twelve years old when he became king' (2 Kings 21:1. See 2 Kings 20 and 21 for the full story). If Manasseh was twelve years old when Hezekiah died fifteen years too late, clearly Manasseh should not have existed. Hezekiah may have died at the end of the fifteen years extension to his life, thanking God for listening to his prayer and extending his life, but he did not know he was leaving behind a son, born after his initial illness, who would turn the nation back to a barbaric form of paganism. It is possible God may have granted what Hezekiah wanted, yet sent leanness to the nation of Judah for generations. To insist on our own way with God is dangerous! He may give it. He is under no obligation to do so, but this is why the true expression of faith in God is the permeation of our prayers with, 'Your will be done'.

Concern with need

When it is our business to engage in the worship of God, to be concerned with doing the work of God, in submission to the will of God, we will discover we have many needs. The requests of this prayer address three areas of need.

a. Physical need: 'Give us today our daily bread'. It is right and legitimate that we acknowledge our dependency on God for our physical needs, not taking them for granted, but asking in humility for our 'daily bread'. This request is not for a stockpile to last the next month! God provides today what we need today. Should we have enough resources for the next month or year, that is entirely legitimate, but it is not what we have a right to and therefore not what we ask him for.

b. Spiritual need: 'Forgive us our debts as we have forgiven our debtors'.

We come to God in constant need for cleansing. The condition attached to this is important, 'as we have forgiven our debtors'. This is amplified at the end of this prayer when Jesus said, 'If you forgive men when they sin against you, your heavenly Father will also forgive you. But if you do not forgive men their sins, your Father will not forgive your sins' (6:14-15). Forgiveness is free but not cheap. To live with integrity before God we must live with the same integrity amongst people. Those who offend us may not deserve our forgiveness in our estimation, but neither do we deserve God's forgiveness. Forgiveness is not dependent on the offending party but on the offended party. It is God who forgives us. It is we who forgive others. The refusal to forgive others in appropriate circumstances, shuts out the forgiveness of God. The change of mind that characterises our repentance towards God must be a change of mind that characterises our attitude towards others – particularly those who need our forgiveness.

c. Moral need: 'Lead us not into temptation but deliver us from the evil one'. When praying according to the pattern Jesus gave here, we can be sure we will be exposed to temptation and to attacks of 'the evil one'. The implication of this statement is not that God may otherwise lead us into temptation. He is never the author of temptation. James wrote, 'When tempted, no one should say "God is tempting me". For God cannot be tempted by evil, nor does he tempt anyone....' (Jas. 1:13). But for Jesus to include this indicates that our deliverance from temptation is something God himself is involved in. We need forgiveness of our past sin, but we need deliverance from the present evil temptations with which we are constantly bombarded.

One last point on this prayer. It is worth noting that this prayer is entirely in the first person plural. He does not speak of 'My Father ... Give *me* today *my* daily bread ... Forgive *me my* debts, and lead *me* not into temptation', but 'Our Father, give *us* today *our* daily bread ... Forgive *us our* debts, and lead *us* not into temptation'. Looking after ourselves first has little to do with the Christian life generally, and nothing to do with an effective prayer life. Our concerns and our prayers are for others as much as for ourselves, and in so doing, we have confident access to God.

Fasting (6:16-18)
The main point in the three verses about fasting has to do with hypocrisy. It is done either to 'show men they are fasting', or 'obvious

... only to your Father ... who sees what is done in secret and will reward you'. However the assumption is made, as with giving to the poor, and with praying, that fasting will have a place in the discipline of discipleship. He says, 'When you fast' (6:17, 18) not 'if you fast'. Fasting seems to have three functions in Scripture.

a. As an aid to humility: David writes, 'I ... humbled myself with fasting' (Ps. 35:13). Humility is part of holiness, and is often associated with fasting, whereas enough food is often associated with pride. Moses writes about God's dealing with the nation of Israel, 'He humbled you, causing you to hunger....' (Deut. 8:3), then warns them not to forget this, 'Otherwise when you eat and are satisfied ... then your heart will become proud and you will forget the Lord your God who brought you out of Egypt' (Deut. 8:12-14). Speaking of this time centuries later to Hosea, God said, 'When I fed them, they were satisfied; when they were satisfied they became proud; then they forgot me' (Hos. 13:6). Fasting can be a corrective to pride, though it is not the act of fasting in itself as much as the spirit in which the fasting takes place.

Isaiah 58 is a chapter devoted to explaining true fasting in contrast with the idea it is a means to manipulate God. '"Why have we fasted," they say, "and you have not seen it? Why have we humbled ourselves and you have not noticed?"' (Isa. 58:3), and the chapter then shows the fast acceptable to God is not something done for one day in the hope it may put pressure on God to act in some prescribed way, rather it is to express a disposition of humility towards him.

b. As an aid to prayer: This is probably the aspect of fasting most familiar to us. Ezra writes, 'So we fasted and petitioned our God about this and he answered our prayer' (Ezra 8:23). Jonah and Daniel both give examples of fasting in association with prayer (Jon. 3:5, 10, Dan. 9:3-23). There is a reference from the ministry of Jesus where the disciples failed to deliver a boy of demon possession that caused seizures and great suffering. Jesus rebuked them for their lack of faith and said, 'This kind does not go out except by prayer and fasting' (Matt. 17:21).[1]

c. As an aid to discipline: What the Scripture describes as the 'lust of the flesh' (1 John 2:16) expresses itself most frequently in the Bible in an

---

[1] There is some dispute about the genuineness of this verse, it being in only some manuscripts. The NIV relegates it to the margin.

unguarded appetite for food. It was a means by which Eve fell in the Garden of Eden, 'When the woman saw that the fruit of the tree was good for food ... she took some and ate it' (Gen. 3:6). Esau exchanged his birthright, with all the privileges and potential that went with it, for a bowl of stew, and afterwards, 'when he wanted to inherit this blessing, he was rejected. He could bring about no change of mind, though he sought the blessing with tears' (Heb. 12:17). The children of Israel complained most in the wilderness about the food! It was one of their main stumbling blocks that brought about the judgement of God on several occasions (e.g. Num. 11:4-34). Even Jesus himself, when tempted by the devil in the wilderness was tempted first in the area of food, 'If you are the Son of God, tell these stones to become bread' (Matt. 4:3).

To be in control of our eating habits is to be in control of so much else. I have discovered in personal counselling and talks with other people that gluttony and an inability to cope with sexual temptation are closely related. That is not surprising, they have a similar root in a physical appetite that has come to master rather than to serve the person. Paul speaks of abstinence of sexual relationships in marriage as part of giving oneself to prayer and fasting (see 1 Cor. 7:5 AV)

The primary theme of this section concerning Giving, Praying and Fasting is not the techniques engaged in each, or the results that may be obtained, but the spirit and attitude in which they are done. God himself is the motivation and the One whose pleasure we are to seek.

13.

Laying up treasure
(6:19-34)

Everyone is laying up treasure in some way. It may not be expressed in the range of our assets or the size of our bank balance, but there is something in our lives which gives us reason to get out of bed in the morning and motivates us to live! It is that which reveals our true treasure, for Jesus said, 'Where your treasure is, there your heart will be also' (6:21). Whatever controls the heart is our treasure, and the person without a treasure is a sad person indeed. The treasure we have is either 'earthly' (6:19), or 'heavenly' (6:20). There can be no compromise between the two, 'You cannot serve God and money' (6:24). But the reality is that we straddle both spheres and no matter how heavenly our interests may be, we live on earth subject to its demands, its pressures and its values.

The reason why this is such an important issue to come to terms with is shown in the progression of thought from verses 19 to 24. Initially Jesus speaks of 'treasures on earth' (6:19) in contrast with 'treasures in heaven' (6:20). He then says, 'The eye is the lamp of the body' (6:22), evidently speaking of vision. He says, 'if your eyes are good your whole body will be full of light. But if your eyes are bad, your whole body will be full of darkness' (6:22-23). The thrust of this is to say that our vision, the issues on which we set our sights and the goals that motivate us in the present, is either good and brings light, or bad and brings darkness. He has spoken of an *alternative treasure*, now of an *alternative vision*, and next of an *alternative master*, for he follows it with, 'No one can serve two masters. Either he will hate the one and love the other, or he will be devoted to the one and despise the other. You cannot serve God and Money' (6:24). It is important we understand this development. What begins as *treasure*, presents itself as something which serves us and furthers our interests. That is the nature of treasure. It is a servant to us. In our pursuit of it, our treasure becomes our *vision*, the goal on which our sight is set, the motivation that drives us. In time, what began as our treasure and grew into our vision, becomes our *master*. Instead of it serving us (treasure), we serve it (our master).

To ask the questions, 'What is your treasure?'; 'What is your vision?' or, 'What is your master?' is to ask the same question. Our treasure, vision and master are one. Freedom of choice in life is limited to one fundamental option – we choose our master. Thereafter, everything we do is a consequence of that. The idea of free will is something of a myth. None of us is really free beyond the choice of our master. From then on we never act in independence of our master, for our values (treasure), our goals (vision) derive from the mastering principle.

Paul expressed this idea when he wrote, 'Don't you know that when you offer yourselves to someone to obey him as slaves, you are slaves to the one whom you obey – whether you are slaves to sin, which leads to death, or to obedience, which leads to righteousness?' (Rom. 6:16). In examining Jesus' teaching about treasure, we are examining the nature and the consequences of our master.

This is the consistent message of Chapter 6, for in the preceding verses Jesus speaks of the motivation to perform 'acts of righteousness' as being either earthly, 'before men', and temporary, 'you have received your reward in full'; or, being heavenly, 'before God' and permanent, 'your Father ... will reward you'.

The options narrow down to two. Our treasures may be: Earthly ('treasure on earth' [6:19]); concerned with human approval ('before men' [6:1]), and temporary ('where moth and rust destroy, and where thieves break in and steal' [6:19]). Alternatively, they may be: Heavenly ('treasure in heaven' [6:20]); concerned with divine approval ('your Father who is unseen' [6:6]), and permanent ('where moth and rust do not destroy and thieves do not break in and steal' [6:20]). We will examine what Jesus says about both.

Features of earthly treasures
There are two fundamental characteristics of treasure laid up on earth. They are temporary and they are troublesome.

1. They are temporary

'Do not lay up for yourselves treasures on earth, where moth and rust destroy, and where thieves break in and steal' (6:19). Treasures on earth are good for this life only, and are vulnerable to decay and theft. Paul made a very obvious statement when he wrote, 'For we brought nothing into the world, and we can take nothing out of it' (1 Tim. 6:7).

I remember being in New York City some time ago and reading in the newspaper one morning of a famous man, reputed to be one of the richest in the world, lying ill in hospital in that city and expected shortly to die. Alongside the main article was an insert entitled, 'How much is he worth?', estimating his assets and worth. Early that morning he died. Later the same day I picked up a late edition of the same paper which carried a headline announcing his death and included the same insert as the morning paper, but with one change. Instead of being entitled, 'How much *is* he worth?', it was entitled, 'How much *was* he worth?'. The exact same details followed, but what in the morning had been present tense was now past tense. Interestingly, although he was one of the world's richest men, he left no more nor less than I will leave one day – he left everything!

To be wrapped up in the treasures of earth as the goal and mastering principle of life, is to hold an extremely shallow understanding of who we are, and of our true significance.

We must be clear about what Jesus says here concerning the role of material possessions. He is not forbidding them or declaring material things inherently bad. God created material things for our good. Writing about the dangers of riches, Paul couples his warnings with the affirmation that, 'God ... richly provides us with everything for our enjoyment' (1 Tim. 6:17). We are encouraged to store goods to meet needs. Solomon wrote, 'Go to the ant you sluggard; consider its ways and be wise! It has no commander, no overseer or ruler, yet it stores its provisions in summer and gathers its food at harvest' (Prov. 6:6-8). We are to wisely store in the good times what we need for the harder times. To provide for our families is an obligation, which to ignore is to have, 'denied the faith and be worse than an unbeliever' (see 1 Tim. 5:8). Jesus did not say, 'Do not store up treasures on earth', but 'Do not store up *for yourselves* treasures on earth'. If it is motivated by selfishness rather than service, there is a fault. Material things are in themselves neutral, being neither inherently good nor bad. It is the role they play within our value system, when they become the vision and motivation of our lives, that makes them dangerous and destructive.

2. They are troublesome

Five times in this passage Jesus uses the word, 'worry'. He speaks of worry about food (6:25, 31), clothing (6:28, 31), and life itself (6:25, 27, 31). It is entirely logical to equate worry with the accumulation of material treasure! The logic runs like this: The more we have, the more we can lose. The more we can lose, the more we have to protect and look after. The more we have to look after, the more damage we will experience by losing it. The more damage we may experience through losing, the more worried we become about losing it. The very thing which in our naiveté we assumed would bring security actually produces insecurity.

I was once staying as a guest in a wealthy area of an Asian city renowned for its extremes of poverty and riches. Against the outer wall which surrounded the grounds attached to the luxurious house in which I stayed, were makeshift, mud-walled, thatched dwelling places of the poor. The home in which I stayed had steel bars at every window, multi-locks on every outside door, alarm systems at the gate and connected to every possible access point, broken glass cemented into the wall surrounding the property and the inhabitants carried loaded hand guns as they went around their business. Meanwhile the wooden shacks outside, the slum communities down the road had doors hanging off their hinges and any locks that existed were useless against a determined intruder. This is not to advocate poverty as a virtue or to be unconcerned about the needs of the poor, but to note the irony of pursuing riches as a source of security! The reality is however, that to make material prosperity either a goal, or a value by which we measure our significance, is to instantly and inevitably become characterised by 'worry'. The moment we lose it, we lose everything it represents to us.

There is another illusion associated with materialism, found in the idea that the more we possess, the more content we will be. The reality is that contentment has little to do with material accumulation, for as Jesus warned, 'Be on your guard against all kinds of greed; a man's life does not consist in the abundance of his possessions' (Luke 12:15). Subsequently, when we accumulate more and don't find the contentment we had hoped to find, we think we need even more and find ourselves locked into an insatiable appetite that will never be satisfied in that area. The big lie of our day is the assumption, 'man's life does consist in the abundance of his possessions', which is the exact reversal of what Jesus said. This pursuit of material satisfaction has led undoubtedly to the fragmentation of personal, family and national life so evident around us today, and which is so clearly forewarned by Jesus in his Sermon on the Mount. When 'treasure on earth' is our goal, 'worry' is our experience.

Features of heavenly treasures
If the features of laying up treasures on earth are that they are temporary and troublesome, the features of laying up treasures in heaven are the exact opposite: they are permanent and peaceful.

1. They are permanent
'Store up for yourselves treasures in heaven, where moth and rust do not destroy, and where thieves do not break in and steal' (6.20). To lay up treasure in heaven is to live on earth with heaven in mind. Jesus does not lay down rules, he lays down principles. The issues that govern our values, goals and behaviour should not be those confined to this life only, played out 'before men' as their umpire. They should have eternal issues at heart, and be played out before God as their umpire.

The very same possessions, the same living standards, the same occupation, the same bank balance can be laying up treasure on earth, or laying up treasure in heaven. It is not the substance of our possessions that is the issue, it is the audience before whom we live. Whether we consciously recognise it or not, to play on the material stage is to derive our satisfaction from what we can be before people. The term, 'Keeping up with the Jones' epitomises this. It leads us into spending money we don't have, to buy things we don't want, to impress people we don't like! To lay up treasure in heaven is to derive satisfaction from pleasing God. One is played out before the world, the other is played out before God.

Materialism does not relate to how much we actually possess, but to what our attitude to material things is. True spirituality does not relate to our profile in the Christian community but to our disposition towards God, which, incidentally, is most true in secret.

It is there we invest in things which money cannot buy, and which death cannot destroy. Everything that will die when we die, should be given appropriate status now, and that which holds its currency beyond death is what we should invest in now.

The nature of 'treasures in heaven' is not specified, but presents an interesting dilemma. If heaven is a place where, 'He will wipe away every tear from their eyes ... there will be no more death or mourning or crying or pain' (Rev. 21:4), and if there are treasures to be gained and treasures therefore to be missed, what will be the benefits of gaining treasures, and the penalties of not accumulating them? We may only speculate, and as heaven is to be so other-worldly than earth, we may be unable to comprehend fully even if we were told.

I did once hear the interesting idea that treasure and reward in heaven may be in a greater appreciation of Christ. Two people may look at a work of art and see exactly the same thing, or listen to a piece of music and hear exactly the same sound, but in both cases with a completely different level of appreciation. The one whose appreciation is limited does not consciously feel any lack. He simply looks at the picture or listens to the music and moves on to something else. The other may be lost in rapture at what he sees or hears, and finds deep pleasure and meaning in the artistry. He is enriched with an appreciation unknown to the other person. Perhaps there will be those in eternity whose appreciation of the Lord Jesus Christ will differ. Those with less appreciation will not be conscious that their capacity is less, but they will only live in the shallows of what the other will enjoy. Whatever may be true, to lay up treasure in heaven is to enjoy forever the consequences of a disposition toward God concerned for his will, his interests and his pleasure.

2. They are peaceful

The five statements of 'worry' (6:25-34) that characterise the person whose treasures are on earth, are removed for the person whose treasure is in heaven.

They do not worry about food (6:25, 31). Food is necessary to the body and we are obligated to work for our food. The difference is that, 'pagans run after these things' (6:32). In contrast, we are to 'seek first his kingdom and his righteousness and all these things will be given you as well' (6:33). The goal is the kingdom and righteousness of God, and in consequence other issues, including food, will find their true perspective and we will find their provision. When our treasure is on earth, earthly considerations inevitably dominate our values, with food taking on greater aesthetic and social significance. When our treasures are in heaven, we may enjoy these material provisions as fully if not more fully than anyone else, but they hold a different status. They serve us, rather than master us.

When Jesus said about this, 'Look at the birds of the air; they do not sow or reap or store away in barns, and yet your heavenly Father feeds them' (6:26) he is not saying we are not responsible to provide food for our families. Birds don't sit in their nests, mouths open, while God rains food on them! Birds work hard to gather food for themselves and their young, but the role of the heavenly Father is in providing the food to be gathered. Paul tells the Thessalonians that he gave them a rule, 'If a man will not work he shall not eat' (2 Thess. 3:10). The rule is not if a man 'cannot' work (there are some who are physically unable and others for whom there is no work to do), but in principle we are obligated to earn our own keep and provide our own needs. The point here is that when our goal is God's interests we do not worry about that provision, any more than the birds do.

They do not worry about clothes (6:28-30). In a materialistic society clothes take on great significance, as they portray an external image to the world whose approval is a determining factor in our behaviour. Image becomes everything! In contrast to this source of anxiety, Jesus said, 'See how the lilies of the field grow. They do not labour or spin. Yet I tell you not even Solomon in all his splendour was dressed like one of these. If that is how God clothes the grass of the field which is here today and tomorrow is thrown into the fire, will he not much more clothe you, O you of little faith' (6:28-30) True beauty is not created on the surface, it is the outward expression of the inward person. It is the inner person that finds its peace and security in God.

They do not worry about the length of life (6:27, 34). When living with an eternal dimension in view, death has lost its threat. For those whose treasure is on earth, death is the ultimate threat for it ends everything. For those whose treasure is in heaven, death presents no fear, for it cannot touch that which is most important. Paul, quoting from the prophet Hosea, wrote, 'Death has been swallowed up in victory. Where, O death, is your victory? Where, O death, is your sting?' (1 Cor. 15:55). We may live with the confidence that not only does God control our death (see Matt. 10:28-31), but that death is only a gateway. The grave for a Christian is the place where he or she puts on new clothes, 'the perishable must clothe itself with the imperishable, and the mortal with immortality' (1 Cor. 15:53). All that can die – will die! But the most important things can not and will not – they will be forever with God.

The key in this section is to, 'Seek first his kingdom and his righteousness and all these things will be given you as well' (6:33). Once we have settled the issue of whether our real treasure is in heaven (6:20), our vision is good (6:22) and our master is God (6:24) there are really no other key issues to face. Everything else, 'will be given you as well'.

14.

Establishing priorities
(7:1-28)

If there is a unifying theme running through the concluding section of
the Sermon on the Mount, Chapter seven, it is that a series of choices
is presented in five important areas of life. They are to do with right
judging (7:1-6), correct asking (7:7-12), good travelling (7:13-14), true
prophesying (7:15-23) and proper foundations (7:24-27). In each case,
there is a right and wrong way to respond.

Right judging (7:1-6)
It is the easiest thing in the world to judge. When Jesus says, 'Do not
judge, or you too will be judged. For in the same way you judge others,
you yourself will be judged ...' (7:1-2) he is not talking of the ability
to make value judgements about a person or their actions, for that is
part of our God-given critical faculty. He is speaking of something
that is condemnatory and destructive.

There is something about judging others that we enjoy! Pulling
someone else down makes us feel good. Solomon describes gossip this
way, 'The words of a gossip are like choice morsels; they go down to
a man's inmost parts' (Prov. 18:8). It is the fact that something within
us enjoys judging which causes Jesus to describe the act of judging
as a symptom of some kind of need in the judge. He says, 'Why do
you look at the speck of sawdust in your brother's eye and pay no
attention to the plank in your own eye?' (7:3). To be able with some
enthusiasm to pick out the speck in the other's eye, is to advertise
a plank in one's own eye! It may be pride, which delights in putting
others down so that in contrast we may be built up. It may be guilt
which so often finds satisfaction in condemning in others what we
refuse to condemn in ourselves. It is well known we often dislike

most in others what is true of ourselves. Greedy people do not like greedy people. Selfish people are deeply irritated by selfish people. Proud people cannot stand proud people. The reason may be fairly obvious. They understand what these people are doing, and they subconsciously, if not consciously, are despising their own behaviour which they either refuse or seem unable to deal with, so condemn it in the other. It is a symptom of their own guilt.

Jesus is not teaching us to take a disinterest in each other's sins and failings, but that we must establish a priority in looking into our own hearts and dealing with sin in ourselves before attempting to help another, 'First take the plank out of your own eye, and then you will see clearly to remove the speck from your brother's eye' (7:5). There is a valid and important role in a relationship with a 'brother' that allows for rebuking one another. Jesus said on another occasions, 'If your brother sins, rebuke him, and if he repents, forgive him' (Luke 17:3), 'If your brother sins against you, go and show him his fault ...' (18:15). He stated earlier in the Sermon on the Mount, 'If you are offering your gift at the altar and there remember that your brother has something against you, leave your gift in front of the altar. First go and be reconciled to your brother; then come and offer your gift' (5:23-24). This is not a call to avoid confrontation with a brother over evident sin, but to first examine ourselves and in the measure to which we are dealing with failure in our own lives, help remove the speck from their eye. This is not to condemn them for their sin, but to help remove it and get them back on track! The coward loves to condemn others for their sin, and to feel quite sanctimonious in doing so, but it takes courage to help get a person back on track and to restore them. In each of the occasions when Jesus talks about going and confronting someone with their sin, it is a 'brother' he speaks of. Someone with whom there is a relationship, and to whom there is a measure of accountability. The purpose is always remedial, to correct and restore.

To receive the helpful rebuke and criticism of others is a mark of wisdom, 'Rebuke a wise man and he will love you' (Prov. 9.8). However the opposite is also true. 'Whoever corrects a mocker invites insult; whoever rebukes a wicked man incurs abuse. Do not rebuke a mocker or he will hate you' (Prov. 9:7-8). Perhaps this is the context of the statement that follows immediately Jesus' teaching about removing the speck from a brother's eye, 'Do not give dogs what is sacred; do not throw your pearls to pigs. If you do, they may trample them under their feet, and turn and tear you to pieces' (7:6). Discretion is the better part of valour, and should someone refuse to accept a rebuke, not only will they resist the intrusion into their lives, but they may turn the accuser into a victim and 'tear him to pieces'. This statement of Jesus is not a rule of obligation to rebuke a failing brother, but a statement of the principle that if we are going to do it, you must first examine your own heart. It may be sobering to remember, 'the same way you judge others, you will be judged, and with the measure you use, it will be measured to you' (7:2).

Correct asking (7:7-12)

All through life we are faced with need, and theoretically at least, we know God has the solution to those needs. For that reason, a constant feature of life is to, 'ask', to 'seek' and to 'knock' (7:7). The promise is that 'everyone who asks receives; he who seeks finds; and to him who knocks the door will be opened'. It follows therefore that the only people who do not receive are those who do not ask. The ones who do not find are those who do not seek. Those to whom the doors remain closed are the people who do not knock. This is the privilege and right of access to God that is open to every Christian.

However, the spirit of trust in which we ask is a key characteristic of effective intercession. Jesus asks, 'Which of you, if his son asks for bread, will give him a stone? Or, if he asks for fish, will give him a snake?' (7:9). The illustration is almost absurd! No decent father will give his son a stone sandwich in place of bread, or give his child snake and chips when they expect fish and chips! But that is exactly a fear we may have of God, 'If you then, though you are evil, know how to give good gifts to your children, how much more will your Father in heaven give good gifts to those who ask him' (7:11). We do not need to detail the fine print in our intercession, we need to simply bring God in with the assurance he knows what he is doing and does what is right! When bringing a need before God we often fear the stone for bread, and the snake instead of the fish, for deep down we assume God may not be kind to us. It is true he may not give us what we ask, for he is too wise, too kind and too knowing for that, but he does give us what is right! It is in this spirit and with this confidence we are invited to ask, to seek and to knock. Our poverty can so often be attributed to one source, 'You do not have because you do not ask God' (Jas. 4:2).

At the end of this is what has become known as 'the golden rule', which may not seem particularly relevant at first, 'In everything do to others what you would have them do to you, for this sums up the Law and the Prophets' (7:12). In its context it may mean that this is equally true of God. He treats us well. We would want others to treat us well and are therefore to do the same to them, but an even more important reason is that this is exactly how God treats us. It is bread, not stone, fish, not snake he gives. The doors open when knocked, we find when we seek and we receive if we ask. God is actually on our side! He loves us and is committed to us and we enjoy that in the measure we in turn love and are committed to him. This does 'sum up the law and the prophets'. Our response to the love of God in reciprocated love for him creates the relationship and framework from which all else derives.

Good travelling (7:13-14)

Life is like a road. We are all going somewhere! None of us is static. The only issue is knowing where are we going! There are just two alternatives. Jesus spoke of a broad road and a narrow road. 'Enter through the narrow gate. For wide is the gate and broad is the road that leads to destruction, and many enter through it. But small is the gate and narrow the road that leads to life, and only a few find it' (7:13-14). One has a wide gate, a broad road and plenty of company. Its only problem is that it leads to destruction. The other has a small gate, a narrow road and only a few people on it, but it leads to life. As we noted in introducing the Sermon on the Mount, this is not primarily an evangelistic sermon, preached with a view to inviting people to become disciples of Jesus, but is addressed to those who are already his disciples, instructing them in the means of being the disciples he had called them to become.

I have heard this passage used evangelistically to good effect, the broad way being that of the person outside of Christ, and the narrow way as being the Christian life. The context would not suggest that as the likely interpretation. This is addressed to believers, warning them of the danger of a broad road that leads to destruction, and inviting them to a narrow way which leads to real life. There is a road to destruction along which a Christian may go. It is not the eternal destruction of the soul, but the destruction of all that might otherwise have been the fruit of their lives. For example, Jesus said, 'If anyone does not remain in me, he is like a branch that is thrown into the fire and burned' (John 15:6). Paul wrote, 'But each one should be careful how he builds. For no-one can lay any foundation other than the one already laid, which is Jesus Christ. If any man builds on this foundation using gold, silver, costly stones, wood, hay or straw, his work will be shown for what it is, because the Day will bring it to light. It will be revealed with fire, and the fire will test the quality of each man's work. If what he has built survives, he will receive his reward. If it is burned up, he will suffer loss; he himself will be saved, but only as one escaping through the flames' (1 Cor. 3:10-15). There is a fire of destruction through which believers need to go, though should their works be 'burned up', they will themselves 'escape through the flames'. This is the end of the broad road of which Jesus warns.

If comparing the two roads side by side, the broad road would appear the more attractive. To be 'narrow' is not a popular concept! Most would like to be considered broad and tolerant, and would consider it a mark of maturity. However in this passage to be narrow is to be virtuous for it is to be aiming at a target and going for it. Some years ago I visited the flight deck of a Boeing 747 on a flight from Western Canada to London. I asked the Captain if it was somewhat boring to fly a plane once it was in the air. He told me that he was constantly checking his position and direction and how that the routing to London was an extremely narrow one. One degree off course on the compass bearing would take us hundreds of miles in the wrong direction. I was very glad we had a pilot who was interested in a narrow way! I wouldn't want a Captain who was satisfied all routes went to London, put his feet on the instrument panel and went to sleep! It is in this sense the road to life is narrow.

Paradoxically perhaps, it is in travelling the narrow road that true freedom is found. Jesus said, 'If you hold to my teaching ... you will know the truth and the truth will set you free' (John 8:31-32). My car works best when I put petrol in the tank, not coca cola, oil in the engine not syrup, thirty pounds of air pressure in the tyres, not thirty pounds of bananas! To insist on petrol, oil and air may appear restrictive and rather narrow, but it is the way the car was designed and in keeping to the instructions it is free to function as intended. It is in narrowing our interests to those of Jesus Christ that we find real freedom and real life!

There is freedom within the truth, as I have the freedom when and where to drive my car, but there is no real freedom outside of the truth. The broad road takes down the perimeter fences and invites us to live pretty well as we please. It may even sound mature, but is in fact folly. Its end is destruction!

True prophesying (7:15-23)
Here Jesus gives solemn warning about the kind of spiritual leaders you may meet on the broad road – the false prophets. He talks of two things: The clothes they wear, and the fruit they bear.

1. *The clothes they wear.* 'They come to you in sheep's clothing, but inwardly they are ferocious wolves' (7:15).

The art of falsehood of course is to appear genuine! To print counterfeit currency you would not print a two pound note! The game would be up before you start! Counterfeit must have some marks of the genuine article if it is to stand any chance of deceiving anyone. These false prophets cover themselves well. They imitate the real thing and learn its language, 'Lord, Lord' (7:21), and perform its works, 'Many will say to me on that day, "Lord, Lord, did we not prophesy in your name, and in your name drive out demons and perform many miracles"' (7:22). They have become accomplished performers of miracles, can drive out demons and exercise what appear to be spiritual gifts, but they are evil! They plead with God on the Day of Judgement, referred to by Jesus as 'that day', and they argue their case in the delusion their deception may have extended even to him! But he who is never deceived replies, 'I never knew you. Away from me, you evildoers' (7:23).

Cults and aberrations of true Christianity rarely identify themselves as such in their initial stages of development. They generally appear as having rediscovered a neglected emphasis, and are careful to use legitimate language. Many of the more disastrous cults of recent decades had their roots in evangelical Christianity, and drew initial recruits from evangelicalism, deceiving people with familiar terminology, but which was describing something that proved alien. They were wolves in sheep's clothing.

2. *The fruit they bear.* 'By their fruit you will recognise them' (7:16).

The ultimate test of spiritual reality is fruit. Fruit takes a while to mature, and it is wise to test any new idea or movement which is ambiguous in its genuineness, not on the initial, usually sweet smelling blossom, but on its maturing fruit. The ultimate test of that fruit is its conformity to the person of Jesus Christ. He is the truth! If something is true in any ultimate sense, it was true of Christ. He is the embodiment of the Christian life. The goal of the Holy Spirit within the Christian is nothing else and nothing less than a conformity to his character. The fruit of any movement is not to be measured in whether it does people good, for any movement would die a swift death if it did not have its beneficiaries! Most sects, cults and pseudo spiritual movements give people a sense of goodness at some point. But the measurement by which the genuine article may be measured is that its basis of truth is also true of Jesus Christ.

Proper foundations (7:24-27)

This final story in the Sermon on the Mount is possibly its most familiar. It is the story of two men who built two houses that to all appearances were equal – until a storm broke. The rain came down, the streams rose and the winds blew and beat against each house. One of them remained firm and erect. The other fell with a great crash. The difference between the two was the foundation on which they had been built. One was built on sand, the other on rock. I frequently hear the assumption made that the rock represents Christ and the sand, in contrast, represents anything other than Christ. This is not the case. The wise man who built his house on the rock was the man who 'hears these words of mine and puts them into practice' (7:24). The foolish man who built his house on sand was the man who 'hears these words of mine and does not put them into practice' (7:26). The rock is obedience. The sand is disobedience.

It has been well said that the greatest need of many Christians is not to know more, but to obey what they already know. To listen without obedience is deception, says James when he writes, 'Do not merely listen to the word and so deceive yourselves. Do what it says' (Jas. 1:22). Spiritual growth is more than an intellectual process, it is a volitional process. The word of God is only effectively read and understood from a disposition of submission and obedience. The more we know the more our capacity for sin increases. James again writes, 'Anyone who knows the good he ought to do and doesn't do it, sins' (Jas. 4:17). It is a sobering thought that every new lesson we learn which does not meet with a response of submission creates

125

new possibilities of sin. Understanding carries responsibility. It is submission to the word of God and obedience to the will of God which are the foundation of our security and stability.

15.

Miracles and faith
(8:1–9:34)

The Sermon on the Mount is immediately followed in Matthew's record by demonstrations of power. Jesus came down the mountainside, followed by large crowds, where he met and healed a man with leprosy. Having preached the ethic of the kingdom in the Sermon on the Mount, he now demonstrated the dynamic of the kingdom in his power to heal. Chapters eight and nine record ten distinct miracles by Jesus, interspersed with some teaching on discipleship. There are twenty specific miracles of Jesus recorded in Matthew (of the thirty five different miracles in all four gospels), half of which are in these two chapters. Additionally there are eleven references to groups of unspecified miracles performed by Jesus in this gospel,[1] and two by his disciples.[2] Most of the miracles in Chapters eight and nine are to do with healing, with additional unspecified cases of exorcism and healing the sick (8:16).

The ten specified are:

1. Cleansing a man with leprosy (8:1-4);
2. Healing the centurion's servant who lay paralysed in his home (8:5-13);
3. Healing Peter's mother-in-law of fever (8:14-15);
4. Calming a storm on Galilee (8:23-27);
5. Exorcising two violent demon possessed men and driving the demons into a herd of pigs (8:28-34);

---

[1] See Matthew 4:23; 8:16; 9:35; 11:4-5; 11:20-24; 12:15; 14:14; 14:36; 15:30; 19:2; 21:14.
[2] See: 10:1; 10:8.

6. Healing a paralysed man brought to Jesus on a mat (9:1-8);
7. Raising a dead girl to life (9:18-26);
8. Healing of a woman who had been bleeding for twelve years and who came up behind him in a crowd and touched the edge of his cloak (9:20-22);
9. Restoring sight to two blind men (9:27-31);
10. Driving demons from a dumb man, enabling him to speak (9:32-33).

These include demonstrations of power in the biological, physiological, natural and spirit worlds.

These miracles were not theatrical manifestations of his deity, designed to impress or prove something. It is popular to use Jesus' miracles as evidence of his deity, but miracles were not unique to Christ. Moses performed miracles, as did Elijah, Elisha, Peter, Stephen, Philip and Paul, none of which suggest they were divine, for they were not. The miracles of Jesus do not in themselves prove his deity, but according to Peter on the Day of Pentecost, they demonstrate his credibility as a man sent by God, 'Jesus of Nazareth was *a man* accredited by God to you by miracles, wonders and signs which God did among you through him' (Acts 2:22). If the miracles are regarded in themselves as evidence of his deity, we are presented with a problem with the equally remarkable miracles of other people in Scripture. In reality, the miracles prove the humanity of Jesus for they demonstrate his dependence upon his Father. Jesus claimed that as a man he was capable of accomplishing nothing alone. He said, 'I tell you the truth, the Son can do nothing by himself; he can do only what he sees his Father doing, because whatever the Father does the Son also does' (John 5:19. See also John 5:30; John 8:28). His own explanation for his own activities was, '... it is the Father living in me who is doing his own work' (John 14:10). Jesus demonstrated his true humanity by his dependency upon his Father, and it was the Father's activity in the Son which was his own explanation for his words and actions.

We will look at two interesting features in this record worth considering. One is the variety of ways Jesus performed each miracle, and the other, in contrast, is the common denominator in the response of the people to him.

1. The variety of ways Jesus performed his miracles

There is great variety in the way Jesus dealt with the people he healed. He reached out his hand and touched the leper, he spoke about the centurion's servant without meeting him in person, he touched the hand of Peter's mother-in-law, he stood up and rebuked the wind and waves in the storm, he spoke to the demons in the two violent men, he spoke to the paralytic on the mat without physically touching him, the woman in the crowd took the initiative and reached out to touch him, and he took the dead girl by the hand and pulled her to her feet. His approach in each case was different, and this is exactly true to his nature.

We must guard against ever reducing Jesus Christ to a formula or a predictable pattern. There were those who assumed, that having experienced healing by Jesus touching them, that this was the pattern and formula he followed. Mark records an incident when some people brought a blind man and, 'begged Jesus to touch him' (Mark 8:22). They did not ask Jesus to heal him, they begged him to touch him! They had presumably seen Jesus in action and reduced his working to a pattern, and begged him to apply the formula to this blind man and touch him. Instead Jesus took the man outside and, to the astonishment of the people, spat in his eye, and he was healed! Around the same time a deaf and dumb man was brought to Jesus with the same request – 'they begged him to place his hands on the man' (Mark 7.32). They did not ask Jesus to heal him, but to place his hands on him! He took the man aside, put his fingers into the man's ears and spat on the man's tongue! He said, 'Be opened' and the man could both hear and speak!

We cannot tie Jesus Christ to a predictable formula which can be turned on or off at will. He has the freedom to be original in his dealings with people. The issue is never *how* a person was healed, but always *who* is doing it! God deals with us differently. Some of us are intimidated by that, and either want everyone else to have the same experience of God we have had, or feel something is lacking because we have not had identical experience to someone else. The issue is never the nature of our experience in itself, it is always the origin of the experience – God has been at work.

2. The common factor in people's response to Jesus

However, if there is a variety of ways in which God dealt with the people, there is a common factor in their response to him, and that factor is *faith*. The word is explicitly used on several occasions, and implied in others. To the centurion Jesus said, 'I have not found anyone in Israel with such great faith' (8:10); in the storm on Galilee Jesus said to the disciples, 'You of little faith, why are you so afraid' (8:26); of the friends bringing the paralytic to Jesus it says, 'When Jesus saw their faith ...' (9:2); to the woman who touched his garment he said, '... your faith has healed you' (9:22); and to the two blind men Jesus said, 'According to your faith will it be done to you' (9:29). The idea is implicit in the statement of the leper who said, 'If you are willing you can make me clean' (8:2); and the father of the girl who died, when he said 'My daughter has just died. But come and put your hand on her and she will live' (9:18).

Faith is the indispensable ingredient in a working relationship with God. Faith is not a mystical power, where the act of believing something makes it come true, nor is it a form of wishful thinking needed when the facts are shaky and you go out on a limb and believe something for which there seems insufficient evidence. Faith is a disposition of trust towards an object that allows that object to work on our behalf.

For example, faith in a car is a disposition of trust towards the car that permits the car to take me down the road. Faith in an aircraft is a disposition of trust towards the plane that permits it to fly me through the air. The evidence of faith is not seen in what we do for the object of our faith, but in what we allow the object of our faith to do for us. It is the car that takes us down the road. It is the plane that flies us through the air. Faith in God is a disposition of trust towards God that enables God to work on our behalf. It is not seen in what we may do for God, but in what God does for us.

The faith exercised by those healed by Jesus was a disposition towards him that trusted him to do for them whatever he wished to do. Faith does not prejudge what God may do, it is the attitude of trust that allows him to do whatever he may choose to do, by whatever means he may choose to do it. If for some good reason God permits us to remain sick (cf. Paul in Gal. 4:13) or he chooses to heal is his business. Both results in this case would be a result of faith. Faith in God does not only produce good and wonderful results. There are many times when that is the purpose and will of God, but many times when equally it is not. Hebrews chapter eleven is the classic chapter on faith in the New Testament. It lists all the great people of faith such as Abel, Enoch, Noah, Abraham, Jacob, Joseph and Moses and all the wonderful exploits accomplished in their lives, 'by faith'. However, equally, 'Some faced jeers and floggings while still others were chained and put in prison. They were stoned, they were sawn in two, they were put to death by the sword. They went about in sheepskins and goatskins, destitute, persecuted and mistreated ... They wandered in deserts and mountains and in caves and holes in the ground. These were all commended for their faith, yet none of them received what had been promised' (Heb. 11:36-39). It is not the consequences of our faith in God that measures its effectiveness. Faith in God allows God to be God and when living by faith we live with the certainty of his will being accomplished, whether it involves miraculous intervention or not.

The disposition of trust in Jesus does not prejudge his actions. Knowing his will in a particular situation is not a prerequisite to exercising faith in his ability to perform it. It is sometimes stated that faith is not saying, 'God can', but 'God will', but this passage would suggest the reverse is true. The leper came to Jesus and said, 'Lord, if you are willing you can make me clean' (8.2). He was saying in effect, 'I know you are able, but I do not at this moment know if you are willing'. Jesus response was to say, 'I am willing. Be clean'. He said to the two blind men, 'Do you believe I am able to do this?' (9:28). He did not ask, 'Do you believe I am willing to do this?'. To believe he is willing is to prejudge his actions, which is legitimate if he has disclosed his will, but is not legitimate if he hasn't.

To believe he is able, is to have every confidence in his ability, but not necessarily to be aware of his intentions. When the blind men answered, 'Yes Lord', Jesus touched their eyes and said, 'According to your faith will it be done to you'. Their faith was a confidence in his ability, and the readiness to let him work according to his own agenda and purpose. How God works in our circumstances is his business, but the reality of his working is always in response to faith.

Discipleship: the cost and consequences
Interspersed in the ten miracles of chapters eight and nine are accounts of the calling of Matthew to be a disciple (9:9-13) and the offer of two others to follow Jesus (8:18-22). We have some detail in the four gospels of the calling of six of the twelve apostles – Philip, Andrew, Peter, James, John and Matthew. To each of them the two key words

in Jesus calling his disciples are his invitation to, 'Follow me', or in the case of those who would be his disciples (8:18-22), the promise they make to 'follow you'.

The words, 'Follow me' sound an incomplete invitation. If someone were to give the same invitation to you or me we would almost certainly respond by asking, 'Where are you going?'. It is interesting these men did not ask that question! The issue in discipleship is never *where* we are going, it is *who* we are going with. Had the disciples asked where they were going, and had Jesus answered honestly, they probably would not have gone! To James he could have said, 'You are going to be executed by Herod while still young'. To Peter he could have said, 'You will be crucified upside down by the Romans'. As far as we know, ten of the twelve apostles were martyred, Judas committed suicide on the day Jesus was crucified, and only John survived to die as an old man in his bed!

Our own well being and comfort has little to do with discipleship. To be a disciple of Jesus Christ is to be fully caught up in his programme and to live by his agenda. This may or may not include tough circumstances, but the option of it doing so remains ever present. When a teacher of the law came to Jesus and said, 'Teacher, I will follow you wherever you go,' Jesus' reply was to say, 'Foxes have holes and birds of the air have nests, but the Son of Man has nowhere to lay his head' (8:18-20). This response of Jesus was not to give particular virtue to homelessness, but rather to indicate that discipleship does not have as its main goal the fulfilment of the disciple, but the fulfilment of the Master's purposes, for which his own well being may have to be relinquished. We cannot bring conditions into discipleship or place boundaries on our obedience and still regard it as true discipleship.

Another man came and said to him, 'Lord, first let me go and bury my father', but to him Jesus replied, 'Follow me and let the dead bury the dead' (8:21-22). It is almost certain that the man was not implying his father lay dead and in need of burial, but that he needed to wait until his father had died so as to be free from family obligations before being available to follow Jesus. The response of Jesus is to say that his first obligation was to obey him and let the consequences be what they are. We must not wait until other obligations are worked out before giving obedience to Christ. We surrender exclusively to him as the first call on our lives, and all other obligations work their way out of that prior relationship. This sounds hard, almost shocking, language, but we dare not tame the demands of Jesus. If nothing else, discipleship is serious, costly business.

Immediately after these two encounters Matthew writes, 'Then he got into the boat and his disciples followed him' (8:23). The wording implies they acted as instructed, 'followed him', but 'Without warning a furious storm came up on the lake so that the waves swept over the boat'. In following Jesus they were led into a furious storm. And so it may be! To be a disciple of Jesus Christ is not to be exempt from hardships and difficulties, rather it is to be equipped to live within them securely. When the disciples woke up Jesus who had fallen asleep in the boat, he rebuked them, 'You of little faith, why are you so afraid'. In 'following Jesus' their security was not to lie in their circumstances and therefore to be vulnerable to changes in circumstances, their security was to be in Christ. This is the fundamental ingredient in the life of discipleship to which we are called!

16.

The disciples in preparation
(9:35–10:4)

The second teaching section of Matthew records the gathering together of the twelve disciples, equipping them with authority over evil spirits and sickness, and sending them out to preach to the 'lost sheep of Israel'. The passage may be divided into five sections:

The preparation (9:35–10:1)
As Jesus travelled through towns and villages, preaching, teaching and healing, Matthew records the effect of the crowds on him, 'When he saw the crowds, he had compassion on them, because they were harassed and helpless, like sheep without a shepherd'. There is both an objective vision and a subjective compassion. Objectively he, 'saw the crowds ... like sheep without a shepherd'. That was his vision. Subjectively, 'he had compassion'. Compassion comes from seeing people in their true state. Praying for compassion is not likely to be very effective! Opening our eyes to see people as they really are is the source of true compassion.

What follows is a key to understanding effective evangelism. 'Then he said to his disciples, "The harvest is plentiful but the workers are few. Ask the Lord of the harvest therefore, to send out workers into his harvest field"' (9:37-38). The response to seeing the harvest was not to say, 'Go into the harvest field', but 'Ask the Lord to send workers into his harvest field'. There is a 'Lord of the harvest field' who knows his business in the world, and who knows exactly the state of the harvest. Our task is not so much to run around and try and do everything, but to allow him to direct our path and bring us in touch with the right people in the right place at the right time to reap the ripe harvest! We make a very big mistake when we think of technique as the secret of evangelism. Various techniques may have validity and help us in our evangelistic task, but the key to evangelism is to be found in relating to the role of Jesus Christ as Lord of the harvest.

It is very difficult to establish a strategy for evangelism from the New Testament without recognising the indispensable role of God in putting people in contact with the right people at the right time. When an angel appeared to Philip in Samaria (Acts 8) and told him to go south to a desert road, Philip did not know that an Ethiopian eunuch would arrive at the same place at the same time on a journey home from Jerusalem to Ethiopia – but God did. Furthermore he would just happen to be reading the passage from Isaiah which foreshadows Christ and says of him, 'He was led like a sheep to the slaughter'. Philip was able to jump on board the chariot, explain the passage, lead him to Christ and baptise him before he continued his journey. No organised technique would bring that about!

The key ideas here are vision, compassion and intercession. The *vision* of Jesus, 'When he saw the crowds', led to *compassion*, 'he had compassion on them because they were harassed and helpless, like sheep without a shepherd', which led to *intercession*, 'Ask the Lord of the harvest therefore to send out workers into his harvest field'. Breaking any one of those links renders the process ineffective. The next statement says, 'He called his twelve disciples to him and gave them authority to drive out evil spirits and to heal every disease and sickness' (10:1). The ones he told to ask the Lord of the harvest to send out workers, are the same ones he then sent out to do the job. Vision, compassion and intercession lead to action!

The people (10:2-4)

Matthew gives a list of the twelve disciples at this point. What we know of these men is quite limited, but the overwhelming picture of them is their sheer ordinariness. We must not instal them in stained glass windows with a halo around their heads and present them as somehow other-worldly. It is worth summarising some of the information we have of these men in the Gospels, to discover a picture of the raw material with which God delights to work!

Of the four lists of the twelve apostles in the New Testament,[1] there are one or two details in common. Peter always heads the list, and Judas Iscariot closes it, apart from the list of those waiting for

---

[1] See also Mark 3:16-19; Luke 6:14-16; Acts 1:13.

Pentecost, when Judas is already dead. The selection of these twelve is an important landmark in Jesus' ministry. It is difficult to be exact in knowing at what stage in the three year public ministry of Jesus these twelve were selected out of the larger number of disciples who followed Jesus, but the likelihood is they were with him as a completed unit for most of his ministry.

Mark records that Jesus, 'appointed twelve – designating them apostles – that they might be with him and that he might send them out to preach and to have authority to drive out demons' (Mark 3:14-15). To be with him, and to be equipped by him for ministry which would come to its fore after his ascension was clearly his purpose. How many disciples there were from which to choose the twelve we do not know, but on another occasion we know he sent out seventy two other disciples with similar instructions and in a similar context to this occasion in Matthew 10 (see Luke 10:1).

Who were these men whom Jesus chose to work through?

Simon who is called Peter

Peter is first in the list and is the most vocal of all the disciples. His name was Simon and it was Jesus who called him Peter, meaning rock (John 1:42). We know he was the son of a man named John (John 1:42) or Jonah (Matt. 16:17), was a brother to Andrew (John 1.40), came from Bethsaida on the north shore of Galilee (John 1:44) where he worked as a fisherman, was married at the time he became a disciple, and at one stage it appears his mother-in-law lived with him (Matt. 8:14-15), and his wife later accompanied him on his missionary travels (1 Cor. 9:5). He is not only the first named in the list of disciples, but was part of an inner circle of three that included James and John who were alone together with Jesus on several important occasions.

The larger than life image of Peter is as an extrovert talker. He speaks in the gospels on more occasions than all the other disciples put together, very often to say the wrong thing! It was to him Jesus said, 'Get behind me, Satan. You are a stumbling block to me; you do not have in mind the things of God, but the things of men' (16:23). It was Peter who promised Jesus he would never fall away, promising, 'Even if I have to die with you, I will never disown you' (26:35). That same night he denied knowing Christ on three occasions, cursing and swearing to affirm his innocence of any knowledge of him. Jesus had said aptly to him in the Garden of Gethsemane, shortly before his denial, 'The spirit is willing but the body is weak' (26:41). It was to him Jesus especially spoke after his resurrection (Mark 16:7) and made a special appearance (Luke 24:34).

Andrew

Andrew was the brother of Peter. He was formerly a disciple of John the Baptist, who left John for Jesus when John announced Jesus as the 'Lamb of God' (John 1:35-40). He first went and found his brother and introduced him to Christ. He was a fisherman in partnership with his brother, and having come from Bethsaida later lived with Simon Peter and his wife in Capernaum (Mark 1:29). He said or did little that was marked out as great, but he was the disciple who brought the boy with five loaves and two fishes to Jesus, which Jesus then multiplied to feed the five thousand (John 6:8-9). Perhaps he was a kindly man to whom the boy felt attracted, but he had little grasp of what Jesus might do with the food, apologising as he brought it, 'but how far will they go among so many?'. Tradition has it Andrew ended his life crucified in Achaia.

James and John

James and John were brothers, the sons of Zebedee and Salome, who worked as fishermen in Galilee in partnership with two other brothers called to be disciples of Jesus, Andrew and Simon (see Luke 5:10). They formed, with Simon Peter, the inner core of Jesus' disciples, the three being present with Jesus at the raising of Jairus' daughter (Mark 5:37), the transfiguration (Matt. 17:1) and in the Garden of Gethsemane (Matt. 26:37).

John has a reputation as the 'apostle of love', primarily from his own writings that form part of the New Testament. However, in reality the image of these two brothers in the gospel records is quite the opposite. They come across as hard, arrogant and self-seeking!

On a journey to Jerusalem, Jesus once sent some messengers ahead of him who went into a Samaritan village to get things ready for him, but the people did not welcome him. James' and John's reaction to this was to ask, 'Lord, do you want us to call fire down from heaven to destroy them?' (Luke 9:51-54). This is hardly the apostle of love talking!

Another time John complained to Jesus, 'we saw a man driving out demons in your name and we told him to stop because he was not one of us' (Mark 9:38). John made the deduction many have erroneously made since: If someone is not 'one of us', he is not one of God's! The reverse is true: If someone is one of God's he is 'one of us', whether we actually like it or not.

The two brothers once made an incredible request of Jesus, 'Let one of us sit at your right and one at your left in your kingdom'. Their understanding almost certainly was of Jesus setting up a kingdom of Israel, as was anticipated by most of the Messiah, and they wanted the prominent places alongside him, one on his right and one on his left. Jesus said, 'You don't know what you are asking. Can you drink the cup I drink or be baptised with the baptism I am baptised with?' Their incredible answer was, 'We can'! (Mark 10:35-45). To this Jesus told them, 'Whoever wants to be great among you must be your servant, and whoever wants to be first must be slave of all'. This is John and James at their most arrogant. Interestingly Matthew's record of the same or a similar incident has their mother bringing James and John to Jesus with the same request. Perhaps when Jesus did not grant them their request they thought it might help if their mother came and asked!

Jesus gave a nickname to James and John, 'Boanerges, which means Sons of Thunder' (Mark 3:17). These aptly described sons of thunder prior to Pentecost, became John, the man of love, who left us the legacy of five New Testament books or letters, and James who was the first disciple to be martyred, killed by a sword under Herod's orders in the early days of the church (Acts 12:2). Reliable tradition tells us John died as an old man in Ephesus and possibly the only one of the eleven apostles (not including Judas) who died a natural death.

Philip

Philip was one of the first disciples of Jesus, having been a disciple of John the Baptist, with Andrew. He was from Bethsaida in Galilee, and was called to be a disciple the day after Jesus called Andrew and Peter. He was then instrumental in bringing Nathanael to Jesus (John 1:43-51). He only speaks twice after his initial call. Once when Jesus did a test on him at the time of the feeding of the five thousand. John's record states, 'When Jesus looked up and saw a great crowd coming toward him, he said to Philip, "Where shall we buy bread for these people to eat?"' The next verse explains what lay behind the question, 'He asked this only to test him, for he already had in mind what he was going to do' (John 6:6). Jesus was not looking for advice, but testing how much Philip was learning. Philip's response in effect was to look into his pocket, perhaps find out how much money Judas had in the bag, and come back with the response, 'Eight months' wages would not buy enough bread for each one to have a bite', or as the marginal reading says, 'two hundred denarii would not be enough' (John 6:7). Philip's response was equal to the response of any sensible atheist faced with the same test! He had no sense of the miraculous. It is one thing to be able to explain theological niceties, but the real test of spiritual understanding is found in what we know of the resources available to us in a crisis, when all natural remedy has been exhausted. This is the test of true understanding. Philip in this crisis failed the test!

The second time he spoke was when Jesus explained, "If you really knew me, you would know my Father as well. From now on, you do know him and have seen him". Philip said, "Lord, show us the Father and that will be enough for us'" (John 14:7-8). The implication seems to be, 'Leave the technical jargon and just show me!' He doesn't want the theory, just the real tangible thing! He may have been pragmatic and down to earth but he was missing the whole point.

Bartholomew

This name appears in each list of the apostles, but otherwise is not mentioned in the New Testament. We therefore know no details of anyone of this name. However, it may well be that Bartholomew is another name for Nathanael who is mentioned twice in the gospels. Firstly, when Philip on meeting Jesus for the first time went and found Nathanael and told him he had found the one, 'Moses wrote about in the Law, and about whom the prophets also wrote – Jesus of Nazareth' (John 1:45). Nathanael replied, 'Can any good thing come out of Nazareth?' On then meeting Jesus he believed, exclaiming, 'Rabbi, you are the Son of God, you are the King of Israel' (John 1:49). He is never mentioned again until after the resurrection of Jesus from the dead when seven disciples were together at Galilee when Jesus appeared to them. Nathanael is one of the five named (John 21:2). We may not be certain that Nathanael and Bartholomew are one and the same person, but it is a strong possibility.

Thomas

There are only references to Thomas doing or saying anything in John's gospel. He is best known for his doubting the reality of Jesus' resurrection from the dead, after Jesus had appeared to the other disciples in his absence. Jesus appeared to Thomas a week later, causing him to fall before him and confess, 'My Lord and my God' (John 20:24-29). This comes as something of a climax to John's gospel, with the response of Jesus, 'Because you have seen me, you have believed; blessed are those who have not seen and yet have believed'.

The first time Thomas appears is at the time Jesus received the news that his friend Lazarus had died. Thomas said to the rest of the disciples, 'Let us also go, that we may die with him' (John 11:16). That was not the most constructive contribution!

He asks a question of Jesus which indicated his confusion about what the whole purpose of Jesus was. 'Thomas said to him, "Lord, we don't know where you are going, so how can we know the way"', to which Jesus replied, 'I am the way' (John 14:5). Bishop J. C. Ryle comments on Thomas, 'On each occasion he is mentioned he appears in the same state of mind – ready to look on the black side of everything, – taking the worst view of the position, and raising doubts and fears. He does not know where our Lord is going.... He cannot believe our Lord is risen.... He sees nothing but danger and death if his Master returns to Judea'.[2] The term 'doubting Thomas' may well be an accurate legacy of the man!

Matthew

The call of Matthew is recorded in the gospels of Matthew, Mark and Luke (Matt. 9:9-13; Mark 2:14-17; Luke 5:27-32). In Mark and Luke he is called 'Levi'. Mark also tells us he is the 'Son of Alphaeus' (Mark 2:14). Apart from his call to leave his tax collector's booth, we have no record of anything Matthew did or said. As a tax collector he worked for the Romans and was in consequence hated by the Jews. The gospel that bears his name has been attributed to him since at least the second century and there is no good reason to dispute that. He would have had some basic writing and book keeping skills.

After Jesus had called him, Matthew threw his home open for a banquet attended by Jesus and 'many tax collectors and sinners', giving

---

[2] *Expository Thoughts on the Gospels – John* Volume 2, by J. C. Ryle, James Clarke & Co Ltd 1969.

rise to Jesus' statement in response to the criticism of the Pharisees, 'I have not come to call the righteous but sinners to repentance' (9:13).

James, son of Alphaeus
This second 'James' of the twelve is also called, 'James the younger' (Mark 15:40), presumably to distinguish him from an older James, the brother of John. This reference to him also tells us his mother was Mary, and we know his father was Alphaeus (10:3), though there is no evidence it was the same Alphaeus who was the father of Matthew. We know of nothing he said or did.

Thaddaeus
The Authorised Version calls him, 'Lebbeus whose surname is Thaddaeus', but in the list of disciples in Luke and Acts he is, 'Judas, son of James'. The only time he features in the gospel record is when he is identified as, 'Judas not Iscariot' and asks the question, 'Lord, why do you intend to show yourself to us and not to the world' (John 14:22). Apart from that we know of nothing he said or did.

Simon the Zealot
The second 'Simon' in the list is identified as 'Simon the Zealot'. Some translations at this point call him, 'Simon the Canaanite'. The historian Josephus gives us some information about the Zealots. They were founded by Judas the Galilean who led a revolt against Rome in AD 6, opposing the payment of tribute to the Roman emperor on the grounds it was treason to God, Israel's true King. The revolt was quickly crushed, but its spirit was kept alive for 60 years.[3] The Zealots were the ultimate patriots who put the dignity of their nation before everything. It may well have been Simon who asked the question of Jesus immediately prior to his ascension, 'Lord, are you at this time going to restore the kingdom to Israel' (Acts 1:6). This would have been his interest in particular. We would describe him today as a political activist, and almost certainly he saw his alignment with Jesus and the role of the Messiah as being to the political advantage of Israel.

In every other circumstance, to find a Zealot and a tax collector together in the same group would have been unthinkable. The Zealot would have plunged a knife into the tax collector. They stood at

---

[3] See 'Zealot', *New Bible Dictionary*, Inter Varsity Press.

opposite ends of the spectrum in relation to the Roman empire, yet they are found together as disciples of the Jesus Christ.

Judas Iscariot

The last disciple in the list is Judas Iscariot. He was the treasurer who became the betrayer. Whenever he occurs in the gospel records it is connected in some way with money. When Mary anointed Jesus in Bethany with costly ointment, Judas was indignant and objected, 'Why wasn't this perfume sold and the money given to the poor? It was worth a year's wages'. John adds, 'He did not say this because he cared about the poor but because he was a thief; as keeper of the money bag, he used to help himself to what was put into it' (John 12:2-6)

Jesus knew Judas from the beginning. He said to the twelve disciples on one occasion, 'Have I not chosen you, the Twelve? Yet one of you is a devil' (John 6:70). It was the devil who prompted Judas to betray Jesus (see John 13:2), and when he acted on his decision to do so, 'Satan entered into him' (John 13:27). Judas was not driven by Satan. He was tempted by the devil but when he made his choice to betray Jesus for thirty pieces of silver the devil entered. The devil entering Judas was not the cause of his actions but the consequence of them.

The true nature of Judas came as a surprise to his fellow apostles. When an artist paints a picture of the twelve, Judas is almost always recognisable because he looks gaunt and hollow eyed, he stands to the side and does not make eye contact. You look at him and know you would not trust him. That is not true to the evidence however. Who would make a crook the treasurer! With hindsight, John calls him a thief (John 12:6), but at the time they had no idea. When Jesus told the twelve that one of them would betray him, they didn't turn to each other and whisper, 'It's Judas! I knew he would do this'. Rather, 'They were very sad and began to say to him one after the other, "Surely not I Lord?"' (26:22). When Judas eventually left the gathering in the Upper Room with Jesus saying, 'What you are about to do, do quickly', most of the disciples did not understand what he was doing, 'some thought Jesus was telling him to buy what was needed for the Feast, or to give something to the poor' (John 13:27-29). Judas had conned his closest colleagues.

Only when it was over did the consequences of what he had done truly dawn on Judas. He returned the money and committed suicide on the morning of the day Jesus was crucified (27:1-10).

Some women

Along with these twelve men were a group of women who travelled at least some of the time with Jesus, not designated as apostles, but who provided them with material support. Luke gives a list of some of them when he writes, 'The twelve were with him and also some women who had been cured of evil spirits and diseases: Mary (called Magdalene) from whom seven demons had come out; Joanna the wife of Chuza, the manager of Herod's household; Susanna; and many others. These women were helping to support them out of their own means' (Luke 8:1-3). Even this partial list shows a wide range of women with Jesus. Contrast Joanna, wife of Herod's chief of staff, Chuza, from the top social drawer, with the formerly demon possessed Mary Magdalene. Other women occur in the narrative from time to time, and played a full role in his ministry.

The ordinary and the extra-ordinary

This was a very ordinary crowd of people. They were very ordinary financially, academically, socially and spiritually. They were hardly material for turning the world upside down! Yet although they were a very ordinary group of people they were commissioned by Jesus Christ to do extra-ordinary things, 'He called his twelve disciples to him and gave them authority to drive out evil spirits and to heal every disease among the people' (10:1). The secret of ordinary people doing extra-ordinary things is found in their relationship to Jesus Christ. '*He* called ... and gave them authority.... These twelve *Jesus* sent out...' (10:1, 5).

It is the extra-ordinary Christ working through ordinary people that has extra-ordinary results! He is the *extra* in the *ordinary* that makes the extraordinary! The quality of the end product is determined by its source. The source was not something inherent in the disciples themselves, but in Christ who called them and sent them. This principle holds true in the Christian life, 'The one who calls you is faithful and *he* will do it' (1 Thess. 5:24). The One who calls and commissions is responsible for the consequences. To understand this lifts the pressure of 'performance' and enables us to rest in his sufficiency alone. These disciples were to obey their instructions in dependence on God in such a way that left him responsible for the consequences.

17.

The disciples in action
(10:5-42)

Matthew having named, and Jesus having commissioned his disciples, there are now details given of the procedures, problems and provisions that will characterise their ministry.

1. Procedures (10:5-15)

Jesus first gives his disciples some procedural instructions. They were to limit their mission entirely to the 'lost sheep of Israel', and to avoid going to any Gentiles or Samaritans. This was a temporary instruction, in keeping with the pre-Pentecostal limitations on their message. Later the bounds of both the message and the people to whom it should be preached were to become universal (see 28:18-20).

The message to be preached was 'The kingdom of heaven is near' (10:7), almost identical to that preached by John the Baptist (3:2) and Jesus (4:17). It was a message that centred on the King himself, setting up his kingdom, and was to be accompanied by miracles of healing, exorcism and even raising the dead. There is nothing here about forgiveness of sin, the indwelling and fulness of the Holy Spirit or the eternal repercussions of either accepting or rejecting the King. This message would come in its fulness later.

Peter's explanation on the Day of Pentecost of the miracles of Jesus was that they gave him authenticity by his Father, 'a man accredited by God to you by miracles, wonders and signs which God did among you through him' (Acts 2:22). We have no record of the disciples performing miracles prior to Pentecost, though it is implied they did do so (see 17:17-20), but the widespread miraculous work through the apostles reported after Pentecost authenticated them as those in league with Jesus Christ and therefore with God. It is a mistake to assume miracles were performed by almost any believer after Pentecost, for the facts are they were generally limited to the apostles. Luke records, 'many wonders and miraculous signs were done by the apostles' (Acts 2:43), and 'The apostles performed many miraculous signs and wonders among the people' (Acts 5:12). The apostles were a broader group than just the twelve whom Jesus called, and included Paul, Barnabas, Timothy and others. Only two men performed miracles in the New Testament who were not specifically called apostles, namely Stephen (Acts 6:8) and Philip (Acts 8:6-8). It may well be they could be among the group designated apostles, and as Paul classifies the 'things that mark an apostle' as 'signs, wonders and miracles' (see 2 Cor. 12:12) it is very likely they were. This is not to suggest God does not perform miracles in other contexts or through other people, but to recognise that when he does so it is exceptional rather than normal. Even those today who place miraculous healing high in their understanding of the work of the Holy Spirit are forced by sheer facts to acknowledge that miraculous healing of the kind seen in the ministry of Jesus and the apostles is exceptional rather than normal.

As for the material necessities the apostles were told, 'Do not take along any gold or silver or copper in your belts; take no bag for the journey, or extra tunic; or sandals or a staff; for the worker is worth his keep' (10:9-10). They were not to get bogged down with concerns about material things, but to trust God that as they enriched the lives of those to whom they would minister, they would in turn be enriched.

The instructions to take no material possessions with them were for that particular time and place. Later Jesus would ask them, '"When I sent you without purse, bag or sandals, did you lack anything?" "Nothing," they answered. He said to them, "But now if you have a purse, take it, and also a bag; and if you don't have a sword, sell your cloak and buy one"' (Luke 22:35-36). They had learned the complete trustworthiness of God on the occasion they had gone out with nothing. Having learned that, he then tells them to care for as much of their own needs as they can. It is often in the early stages of our Christian life or particular ministry that we see God work dramatically, only to find as time goes on his provision becomes much more 'ordinary'. This is the pattern here, and probably a general one in Christian experience.

The strategy in discerning where to stay and spend their energies was to look for an initial response of welcome and receptivity that would enable them to form a nucleus of people, stay in their homes and build from there. If no nucleus was found, they were to 'shake the dust off your feet' (10:14) and move on to those who would be more receptive. The point is not that those who do not initially respond should be abandoned. There is a place for stubborn persistence in seeking to introduce people to Christ, but we are workers *with* God rather than workers *for* God. The onus is not on us to persuade and convince, but to be discerning of those individuals and situations in which God is working, and keep in step with him. Jesus said of his relationship with his Father, 'My Father is always at his work to this very day, and I, too, am working ... I tell you the truth, the Son can do nothing by himself; he can do only what he sees his Father doing, because whatever the Father does the Son also does. For the Father loves the Son and shows him all he does' (John 5:17, 19-20). Jesus did not work in independence of his Father in any detail of his life, and as Jesus worked in harmony with his Father, so we are to work in harmony with Christ. That is why he had previously told them not to run out and accomplish whatever they could on his behalf, but to, 'Ask the Lord of the harvest to send out workers into his harvest field' (9:38). He is the Lord of the harvest and knows where the harvest lies, and it is in dependency on him that the disciples were to be directed to the right people in the right place.

2. Problems (10:16-23)

So far, the instructions of Jesus were positive and exciting. The apostles may well have been revelling in the excitement of all they were now going to be doing and experiencing, when Jesus listed a whole catalogue of warnings which began, 'I am sending you out like sheep among wolves'! (10:16). When sheep and wolves meet it is normally the sheep who are vulnerable and get into trouble! It is the disciples who are the sheep, and the world at large who are the wolves! We must be careful not to reverse this and create an understanding that we are the triumphant, aggressive ones, and the world is vulnerable against disciples of Jesus Christ. It is we who get hurt. It is we who must be careful. Jesus identifies three packs of wolves in the following verses.

Firstly, there is the *religious pack of wolves*: '... they will ... flog you in their synagogues' (10:17). Of all the people who should know better it is those meeting in the synagogues with open Scriptures, yet the first source of opposition would come from them! It is a sad fact of the four Gospels, the book of Acts, and the history of the church that some of the most savage attacks come from within the ranks of the supposed people of God. It was the priests, scribes and Pharisees of the day who led the attacks on Jesus. It was the Sanhedrin Council in Jerusalem, presided over by the High Priest, with the Old Testament scriptures in one hand, who condemned Jesus to death and sought the injunction of the Roman governor to do so. It was primarily the religious leaders who opposed the gospel after Pentecost, both from within Judaism in the early record, and from other religious sources as the gospel spread wider throughout the Mediterranean world. Even today, the work of God has to grow against opposition from organised religion at large, but also from within its own ranks. Often it is those who ought to know better, who are blinded by prejudice and history to a sensitivity to God, an understanding of his word and a recognition of his work.

Secondly there is the *governmental pack of wolves*: 'On my account you will be brought before governors and kings as witnesses to them and to the Gentiles' (10:18). This happened in the early church, and James was the first of these men to die at the hands of government leaders when King Herod put him to death in the early years of the church in Jerusalem (Acts 12:2). By the year 64 AD, the Christians had been singled out as the enemy of the Roman empire, and were ruthlessly persecuted, many in Rome being thrown to the lions, with others hiding in the caves and catacombs beneath the city.

The authorities had been able to bring charges against the Christians which satisfied the people they had to be eliminated. They were accused of many things, including being revolutionaries seeking the overthrow of Rome because they preached the 'kingdom of God'; of cannibalism because the words of Jesus, 'This is my body' and 'This is my blood' were twisted into stories of Christians sacrificing fellow humans and eating their flesh and drinking their blood; of gross sexual immorality in their weekly meeting, which they called the Love Feast (the Agape) and were said by their enemies to be orgies of lust. There were many other accusations levelled against them. It is an interesting observation that the church historically has generally grown best when persecuted. This is not to encourage the seeking out of persecution for its own sake, but to be realistic in seeing that when the church is not under pressure it is in danger of being superficial.

Thirdly, there is the *family pack of wolves*: 'Brother will betray brother to death, and a father his child; children will rebel against their parents and have them put to death' (10:21). This is probably the most distressing of all opposition. He speaks of 'brother', 'father', 'children', all in opposition to the point of putting to death, and 'a man's enemies will be members of his own household' (10:36).

Subsequent history proved the truth of these warnings, and therefore showed the cost of true discipleship of Christ. There is no promise of an easy road, in fact the reverse is true. There is promise of a difficult road! Paul warned Timothy, 'In fact, everyone who wants to live a godly life in Christ Jesus will be persecuted' (2 Tim. 3:12). It is a temptation sometimes to think that as a reward for obedience and loyalty to Christ, he will engineer our circumstances to take out the tough and painful experiences, but the facts of history, and the promises of Jesus do not give any ground for this. There is no virtue in experiencing trouble in itself, but we must be realistic in expecting it, and constructive in understanding its role.

When Jesus warned the disciples they would be like sheep among wolves, he added, 'Therefore be as shrewd as snakes and as innocent as doves' (10:16). Snakes do not go looking for trouble. If they perceive it is coming to them they will respond, but they do not go looking for it. Neither should we, which is why Jesus said in this context, 'Be on your guard against men' (10:17)! There is no virtue in trouble, particularly if it has been provoked unnecessarily. The fact it will come is sure, but we are to be as 'shrewd as snakes' in our attention to potential trouble, and when it comes, to be 'as innocent as doves'. The innocence and clean living of the Christian will mean that when people start throwing mud, it is given little reason to stick! The reality of what we are will carry more influence than the cleverness of anything we might say.

3. Provisions (10:19-42)

After the realism of Jesus' warnings, he tells them not to worry or be afraid on four occasions, describing four sets of circumstances: when arrested, when accused, when assassinated and when alone.

When arrested (vv. 19-23)

'When they arrest you, do not worry about what to say or how to say it. At the time you will be given what to say, for it will not be you speaking but the Spirit of your Father speaking through you'. He does not say, 'If they arrest you', but 'When they arrest you'. It is going to happen! No matter how shrewd and innocent the sheep may be, they are going to provoke the wolves. Being arrested seems a normal part of apostolic experience in the book of Acts. Events will take unanticipated turns, and circumstances will catch us off guard! In that situation we may not know what to say or how to react, but 'do not worry', said Jesus for at that time we will experience the Father giving us what to say.

The idea of not having to worry about what to say, is a very attractive one but has a strict context! He does not say, 'When you get up to preach ...' or 'When you face your Bible class ...' or 'When you go to your Sunday school class ...' do not worry about what to say for your Father will speak through you! The context is 'When they arrest you ...'. In a situation where we are caught off guard or taken by surprise we may be sure he won't be, and will provide us with all that we need.

The certainty of being arrested and persecuted as a disciple of Jesus Christ does not mean there is an inherent virtue in it, or that it is something to be courted and desired! The willingness to lose our lives for Christ is part of discipleship (see 10:39), but to court persecution or to regard martyrdom as an accomplishment is not what this is about. Jesus says, 'When you are persecuted in one place, flee to another' (10:23), which, in other words, is to get out of the way when it is appropriate and possible. The sheep are not to tease the wolves!

When accused (vv. 24-27)

Genuine misunderstandings as well as deliberate distortions of our motives and intentions are going to take place. 'It is enough for the student to be like his teacher and the servant like his master. If the head of the house has been called Beelzebub, how much more the members of his household' (10:25). False accusations are to be expected. Jesus had been accused of driving out demons by Beelzebub, the prince of demons (12:24), which is as extreme a distortion of truth as is possible to go. We are to expect it and we are to accept it. Some explanation in response to false accusations may be appropriate, as

Jesus responded to the accusation of driving out demons by Beelzebub (see 12:25-32), but despite the malicious accusations that are made against us, we may be sure truth will ultimately be known. 'So do not be afraid of them. There is nothing concealed that will not be disclosed, or hidden that will not be made known' (10:26). We may wait patiently for the day when everything will be made known, and the truth will be out!

When assassinated (vv. 28-29)

'Do not be afraid of those who kill the body but cannot kill the soul' (10:28). Jesus warns the disciples of the possibility of martyrdom, but assures them they need not fear those whose ability extends to killing the body, but who cannot touch the soul. Most of us would prefer to die at seventy rather than at thirty, enabling us to make the most of this life. In the long ages of eternity it really will not matter. The enemies of God may throw the servants of God to the lions, burn them at the stake, or chop them into a thousand pieces, but they will not and cannot kill the real them, so 'Do not be afraid' said Jesus. Most of us will not face the prospect of assassination, but we do need to face its implications. We are never so ready to live than when we are ready to die. We are never as equipped to live as when we are equipped to die. To have overcome the fear of death is to have overcome the fear of most things in life! Perhaps this is implicit in Jesus' statement later in the same passage, 'whoever loses his life for my sake will find it' (10:39).

Even death at the hands of evil men does not violate the will of God. Jesus told these disciples that not one sparrow will fall to the ground, 'apart from the will of your Father' and 'you are worth more than many sparrows' (10:29-31). If he is involved in the death of a sparrow, how much more is he involved in the death of a person. When John had his vision of Jesus on the Isle of Patmos, he fell at his feet as though dead. The Lord said to him, 'Do not be afraid. I am the First and the Last. I am the Living One; I was dead and behold I am alive for ever and ever! And I hold the keys of death and Hades' (Rev. 1:17-18). The keys of death belong to the Risen Christ. He is never the author of evil, but he sets the bounds on the evil of which we may be victims (for examples of this, see Job 1:12; 2:6). Death will never come to us outside of God's permission, for he holds the keys of death. We die on time!

When alone (vv. 31-42)

This last section highlights the loneliness of being separated from those we love (10:34-36), of Christ taking priority above all other relationships (10:37-39), of being ministered to when in need of a cup of cold water (10:40-42). In each instance, our security is found in being known to the Lord Jesus Christ, and in being identified with him. No matter the human loneliness of the circumstances, Jesus reassures them that, 'even the very hairs of your head are all numbered. So don't be afraid ...' (10:30, 31).

True discipleship is unlikely to involve a comfortable cruise through life without misunderstandings, opposition, persecution and for some, martyrdom. If God does or does not shield us from some or much of this, our security is not to lie in our circumstances, but in Christ himself. Our union with Christ is such that 'he who receives you receives me' (10:40), and 'if anyone gives even a cup of cold water to one of these little ones because he is my disciple, I tell you the truth he will certainly not lose his reward' (10:42). This great promise of his identity with us, and all the security we may derive from that, is dependent in practical experience on the measure to which we identify with him. 'Whoever acknowledges me before men, I will also acknowledge him before my Father in heaven. But whoever disowns me before men, I will disown him before my Father in heaven' (10:32-33).

18.

Stumbling blocks to truth
(11:1-30)

The tenth chapter of Matthew records the commissioning of the disciples by Jesus to go out to teach, preach and heal. The narrative however does not follow the disciples in their exploits but stays with Jesus. 'After Jesus had finished instructing his twelve disciples, he went on from there to teach and to preach in the towns of Galilee' (11:1). In the course of those travels, this chapter records his encountering stumbling blocks over which three kinds of people fell. John the Baptist was the first. I want to call this *the problems of the expectant* (11:1-19). The cities of Korazin, Bethsaida and Capernaum in which Jesus had performed miracles was the second. I want to call this *the problems of the experienced* (11:20-24). The 'wise and learned', contrasted with 'little children' are the third. I would like to call them *the problems of the educated* (11:25-30).

1. John the Baptist – problems of the expectant (11:1-19)
John the Baptist had been put in prison shortly after the commencement of Jesus' ministry (see 4:12 and 14:3-5), and whilst there had received reports of what Christ was doing. He sent his disciples to Jesus to ask him, 'Are you the one who was to come, or should we expect someone else'? (11:2).

It is unlikely John was questioning the identity of Jesus, for he had publicly acknowledged him, baptised him and testified that he had witnessed the descent of the dove and the voice of the Father which marked the beginning of his ministry, and on that basis he stated, 'I have seen and I testify that this is the Son of God' (see John 1:32-34). It is more likely his questioning related to the method and ministry of Jesus. John the Baptist himself had caused a great stir in Judea. He was very much the 'voice of one calling in the desert' (3:3), he was loud and eccentric, wearing clothes of camel's hair, and eating locusts and honey! The whole region of Jordan was stirred by his ministry (3:5). Jesus was different. The prophet Isaiah had foretold of the Messiah, 'He will not shout or cry out, or raise his voice in the streets' (Isa. 42:2). John in his passion for righteousness had preached judgement, Jesus was preaching mercy. John had an expectancy of Jesus' continuing of his own ministry and had publicly declared, 'He must become greater and I must become less' (John 3:30).

This continuity had happened in a way John may not have anticipated when he was arrested by Herod, taken from the scene and inevitably 'became less'. Now in prison, his expectation of the Messiah is being brought into question. Is he really accomplishing the work John expected of him?

Jesus' reply is particularly interesting. 'Jesus replied, "Go back and report to John what you hear and see: The blind receive sight, the lame walk, those who have leprosy are cured, the deaf hear, the dead are raised, and the good news is preached to the poor. Blessed is the man who does not fall away on account of me" ' (11:4-6). His reply very much alludes to the statement Jesus had read from Isaiah the prophet when he first introduced himself as the promised Messiah in the synagogue in Nazareth and which centres around the proclamation of good news to the poor and oppressed (see Luke 4:18-19). On that occasion he concluded his reading in mid sentence with the words, '... to proclaim the year of the Lord's favour', and left his hearers with a sense of the goodness of the good news for those who receive it, but he did not go on to complete the statement in Isaiah with the final clause, 'and the day of vengeance of our God', which declared wrath and judgement on those who did not receive it (see Isa. 61:1-2). John was the great prophet of this period, 'he is the Elijah who was to come' (11:14) and he would have understood the full message of Isaiah and anticipated something of the 'vengeance of our God' which had characterised his own ministry.

In our Bibles, the little comma between proclaiming 'the year of the Lord's favour', and 'the day of vengeance of our God' divides the period between the first and second advent of the Messiah. There is a judgement day yet to come, but in the meantime it is the time 'of the Lord's favour'. In the previous chapter Jesus had said to his disciples they should not be afraid of those who falsely accuse them for, 'There is nothing concealed that will not be disclosed, or hidden that will not be made known' (10:26), but that disclosure is yet to come. John saw the whole picture of the Messianic ministry, and perhaps did not sufficiently appreciate there was both a present and a future aspect to it.

Sometimes our expectancy of Christ and his work can lead to a deep disappointment or even disillusionment. Our reading of parts of Scripture has led us to an understanding that is not true to the whole picture, and we have built an expectancy and trust that has not come to fruition. The question of divine healing is one example. Matthew clearly indicates that physical healing is included in the effects of the cross of Christ when he quotes Isaiah's statement about the suffering Messiah, 'He took up our infirmities and carried our diseases' (8:17 quoting Isa. 53:4), and points to Jesus' miracles of healing as a fulfilment of this. There is a present tense, 'now' aspect to the gospel, and a future tense 'not yet' aspect. Getting the right balance between the 'now' and the 'not yet' is crucial. Healing of diseases and sickness may be included in the atonement, but so is dealing with sin and death. The reality is we still sin, we still die and we still suffer in the present tense of our experience.

But there is a future aspect! The story will one day be complete when 'He will wipe every tear from their eyes. There will be no more death or mourning or crying or pain, for the old order of things has passed away' (Rev. 21:4). This is not to exclude a present working of God in these areas, but to acknowledge that the fulness of our salvation is yet to be realised.

Jesus' last words to John the Baptist are: 'Blessed is the man who does not fall away on account of me' (11:6). If we cannot understand what Christ is doing, trust him anyway! To fall away on the grounds of unfulfilled expectation is to put the failure on to Christ, rather than us, when we may have been misguided. The absolute immovable truth is Christ. We have to conform our belief and our expectancy to him as he is, not the other way around.

There is no greater endorsement of a human being in Jesus' ministry than the one he gives about John the Baptist to the crowd, after John's disciples left them. 'Among those born to women there has not risen anyone greater than John the Baptist'. Yet, said Jesus, despite the greatness of John, 'he who is least in the kingdom of heaven is greater than he' (11:11). John began to preach the kingdom as something 'near' (see 3:2), and from that time on the kingdom had been advancing until its implementation through the death and resurrection of Christ and the gift of the Holy Spirit at Pentecost. The least partaker in that kingdom has more going for them than John ever did. John never saw the love of God and the provision of God in the cross of Christ. He could preach the holiness of God, the righteousness of God, the justice of God and the wrath of God. His message carried the threat of judgement and destruction, but he could never bask in the love of God and the indwelling resources of the Spirit of God which were to be the normal features of those in the kingdom. John was 'filled with the Holy Spirit from birth' (Luke 1.15), but in the Old Testament sense of being empowered for service rather than the fuller post-Pentecostal sense of the Holy Spirit forming Christ in us (see Gal. 4:6 and 4:19).

2. The cities of Korazin, Bethsaida and Capernaum – problems of the experienced (11:20-24)

Jesus came to the Galilean cities in which most of his miracles had been performed, Korazin, Bethsaida and Capernaum, and denounced them, 'If the miracles that were performed in you had been performed in Tyre and Sidon, they would have repented long ago in sackcloth and ashes. But I tell you, it will be more bearable for Tyre and Sidon on the day of judgement than for you' (11:21-22).

Experience brings responsibility. How it will be more bearable for Tyre and Sidon on the Day of Judgement than for these cities, Jesus does not explain, but the fact it is so is not left in doubt. The more we know, the more responsible we become. Some have argued that ignorance of Christ is bliss, and to take the gospel to those who have never heard is to give them the opportunity of rejecting Christ which they would otherwise not have had! That is in conflict with the instruction to take the gospel to all the world, so we cannot argue that point effectively. What is true however, is that, 'From everyone who has been given much, much will be demanded; and from the one who has been entrusted with much, much more will be asked' (Luke 12:48). The context of this statement is knowledge of a master's will. The greater our exposure to God and our knowledge of his will, the greater our obligation of response and obedience.

There is a resistance to God that is not intellectual but volitional. It is one thing to say, 'I can't believe', it is another to say, 'I won't believe'. Doubting Thomas was not filled with intellectual confusion when told of the resurrection of Jesus, but volitional resistance, 'Unless I see the nail marks in his hands and put my finger where the nails were, and put my hand into his side, *I will not believe*' (John 20:25). It is impossible to remain static in Christian growth. It is like riding a bicycle. We either keep moving or we fall off! We do not remain static! We move on in response to increasing understanding of God and his purposes, or our hearts harden and we become more resistant.

The people of Korazin, Bethsaida and Capernaum had seen sufficient to understand he was 'a man accredited by God to you by miracles, wonders and signs which God did among you through him' (Acts 2:22), but they had failed to acknowledge that in repentance, which, said Jesus, Tyre and Sidon would have done long ago. Their rejection of him only heaped on them a sense of responsibility that would lead to greater condemnation on the Day of Judgement.

3. The 'wise and learned' – problems of the educated (11:25-30)

It was at the time of Jesus' condemnation of the cities of Korazin, Bethsaida and Capernaum that Jesus said, 'I praise you, Father, Lord of heaven and earth, because you have hidden these things from the wise and learned, and revealed them to little children'.

Knowledge of God is never attained, it is received! If our resistance to God is not primarily intellectual but volitional, it is also true that our knowledge of God is volitional rather than intellectual. The frustration of the 'wise and learned' is in their assumption they might know God through their wisdom and learning.

It seems a fact that the great influences on our knowledge of God and godliness rarely, if ever, emanate from our universities or theological schools. Paul's own testimony was that the 'surpassingly great revelations' given him by God held the potential to lead him astray, so God allowed him to weaken in order to keep him dependent! (see 2 Cor. 12:7-10). If this was a potential trap in real revelation, how much more is it the potential of academic investigation of God! It was Paul who wrote of the danger that 'Knowledge puffs up', which he contrasted with the fact that 'love builds up' (1 Cor. 8:1). Paul tells the Corinthian believers, 'Not many of you were wise by human standards ... But God chose the foolish things of the world to shame the wise' (1 Cor. 1:26-27). The incredulity of the educated religious leaders in Jerusalem at the impact of the early church was contributed to by their realisation these were 'unschooled, ordinary men' (Acts 4:13).

This is not to down play the validity of academic investigation into spiritual things, but to get that discipline into perspective. We do not in the first place know God through investigation, we know him in the first place by revelation. Revelation does not depend on intellectual capacity but on the disposition of heart, 'you ... revealed them to little children. Yes, Father, for this was your good pleasure' (11:25-26).

This revelation is at the Son's discretion, for 'no one knows the Father except the Son and those to whom the Son chooses to reveal him' (11:27). Does that suggest an arbitrary revelation? To whom does the Son reveal the Father and himself? The answer is in the next statement, 'Come to me, all you who are weary and burdened, and I will give you rest. Take my yoke upon you and learn of me ...' (11:28-29). It is those who are weary of carrying their own burden, who are overwhelmed by their lack of resources, who come in humility and place their own burden on his shoulder and learn to rest! To them he says, 'learn of me'.

Before the mind is ever thrilled with Jesus Christ, the disposition of heart is one of insufficiency in ourselves, which leads consequently to full submission to him. The tests applied by God to people in Scripture were never tests of their intellectual grasp of truth, they were tests of their disposition towards God and the measure to which they looked to him for their sufficiency. (For examples of this see Gen. 22:1ff; Deut. 8:16; Ps. 26:2-3; Ps. 139:23-24; John 6:5-6; 2 Cor. 13:5-6).

19.

Mounting opposition
(12:1-50)

The first time it is suggested Jesus be put to death in Matthew's gospel is in chapter 12. Opposition to Jesus is first recorded in Chapter 9 following the healing of a paralytic when Jesus had said to him, 'Take heart, son; your sins are forgiven'. Some of the Scribes said to themselves, 'This fellow is blaspheming'. This marks the beginning of an escalating desire to get rid of him, which becomes more focused in this chapter in three events which contribute to the growing opposition.

1. *He did what was unlawful.* His disciples plucked grain and Jesus healed on the Sabbath Day (12:1-21).
2. *He did what was improbable.* He drove out demons and the Pharisees concluded it could only be by Beelzebub the prince of demons (12:22-37).
3. *He did what was illogical.* He refused to perform a miracle when asked to do so in order to prove himself (12:38-45).

1. He did what was unlawful (12:1-21)

The Pharisees were provoked by two instances in these verses which violated their interpretation of the Sabbath law. Firstly, his disciples plucked heads of grain and ate them, and secondly, Jesus healed a man with a shrivelled hand. However, it was not so much the actions of Jesus and his disciples that were the source of the provocation, but more the attitude of the Pharisees who were 'Looking for a reason to accuse Jesus' (12:10), and found a convenient one.

We need to understand the perspective of the Pharisees at this point. The name *Pharisee* is derived from a Hebrew word meaning 'separated'. What they originally saw themselves to be separated from is not altogether clear, but most references to the Pharisees involve their strict observance of the law and a sense of being separated from any violation of that law was certainly part of their ethos. However, in order to avoid breaking the law of God, they built fences of lesser laws around the Mosaic law to prevent them getting close to breaking the real law!

The first violation of the Sabbath in this chapter is when the disciples plucked heads of grain and ate them. The commandments forbade work on the Sabbath day, but that was too ambiguous a prohibition for the Pharisees, work had to be defined. Thirty nine specified prohibitions were laid down as defining work on the Sabbath. Amongst them were reaping, winnowing, threshing and preparing a meal, all of which the disciples had done in the process of plucking heads of grain, separating the grain from the chaff, blowing the chaff away, the whole exercise preparing food to be put into their mouths! Normally, a meal was prepared on the day before the Sabbath so that it could be eaten without any preparation taking place.

These laws originally written to protect people from violating the real law had predictably in due course assumed the standing of the Mosaic law. Thus the Pharisees felt entirely justified in accusing Jesus and his disciples of 'doing what is unlawful on the Sabbath'.

Jesus answered the accusation by pointing out what David did when he and his companions were hungry and entered the tabernacle to eat consecrated bread, only lawful for the priests (see 1 Sam. 21), and how the 'priests in the temple desecrate the day and yet are innocent' through their work of sacrificing animals, a task doubled on the Sabbath.

The law was to the Pharisees and Jews an external imposition of demands by which they assumed they would please God. But what has its origins externally only touches the externals. Hence the later diagnosis of Jesus, 'You clean the outside of the cup and dish, but inside they are full of greed and self-indulgence. Blind Pharisee!' (23:25-26). Jesus' concern is with change on the inside, which inevitably expresses itself externally in true godliness, but the externals are the effect rather than the cause. Jesus then said, 'If you had known what these words mean, "I desire mercy, not sacrifice", you would not have condemned the innocent. For the Son of Man is Lord of the Sabbath' (12:7-8). It is not on the basis of sacrificial service *for* God, but the receiving of mercy *from* God that true godliness is received and then expressed in love and kindness.

As if to make his point, Jesus immediately met a man with a shrivelled hand in the synagogue on the same day. He questioned the Pharisees as to whether they would pull one of their own sheep out of a pit if it fell in on a Sabbath day, and then asked the man to stretch out his hand and healed him. A man is of much more value than a sheep, said Jesus, but healing the man so provoked the Pharisees, 'they went out and plotted how they might kill Jesus' (12:14). There is not a better example than this of the law which is designed to reveal the character of God (see notes on 5:17) being made the antagonist of the purposes of God. God is love, and the law, designed to reveal his character in practical terms is rightly understood as it interprets his love, not hinders it.

Following the plot of the Pharisees to kill him, Jesus withdrew from that place. Many followed him, but he warned them not to tell who he was.

2. He did what was improbable (12:22-37)

The open antagonism to Jesus by the Pharisees resurfaces again when he drove out demons from a blind and mute man, enabling him to both see and hear. The Pharisees seeing this realised the miracle could not be denied, but concluded it could only be by Beelzebub the prince of demons that he drove out demons. So blind were they to the realities of who Jesus was and what he was doing, they concluded the explanation for his actions must be demonic. In their thinking it was completely improbable that Jesus would be working by the Spirit of God, for as far as they were concerned, he violated the laws of God. Their own assumptions were not challenged by Jesus. Rather it was by their own assumptions they challenged Jesus.

Jesus' answer to this was to state that if he did in fact drive out demons by the prince of demons then they should rejoice for it indicated civil war was taking place in the demonic realm. To drive out demons by Beelzebub was an absurd idea unless hell itself was in utter turmoil. Conversely, if he drove out demons by the Spirit of God then they should equally rejoice for the 'kingdom of God is come upon you'. Either way, they ought to be glad!

It was following this incident that Jesus made his statement, '... every sin and blasphemy will be forgiven men, but the blasphemy against the Spirit will not be forgiven ... either in this age or in the age to come' (12:31-32). This statement has brought some turmoil to Christian people who wonder if they might have committed this sin. It seems clear, however, that the sin of blasphemy against the Holy Spirit is to so resist him and his revelation of Christ that all possibility of forgiveness is closed to us. If these people failed to see that the liberty, light and relief being brought to those he healed and exorcised was of God, then their resistance to the Holy Spirit was so acute they were closing all opportunity of conviction and cleansing. All other statements of forgiveness in the New Testament are for those who repent and confess their sin (see Rom. 8:1; 1 John 1:9 etc.). It is the refusal to recognise Christ and to repent which is the unforgivable sin. From its context, this is the sin of the Pharisees to whom Jesus addresses himself in this chapter.

Jesus says to these Pharisees that what is externally visible in a person's life has its roots internally. Good or bad fruit derive from a good or bad tree. His fruit is good and they should therefore recognise the nature of the tree to be good. In contrast, their words are bad and 'From the overflow of the heart the mouth speaks' (12:34).

3. He did what was illogical (12:38-45)

Suddenly the Pharisees seem to adopt a sickly sweet disposition towards him when they ask, 'Teacher, we want to see a miraculous sign from you' (12:38). His response seems illogical. Here is his opportunity to demonstrate his true ability and identity, but he refuses to prove himself, saying, '... it is a wicked and adulterous generation who asks for a miraculous sign' (12:39). The only sign given is the sign of Jonah who spent '... three days and nights in the belly of a huge fish', likened to the fact the 'Son of Man will be three days and three nights in the heart of the earth'. The sign of the authenticity of Jesus is his death, burial and resurrection from the dead. To seek beyond that is to align with a '... wicked and adulterous generation'.

Miracles in themselves do not prove the identity of Christ. Others performed miracles in Scripture without any suggestion they were divine. There are Satanic sources of miracles too. Jesus warned, 'For false Christs and false prophets will appear and perform great signs and miracles to deceive even the elect – if that were possible' (24:24). The weakness of miracles as evidence of God working is that they concern themselves with the here and now rather than with the eternal truths that constitute the gospel. We are to believe, not because we benefit from supernatural intervention, valid as that intervention may be, but because Jesus Christ has satisfied God in his death on the cross on our behalf, was buried, and has risen from the dead to impart his Spirit to us. The historical fact of his death and resurrection is the sign to an unbelieving world, and Jesus refused to give any other sign to the Pharisees.

Jesus compares these Pharisees with two events – the people of Nineveh in Jonah's day (12:41), and the visit to Solomon of the Queen of Sheba (12:42). The people of Nineveh had repented at the preaching of Jonah, and the Queen of Sheba travelled from the ends of the earth to listen to Solomon, but these Pharisees had turned deaf ears to Christ. Now that one greater than Jonah and Solomon was here, their excuses were less and their condemnation was greater. Additionally, the Pharisees were Israelites, participants in the covenant God had made with that nation. They had failed to recognise Christ, yet both Nineveh, the capital city of Assyria, and the Queen of Sheba who were outside of the covenant Israel enjoyed with God had recognised and responded to the truth.

The more exposed we are to truth, the greater the benefit as we respond to it, or the harder we become when we fail to respond to it. This latter condition characterised the Pharisees. To make this point Jesus gave a rather surprising and remarkable illustration from demon possession (12:43-45). Demons need bodies through which to act as mediums. When an evil spirit leaves a body it is restless and dissatisfied, looking for a body to inhabit and through which to express its evil intentions. It returns to the body it originally occupied and finds it 'swept, clean and put in order', but at the same time 'unoccupied'. The demon which has been driven out has not been replaced by someone or something else. The evil spirit then returns with seven other spirits to inhabit the man and the final condition is worse than the first. Then said Jesus, 'this is how it will be with this generation'.

The ministry of Jesus amongst the people was to drive out evil as an expression of the rule of his kingdom. 'If I drive out demons by the Spirit of God, then the kingdom of God has come upon you' (12:28). That may bring wonderful relief to people, but it is not the final goal to which he is working. The outcast demon must be replaced by the indwelling Spirit. The Lord Jesus Christ must first drive out the evil but then replace it with himself. These Pharisees had put all of their energy into getting rid of evil, strictly following the rules of the Old Covenant for holiness of life, but failing to understand the need for their sin being replaced with the presence of God. They therefore remained 'unoccupied', and ripe for re-invasion of evil, worse than before. We cannot remain static in these things. We either grow in spiritual maturity and godliness or we grow hardened and embittered against true godliness. What we do not do is remain the same. This generation, said Jesus, had seen the kingdom of God come in power and authority but had not allowed evil to be replaced with God, so were in a worse condition than they were originally.

His mother and brothers (12:46-50)

This chapter concludes with the incident of Jesus' mother and brothers waiting to talk to him outside the building in which he was speaking. Matthew does not tell us why they were there or what they wanted to talk to him about, but Mark's record of this same incident does: 'When his family heard about this they went to take charge of him for they said, "He is mad"' (Mark 3:21). John the Baptist queried Jesus in Chapter 11. His own family do so in Chapter 12.

Mary, the mother of Jesus, had insight into his true identity from the time of his birth, but she kept it very much to herself. As announcements were made at his birth we are told, 'Mary treasured up all these things and pondered them in her heart' (Luke 2:19). At the age of twelve she took him to Jerusalem and on return to Nazareth it says again, 'His mother treasured all these things in her heart' (Luke 2:51). There is no evidence of her speaking about Jesus, or persuading his brothers of his true identity, and she may sometimes have been confused herself by him. At the age of twelve when Jesus explained to Joseph and Mary how he must be about his Father's business, Luke writes, 'But they did not understand what he was saying to them' (Luke 2:50). He was misunderstood in his own home, and misunderstood outside it. Those who hated him accused him of driving out demons by Beelzebub, and those who loved him accused him of being mad. Neither understood him. It must have been a lonely business to remain true in such circumstances.

Jesus' answer to those who told him his family was waiting for him was to point to his disciples and say, 'Here are my mother and my brothers. For whoever does the will of my Father in heaven is my brother and sister and mother' (12:49-50).

True relationships are measured by Jesus in terms of allegiance to his Father. To do the will of God is to be in relationship with Christ. These are not so much the terms of our relationships with each other, but of our relationship with Christ. However, in all human relationships he is to take priority, for '... anyone who loves his father or mother more than me is not worthy of me' (10:37). We are united to each other as believers, by our union with Christ. Outside of a shared union in Christ, unity with fellow human beings will be limited. The reality of that union with him will determine the depth of our unity with each other.

20.

Kingdom parables – the bad news
(13:1-52)

We come to the third main teaching section of Matthew's gospel, the first being the Sermon on the Mount (chs. 5–7), and the second the sending out of the disciples (ch. 10). This is concerned with eight parables told by Jesus, all of which have to do with the kingdom of heaven. The eight parables are as follows:

1. The seed and the soil (13:3-9 and 13:18-23);
2. The wheat and the weeds (13:24-30 and 13:36-43);
3. The mustard seed (13:31-32);
4. The leaven and the loaf (13:33);
5. The hidden treasure (13:44);
6. The pearl of great price (13:45-46);
7. The fishnet (13:47-50);
8. The householder (13:52).

These are presented by Matthew not as a collection of parables neatly edited together by him into one section of his gospel, but as a consecutive presentation given on one occasion. The first four were told to the crowds who gathered around him as he sat in a boat (see 13:1-3), and the last four were told in private to the disciples after leaving the crowd and going into a house with them alone (see 13:36).

At the conclusion of the parables Matthew writes, 'When Jesus had finished these parables, he moved on from there' (13:53) indicating they had been told together and should be understood as such. Each parable is a part of a whole picture, and in order for the whole picture to make sense it is necessary for us to interpret each individual parable as a contributor to the whole. They are not a series of unrelated stories, one here about seed sown into a field, another there about a pearl that cost everything to purchase, but contributions to a whole picture, which, taken together, gives crucial understanding about the workings of the kingdom of God. That is the way we will seek to understand and interpret this passage.

Before looking at the parables themselves, we should look at the surprising answer Jesus gave to the question, 'Why do you speak to the people in parables?'. 'He replied, "The knowledge of the secrets of the kingdom of heaven has been given to you, but not to them. Whoever has will be given more, and he will have an abundance. Whoever does not have, even what he has will be taken from him. This is why I speak to them in parables: 'Though seeing, they do not see; though hearing, they do not hear or understand' (13:10-13).

I was taught as a child that parables were earthly stories with heavenly meanings and I assumed from that they were designed to make heavenly meanings intelligible! There is of course some truth in that, for a parable is a story told in familiar terms to explain something that is not familiar. However, to see parables only as an aide to understanding would not take into account what Jesus said about them. These parables, says Jesus in effect, are going to confuse those who are not his disciples, undermining what they thought they already knew, and will add to the understanding of those who are his disciples! He goes on to quote from Isaiah, 'You will be ever hearing but never understanding; you will be ever seeing but never perceiving. For this people's heart has become calloused: they hardly hear with their ears, and they have closed their eyes. Otherwise they might see with their eyes, hear with their ears, understand with their hearts and turn and I would heal them' (13:14-15 quoting Isa. 6:9-10).

It is important to note that any lack of understanding was not due to the teacher but the hearer. Jesus was not teasing them with deliberate confusion, but pointing out that the confusion was a symptom of something fundamentally at fault within the hearer.

The distinction between 'you' and 'them' (13:11) is a distinction between the disciples and the crowd. The secrets have been given to 'you', said Jesus, but not to 'them'. What the disciples already had, and the crowds did not have, was the grounds on which they would go on receiving more and 'will have an abundance' (13:12), whilst for the others, 'even what he has will be taken from him'.

What is this key ingredient that makes sense of spiritual truth but that otherwise would only compound our confusion? The answer lies in the relationship of the disciples to Jesus Christ. The first ingredient in the capacity to understand spiritual truth is not intellectual capacity but a moral disposition towards God.

Jesus said on one occasion, '... you do not believe because you are not my sheep' (John 10:26). Their incapacity to believe derived not from an intellectual barrier, for he had just said to them, 'The miracles I do in my Father's name speak for me', and were evident to any observer. Their incapacity to believe derived from their relationship with him, 'you are not my sheep'. Their disposition towards him created the incapacity to understand and believe him. Paul wrote, 'The man without the Spirit does not accept the things that come from the Spirit of God, for they are foolishness to him, and he cannot understand them, because they are spiritually discerned' (1 Cor. 2:14).

The fundamental prerequisite to understanding the things of the Spirit is the Spirit himself, and the disposition of submission to him. Alan Redpath has said, 'Capacity to receive God's truth depends upon the surrender of the will. Moral conquest of the will must precede intellectual enlightenment of the mind.'[1] To those men who had left all to follow him, Jesus could say, 'Blessed are your eyes because they see, and your ears because they hear' (13:16).

Before looking at the details of the parables themselves, there are two basic rules we should adopt for interpreting them.

Firstly, each parable will be teaching one central truth. There may be different aspects of that truth which are evident in the parable, but we must guard against being too carried away with details that are outside the purpose of the parable. The simplest interpretation is likely to be the true one, for the very nature of a parable is to explain and reveal truth, not to hinder them (the hindrance, remember, is in the disposition of the hearer).

Secondly, we should assume a consistent use of figurative terms used, both within the parable and its immediate context, and within Scripture as a whole, unless it is specifically stated otherwise. For an example, each of the first three parables have to do with a sower sowing seed into a field. One emphasises the different soils on which the seed lands, another the fact that an enemy sows bad seed amongst the good seed, and the third that the seed is mustard seed. Our first

---

[1] From personal notes taken from an address by Alan Redpath.

assumption ought to be that they are consistent symbols and in each case represent the same things. As the identity of the sower is only given once, we would be wise to make that our starting point for all three, unless the context makes it evident we should not understand it that way.

The first four parables were addressed to the crowds (13:2ff), and present a picture of how the world will see the kingdom of heaven. Conflict, failure and strife run through each of these stories, and they present a picture of an age characterised by set backs, attacks, disappointments and, ultimately, apparent failure. Much of the sown seed lands on unproductive soil. The good seed has the potential to be destroyed by the bad seed sown among it. The mustard seed grows out of proportion into a tree. The yeast in the loaf, a constant picture of evil in the Bible, permeates the whole loaf.

The second four parables were addressed to the disciples (13:36ff), and present a picture of how God sees the kingdom. Conflict, set backs and difficulties still characterise each, but ultimate success is the outcome of them all. The treasure in the field is purchased at great cost, so is the pearl of great price. The good and bad fish are eventually separated from one another, and the householder has always something to give.

The first four parables are:

1. The seed and the soil;
2. The wheat and the weeds;
3. The mustard seed;
4. The leaven and the loaf.

1. The seed and the soil (13:3-9 with explanation 13:18-23)
The first of the parables is probably the best known. A sower sowed seed in his field, some fell on the path and birds came and ate it up. Some fell on rocky places, sprang up but because they had no root, scorched in the heat, withered and died. Some fell among thorns which choked the plants. Others fell on good soil where it produced a crop, a hundred, sixty or thirty times what was sown.

The explanation Jesus gave of this parable does not specify the sower but concentrates on the reaction of the seed to the soil. The identity of the seed and soil is ambiguous on first reading. In the first instance it speaks of the seed falling on the path as being 'sown in his heart' where the evil one comes and snatches it away. In the second instance, where the seed falls on rocky places it speaks of the seed as 'he has no root, he lasts only a short time ... he quickly falls away'. The seed there is 'he', a person. The third instance of seed among thorns speaks of the seed as 'it', but the fourth seed on good soil speaks of 'He produces a crop'.

The general interpretation of this parable is that of Christians preaching the word of God, and the various responses people make to the gospel. I do not think that interpretation gives justice to the wider context of all eight parables or to the interpretation given by Jesus himself. Rather than being a picture of truth being sown into people's minds, it is a picture of people being sown into the world. The detailed interpretation Jesus gave of similar metaphors in the second parable explains, 'The one who sowed good seed is the Son of Man. The field is the world and the good seed stands for the sons of the kingdom' (13:37, 38). That is the interpretation of the second parable, but if we interpret the first parable in the light of the second it makes perfect sense and helps us resolve the ambiguity of the seed appearing to sometimes be truth and sometimes a 'man'. The picture becomes one of the Son of Man sowing people into the world, and the relationship they have with the world into which they have been planted.

Some of us will have difficulties with this because Jesus states explicitly in Luke's version of this parable, 'The seed is the word of God' (Luke 8:11). But is the 'word of God' merely the words of God, or may it equally be something else? The Greek word here, 'logos', is the same word used of Jesus in John's prologue, 'In the beginning was the Word, and the Word was with God, and the Word was God' (John 1:1). The 'Word' is the person of Jesus Christ. The 'word of God' is more than speaking or writing on God's behalf, it is an embodiment of the word. Paul wrote to the Corinthians, 'You show that you are a letter from Christ, the result of our ministry, written not with ink but with the Spirit of the living God, not on tablets of stone but on tablets of the human heart' (2 Cor. 3:3). The word, 'logos' does not appear in this passage, but the same idea is there.

God's strategy in the world is people. He plants people into the world and through them does his work. This parable is not teaching the failure of the word in people's lives, but the strategy by which God carries out his business in the world.

Each combination of seed and soil depicts what some Christians are like in the fulfilment of God's strategy. Some are like seed on the path, some like seed on rocky places, some like seed among thorns and some like seed on good soil. This is not teaching we are hapless victims of our environment, but that the combination of the seed with the different soils provides the possibilities for any one of us.

The shallow seed – sown on the path (13:19)
The first seed is, 'When anyone hears the message about the kingdom and does not understand it, the evil one comes and snatches away what was sown in his heart. This is the seed sown along the path'. He hears the word of God but does not digest it, understand it and appropriate it. He therefore is vulnerable to losing it all as the devil 'snatches away what was sown'. Truth in itself does not do us much good. Writing of Israel after their release from Egypt, the writer of Hebrews says, '... the message they heard was of no value to them, because those who heard did not combine it with faith' (Heb. 4:2). Truth has to be combined with faith in order to become experience, but this one has never taken truth into the realm of experience. He is shallow. The seed planted in the world comes to nothing.

The superficial seed – sown among rocks (13:20-21)
This one 'hears the word and at once receives it with joy. But since he has no root, he lasts only a short time. When trouble or persecution comes because of the word, he quickly falls away'. He begins with great enthusiasm, making a great start, but as soon as trouble comes along he falls away because he has no root. In the right atmosphere he can be jollied along, but he does not stand alone. He has no root and collapses under the pressure of trouble and opposition. He will blow with the prevailing wind. He is superficial. This seed in the world comes to nothing.

The secular seed – sown among thorns (13:22)
This man 'hears the word, but the worries of this life and the deceitfulness of wealth choke it, making it unfruitful'. He too starts well, but he has never been weaned from his secular world view and his measurement of himself by financial standing. He is deceived by wealth, and seduced by the things of the world. He is secular. This seed in the world comes to nothing.

The successful seed – sown on good soil (13:23)

This man 'hears the word and understands it. He produces a crop, yielding a hundred, sixty or thirty times what was sown'. He hears the word like the first seed, he gets excited like the second, he too lives in the world and is subject to all its temptations like the third, but his roots are deep, he survives and reproduces himself. He is successful. This seed in the world accomplishes its purpose.

The purpose of the parable is not to show how some respond to the word and are converted while others don't, but to show how the kingdom of God is to be advanced. Each of us who belongs to Jesus Christ is planted by him in the world for the purpose of producing fruit. But the shallow, the superficial and the secular do not reproduce and fulfil their destiny. Only one of the four kinds of seed is successful.

How does a seed become fruitful? Jesus said, 'Unless a grain of wheat falls into the ground and dies, it remains alone, a single seed. But if it dies, it produces many seeds' (John 12:24). The cost of reproduction is death to self, in order that the life of God might be evident within us and show himself through us.

If we were to look over the fence of the field described in the first parable, we would not be very impressed. There would be such waste and apparent failure. This is a true picture of the church of Jesus Christ, the physical manifestation of the kingdom on earth, as seen from the vantage point of those as yet outside the kingdom.

2. The wheat and the weeds (13:24-30 with explanation 13:36-43)

The second parable tells us that if the Son of Man is sowing his seed in the world, an enemy is sowing his seed in the same field too. 'The kingdom of heaven is like a man who sowed good seed in his field. But while everyone was sleeping his enemy came and sowed weeds among the wheat and went away' (13:24-25).

Jesus explained later to his disciples, 'The one who sowed good seed is the Son of Man. The field is the world and the good seed stands for the sons of the kingdom. The weeds are the sons of the evil one, and the enemy who sows them is the devil' (13:37-39).

Whenever God is at work, we can be sure the devil is at work too. His work is to counterfeit the work of God. The art of counterfeit is to imitate the real thing with something unreal. Within the kingdom of

God, the devil will always offer an alternative to Jesus Christ. It will not always be easy to distinguish between the real and the counterfeit. This is shown in the crucial question of the parable, when the servants asked the owner about the weeds, 'Do you want us to go and pull them up?'. His answer was, 'No, because while you are pulling the weeds you may root up the wheat with them. Let both grow together until the harvest. At that time I will tell the harvesters: First collect the weeds and tie them in bundles to be burned, then gather the wheat and bring it into my barn' (13:28-30). To try to pull up the weeds will invariably involve damaging some of the wheat. There is going to be a harvest time, 'the end of the age', and there are going to be harvesters, 'the angels' (13:39).

There is elsewhere in the New Testament important teaching on how to deal with false teaching in the church, and how to deal with sin in the church. This parable is not about false teaching so much as about false Christians, people who present themselves as part of the real thing but are in fact false.

False Christianity will inevitably lead to false teaching, and when the fruit is evident it may be easier to identify and handle. But we are not to set out on a crusade to purify the church of any false ingredient, and if we did attempt to do so we would fail and do much damage in the meantime. There is a harvest day coming, and that day, 'The Son of Man will send out his angels, and they will weed out of his kingdom everything that causes sin and all who do evil. They will throw them into a fiery furnace where there will be weeping and grinding of teeth. Then the righteous will shine like the sun in the kingdom of their Father' (13:41-43).

The day of separation of the real from the false will come. To the bad seed he presents the prospect of a fiery furnace, where all will be lost and destroyed, and to the good seed he gives the prospect of shining like the sun in the kingdom of the Father. In the end the kingdom will be pure. In the meantime, the kingdom has been infiltrated.

The picture so far is an interesting one. If you walked past this field and saw the good seed scattered around, some on the path, some on rocks, some among thorns and only some on the good soil, and then you saw that alongside the good seed on good soil there were weeds growing, you would not be very impressed. This is the picture so far of the kingdom of heaven as the world will perceive it.

3. The mustard seed (13:31-32)

This parable is very simple. 'The kingdom of heaven is like a mustard seed which a man took and planted in his field. Though it is the smallest of all your seeds, yet when it grows, it is the largest of garden plants and becomes a tree, so that the birds of the air come and perch in its branches'. Jesus gives no explanation of this parable, so we need to tread carefully.

If we remain consistent in our interpretation with the first two parables, which also include the elements of a sower sowing seed in a field, (as Jesus gives no explanation it is proper we should start at this point), then it is a picture of the Son of Man sowing seed into the world, but this time specified as mustard seed, 'the smallest of all your seeds'. The seed then grows into a tree in which the birds of the air come and nest in its branches.

The popular interpretation of this parable is that the kingdom grows from humble beginnings into something good and great which provides a refuge for the 'birds'. I do not think that is how we should understand it.

The key to this parable is in the seed being specifically 'mustard seed' which the parable says 'becomes a tree' and birds nest in its branches. Mustard is a herb and not a tree. It normally grows to about one and a half metres (four feet) and would not be a place you would expect to find a bird's nest! Occasionally a mustard plant might grow to a height of five metres (fifteen feet), but that would be abnormal. It is not a picture of natural growth but of something unnatural portraying a false greatness. The birds nesting in the branches are not something good but bad. In the first parable it was the birds who came and ate up the seed on the path, and then Jesus described them as representing 'the evil one' (13:19). There is a similar image in a vision given to the Babylonian king, Nebuchadnezzar, in which a tree, representing himself, grows large and strong, 'with its top touching the sky, visible to the whole earth ... and having nesting places in its branches for the birds of the air' (Dan. 4:20-21). The tree demonstrated Nebuchadnezzar's arrogance, and in due time a messenger of God came and chopped the tree down and Nebuchadnezzar himself was humbled and reduced to poverty.

It would seem to me that what Jesus is saying here is this – Instead of being characterised by humility and gentleness, the kingdom of heaven in its manifestation on earth has become rich, powerful and in some instances authoritative and arrogant. Its strategies are in danger of not deriving from obedience to Jesus Christ, dependency on the Holy Spirit and child-like trust in a heavenly Father, but marketing tactics, high profiled publicity, public relations expertise and an attempt to woo others with our bigness and noise! It has become a nesting place for the birds!

This parable does not teach the failure of the church as a manifestation of the kingdom of God, but it does predict its distortion and corruption, which history and current experience show only too well to be true.

4. The leaven and the loaf (13:33)

This final brief parable sums up to the crowd the picture given of the kingdom so far. 'The kingdom of heaven is like yeast that a woman took and mixed into a large amount of flour until it worked all through the dough.' This parable has sometimes been seen as a picture of the spread of goodness through the world. It is more likely the complete opposite.

Yeast in Scripture is a consistent picture of evil. From the time of the Passover when God brought Israel out of Egypt, bread eaten in celebration of God's goodness was to be without yeast. Jesus speaks of the 'yeast of the Pharisees and Sadducees' which the disciples understood him to mean he was 'not telling them to guard against the yeast used in bread, but against the teaching of the Pharisees and Sadducees' (16:6, 12).

Paul exhorted the Corinthian church, 'Your boasting is not good. Don't you know that a little yeast works through the whole batch of dough? Get rid of the old yeast that you may be a new batch without yeast ... not with the yeast of malice and wickedness, but with the bread without yeast, the bread of sincerity and truth' (1 Cor. 5:6-8). The context of this statement includes the need to deal with sexual immorality in the church as well as malice and wickedness.

If yeast is consistently used to depict evil in Scripture, this parable is unlikely to be an exception. It is not that the 'kingdom of heaven is like yeast ...', but 'the kingdom of heaven is like yeast ... mixed into a large amount of flour until it worked all through the dough'. It is the whole picture that is likened to the kingdom of heaven. Evil is contagious, righteousness is not. In the Old Testament, the prophet Haggai asked the priests this question: ' "If a person carries consecrated meat in the fold of his garment, and that fold touches some bread or stew, some wine, oil or other food, does it become consecrated?" The priests answered "No". Then Haggai said, "If a person defiled by contact with a dead body touches one of these things, does it become defiled?" "Yes" the priests replied, "It becomes defiled." Then Haggai said, "So it is with this people ..." ' (Hag. 2:12-14). Cleanliness does not spread, dirt does. Righteousness is not contagious, but sin is. The yeast permeates to every part of the dough. That is why we are given no hope of perfection in the present tense of our life on earth, either in our personal lives or in the corporate life of the church. As long as we live within a fallen environment we are vulnerable to contamination by sin and subject to failure. Only in heaven is there prospect of being free from the contamination of sin.

This is not to put a pessimistic view of the kingdom of heaven, in its expression on earth, but to be utterly realistic, as history and contemporary experience have only served to confirm.

But this is the view of the kingdom given to the crowds. It is the perspective from outside the kingdom. It is not attractive. It will rarely be held up to view as the ideal of society. It will not draw people in its natural state. The world will always have reason to criticise and disregard it.

But let's now go inside the house with Jesus and his disciples and see the kingdom from God's point of view. It is a different story!

21.

Kingdom parables – the good news (13:44-52)

The first four of the eight parables about the kingdom of heaven in Chapter 13 were addressed to the crowd, and depict the kingdom as the world at large will see it. It is not an impressive picture. The kingdom has been spoiled by good seed falling on non-productive ground, by bad seed that has been sown alongside the good seed, by the distortion of a mustard plant that has grown into a tree harbouring evil things, and by the spread of evil through every part, depicted by the spread of yeast throughout the whole loaf. This is not a pessimistic picture so much as a realistic picture and is the reason few people will be attracted to seek for God on the basis of organised Christendom. That which purports to represent God and his interests in the world today has suffered distortion, corruption and gives much outward evidence of failure.

At the end of these first four parables, Matthew writes, 'Then he left the crowd and went into the house. His disciples came to him and said, "Explain to us the parable of the weeds in the field"' (13:36). Alone with his disciples in the house Jesus gave them the explanation they asked for, then told them four more parables:

1. The hidden treasure (13:44);
2. The pearl of great price (13:45-46);
3. The fishnet (13:47-50);
4. The householder (13:52).

This is now a different picture. Difficulty and obstacles may exist in each of these pictures, but victory is the outcome of them all.

5. The hidden treasure (13:44)

'The kingdom of heaven is like treasure hidden in a field. When a man found it, he hid it again, and then in his joy went and sold all he had and bought that field.' To find treasure in a field may not be that unusual, for it was quite normal for people to protect their valuables by digging a hole and burying them in the ground. There were no banks or safe deposit boxes as there are today, and this practice served that purpose. In the parable of the talents, the servant who did not get a return on his talent explained to his master, 'I was afraid and hid your talent in the ground' (Matt. 25:25). This was his means of protecting it. In this parable Jesus tells how a man finds a treasure that has been hidden in a field. In his joy, he goes and sells everything he has to purchase the field and obtain the treasure.

Jesus offers no explanation of this parable. However there are two symbols that are already familiar from the earlier parables. These may or may not carry the same meaning in this parable, but to compare them may be a good place to start. The two are 'the field', and 'a man'. In the earlier interpretation of the parable of the wheat and the weeds, Jesus said, 'the field is the world', and the man who sowed good seed was the 'Son of Man' (13:37-38). Two symbols have previously represented the Lord Jesus Christ doing something in the world. There are two additional new features: the treasure, and the act of purchasing the treasure.

If we interpret this according to the symbols already used, the man who sells everything to purchase the field is the Son of Man, who finds treasure in the world and gives up everything in order to purchase it. If we follow this through, it will conflict with the most common interpretation of this parable which sees the treasure (and similarly the pearl in the next parable) as a type of either Christ or salvation, and the man who sells everything to obtain the treasure as the penitent sinner who comes to Christ. Although that is a common understanding, I do not think it can be sustained if examined carefully in the light of the whole picture being given by Jesus in the eight parables. Rather than being a picture of how the sinner obtains Christ, it is a picture of how Christ obtains the sinner. It is Christ finding a treasure in the world, and giving up everything in order to purchase it for himself.

What can be described as God's 'treasure' in the world? On what has he set his heart to the extent he gives up everything to purchase it?

The answer must be that God's treasure is people! The Psalmist asks the question, 'What is man that you are mindful of him, the son of man that you care for him? You made him a little lower than the heavenly beings and crowned him with glory and honour' (Ps. 8:4-5). God, says David, 'crowned' man with 'glory'. Job asks the question, 'What is man that you make so much of him, that you give him so much attention' (Job 7:17). Job is actually complaining in that statement about his sense of being constantly under the scrutiny of God, but his point is important. God gives human beings a lot of attention!

If the treasure is human beings, the parable states, 'When a man found it ...'. To have found it implies he was looking. This is how the activity of the Lord Jesus Christ is described when Jesus said of himself, 'The Son of Man came to seek and to save what was lost' (Luke 19.10). It is a wonderful thing to be described as being 'lost', for to be lost is to be wanted! We do not speak of rubbish being lost, we only speak of precious things being lost.

To obtain the treasure the man gave all that he had. This was the activity of Jesus in making our salvation possible. Paul wrote, 'For you know the grace of our Lord Jesus Christ, that though he was rich, yet for your sakes he became poor, so that you through his poverty might become rich' (2 Cor. 8:9). Again he writes of Christ, 'Who, being in very nature God, did not consider equality with God something to be grasped, but made himself nothing ...' (Phil. 2:6-7). In the laying aside of all that was rightfully his in order to procure our redemption, the Lord Jesus Christ has purchased us. 'You are not your own; you were bought at a price' (1 Cor. 6:19-20).

In the book of Revelation, the apostle John sees a Lamb, looking as though it had been slain, with the elders fallen down before him singing a song which included, 'With your blood you purchased men for God from every tribe and language and people and nation' (Rev. 5:9). Jesus Christ not only died for us, but with his blood he purchased us outright, and to be a Christian is to acknowledge we are not our own. Our salvation may be free, but it is not cheap! It has been at great cost to the Lord Jesus Christ.

The man in the parable did not begrudge the purchase. On the contrary, '... in his joy went and sold all that he had and bought that field'. This too fits a description of Christ, 'who for the joy set before him endured the cross, scorning its shame' (Heb. 12:2). It was in joy he made the transaction which purchased us for himself.

This picture seems clear. The treasure is people, the field is the world, the man is Christ, the giving up all to purchase the treasure is his act of redemption, and his joy is in his having obtained the treasure, the purchase of his redeemed people. There are difficulties and hardships in this parable. The field has to be bought. A cost has to be paid. But the end result is that the treasure has been obtained. This is the kingdom from God's point of view.

6. The pearl of great price (13:45-46)

'Again, the kingdom of heaven is like a merchant looking for fine pearls. When he found one of great value, he went away and sold everything he had and bought it.' This parable is very similar to the last one. The main difference is in the treasure which he purchases by selling everything. It is specified here as being a 'pearl'. Because Jesus did not give an explanation of this parable we must tread carefully, but as the pearl is the distinguishing feature in this parable I think it must be the key to our understanding.

A pearl is the only precious stone that is produced by a living organism. A grain of sand or other irritant gets under the skin of the oyster, hurting and injuring it. The oyster responds by covering the injury with a substance called nacre (more popularly known as 'mother of pearl'), pouring on layer after layer of this substance until the pearl is formed as a beautiful jewel.

I do not accept the common interpretation that sees Christ as the pearl of great price, for no price can be put on him nor do we have to pay for him! It is true that to be a disciple of Christ a person must 'give up everything he has' (Luke 14:33), but by no stretch of the imagination is that a purchase. We are to give up everything because Christ comes to *be* everything and there must be no competition for his place in our lives. But there is no purchase of Christ or of salvation. Rather, as in the last parable, it is Christ who purchases us!

There is a very beautiful aspect of the gospel in this image of the pearl. We, who by our sin have offended against a holy God, are being changed by the One we have offended into something beautiful. Paul writes of this transaction where our injury of God is the means by which he turns us into something beautiful: 'God made him who had no sin to be sin for us, so that in him we might become the righteousness of God' (2 Cor. 5:21). Jesus Christ was made sin, in order that we, for whom he was made sin, might become the righteousness of God.

This is like the formation of a pearl! The pearl is the response of the injured to the injury done. God's response to our sin is the gift of his righteousness in which he moulds us into his own image. There is a moment of redemption when a person is brought into relationship with Christ, but there is a continuing process of growth in righteousness as we are moulded into his own image. Paul again writes, 'And we, who with unveiled faces all reflect the Lord's glory, are being transformed into his likeness with ever-increasing glory, which comes from the Lord, who is the Spirit' (2 Cor. 3:18). There is an 'ever-increasing' glory, an ever-increasing beauty which is the mark of the work of God within us.

Perhaps another important distinction between the two parables is that in the first story the treasure in the field is described very generally, rather than the specific description of the pearl in the second story. If the field is the world, it is true to say that Christ died for the whole world (see 1 John 2:2), and his work has general application to the whole human race. However, in the parable of the pearl the man is looking for fine pearls and, '... when he found one of great value he went away and sold everything he had and bought it'. It is wonderfully true that Christ died for the whole world, but it is also true that he singles us out individually for the gift of his grace, drawing us to himself, one by one.

Again this parable contains aspects of conflict and difficulty. The pearl is produced at a cost to the oyster, the pearl is obtained at a cost to the purchaser, but the end result is the pearl is obtained and the man is satisfied. This is the kingdom as God sees it.

7. The fishnet (13:47-50)

'Once again, the kingdom of heaven is like a net that was let down into the lake and caught all kinds of fish. When it was full, the fishermen pulled it up on the shore. Then they sat down and collected the good fish in baskets, but threw the bad away. This is how it will be at the end of the age. The angels will come and separate the wicked from the righteous and throw them into the fiery furnace, where there will be weeping and gnashing of teeth.'

The images are new in this sequence of parables, though the work of fishermen was familiar to the disciples. It was from this trade that Jesus had called Andrew, Peter, James and John and said to them, 'Come, follow me, and I will make you fishers of men' (4:19). The casting of the net into the sea would seem to represent the evangelistic ministry of the church. The particular net is the large dragnet which is either drawn along by two boats, or with ropes from the shore. All kinds of fish and creatures of the sea, good and bad, are caught in the net and hauled up together.

This picture may be particularly apt in forms of mass evangelism where crowds are confronted with the gospel, and are invited to Christ at once. It becomes easy for people to make the same outward response to the invitation, but for a variety of mixed motives. The good and bad become mingled together in the one net. True as that picture of evangelism might be however, the catching of the fish is not the main point of the story.

Jesus gave an interpretation to this parable which focused entirely on the separation of the good and bad fish when they had pulled up on the shore. The collection of the good fish and the destruction of the bad fish will be the function of the angels at the end of the age. The good and bad will not remain all mixed together at the end. This is a similar statement to one Jesus made in his interpreting the earlier parable of the weeds and the wheat. There he stated that 'the Son of Man will send out his angels, and they will weed out of his kingdom everything that causes sin and all who do evil. They will throw them into the fiery furnace, where there will be weeping and grinding of teeth. Then the righteous will shine like the sun in the kingdom of their Father' (13:41-43). In that parable, addressed to the crowds, the final image is of the good seed stored safely in the barn, where they will shine like the sun in the kingdom of their Father. In this latter parable, addressed to the disciples, the final image is of the bad fish thrown into the fiery furnace where there will be weeping and grinding of teeth.

To the crowds he emphasised the prospect of heaven, to the disciples he gave a vision of hell. The prospect of hell is not a popular one, but it is an unambiguous one in the teaching of Jesus. The word 'hell' occurs seven times on the lips of Jesus in Matthew's gospel,[1] and we dare not belittle the reality and seriousness of this. The parable is not primarily teaching about hell, but showing that ultimately the separation of the good from the bad will take place. No matter how compromised the earthly expression of the kingdom appears here and

---

[1] See 5:29; 5:30; 10:28; 16:18; 18:9; 23:15; 23:33.

now, the day will come when there will be an ingathering of the true kingdom and a destruction of those who are not part of it.

8. The householder (13:52)

"'Have you understood all these things?" Jesus asked. "Yes," they replied. He said to them, "Therefore every teacher of the law who has been instructed about the kingdom of heaven is like the owner of a house who brings out of his storeroom new treasures as well as old." '

This brief parable of the householder begins with a question, 'Have you understood all these things?' They had all heard them, and could possibly recount each of the parables if asked to do so. But did they understand them? Did they understand that some of the good seed sown in the field will ultimately come to nothing? That alongside the good seed, there will be weeds sown by an enemy which will threaten to choke the good? That the little mustard seed, though small in its beginnings, will grow into a tree which may appear impressive but is a distortion harbouring evil? That as yeast permeates a loaf, so the kingdom will be contaminated by sin? These first four have all taught the reality of human failure within the kingdom, and the disciples need to understand that this is what will be true. But, despite these discouraging images as the world will see the kingdom, there is an understanding from God's point of view that is very different. Do they understand that despite the set backs and difficulties, the treasure is going to be obtained? That the pearl is purchased? And that the good and bad fish will be separated at the end of the age?

They reply to the question, 'Yes'. If they have fully understood these things, said Jesus, they will be like the owner of a house who brings out of his storeroom new treasures as well as old. They will never give up in discouragement, for despite the difficulties and opposition they know there are always new and old treasures to bring out. If 'treasure' here is equal to the 'treasure' of the fifth parable, then there will always be new and old treasures, new people for whom Christ died to be brought to him as Saviour, and established believers to be nurtured and brought to maturity. There are no grounds for disillusionment or disappointment if we see things from the perspective of the Lord Jesus Christ. There is always confidence, always hope, always new treasures and always something to do.

Rejection in Nazareth

When he had finished these parables, Jesus moved on to his home town of Nazareth (13:53). He had left Nazareth at the beginning of his ministry, on account of their rejection of him there (Luke 4:16-31, and Matt. 4:13) and made his base in Capernaum on the north shore of Galilee.

This is the only time recorded in the gospels that Jesus returned to Nazareth. He began to teach in the synagogue, no doubt the one in which he had been brought up (this is the last record of Jesus ever teaching in a synagogue), and despite their amazement at the wisdom with which he spoke and the miracles he performed (13:54), they soon 'took offence at him' (13:57).

It was no doubt difficult for the local people. They had known Jesus as a boy, he had worked as their carpenter, they knew his family history, he had sat amongst them in the synagogue every Sabbath day, and they knew he had never trained as a teacher of such things. People are usually more receptive when someone comes to them with a clean sheet, carrying no history, and with no presuppositions made about them. Jesus' home town of Nazareth was the most difficult town of all the places in which he ministered, and he said before leaving them, 'Only in his home town and in his own house is a prophet without honour' (13:57). Thus Jesus' time in Nazareth, the place that had been his boyhood home and his place of work, concludes with the sorry statement, 'And he did not do many miracles there because of their lack of faith' (13:58).

22.

A day in the life of Jesus
(14:1-39)

Three main events take place in Chapter 14, linked together by Matthew as following on from each other during the same day. First, the news reached Jesus of Herod's suspicion that he was John the Baptist raised from the dead (vv. 1-12). On hearing this he withdrew privately by boat to a solitary place, only to be followed on foot by a crowd of five thousand, on whom he had compassion, healed their sick, then fed miraculously with five loaves and two fishes (vv. 13-21). He then made the disciples get into the boat and sent them across to the other side whilst he went up into the hills alone. A great storm broke out on the lake with wind and waves buffeting the boat. In the early hours of the morning Jesus came to the disciples walking on the water (vv. 22-35).

In each of these incidents Jesus deals with apparent obstacles along the way. We will examine them as follows:

1. Herod's antagonism   14:1-11
2. The People's enthusiasm   14.:2-21
3. The Disciples' stubbornness   14:22-35

1. Herod's antagonism (14:1-12)

Chapter 13 concludes with the fact Jesus, '... did not do many miracles there (in Nazareth) because of their lack of faith' (13.58), but Chapter 14 opens with Herod the tetrarch being impressed by reports of his miraculous powers. The miracles denied in Nazareth had been evident in other places and the rumours and reputation of Jesus were spreading. Herod, on hearing these reports concluded, 'This is John the Baptist; he has risen from the dead' (14:2). This idea that Jesus was a resurrected John the Baptist was not original to Herod, for it was one of the popular explanations of Jesus at this time (see Mark 6:14-16, and Matt. 16:14). The thought however alarmed Herod. He had been responsible for the death of John the Baptist after being caught in a quandary over him. John the Baptist had repeatedly told Herod he was wrong to be committing adultery with his brother Philip's wife, Herodias, whom he had taken from his brother and married. The fact he was married to her had not legalised the adultery or diminished his guilt before God. This had clearly awakened Herod's conscience for he 'feared John ..., knowing him to be a righteous and holy man' (Mark 6:20). His brother's former wife had no such conscience and wanted to have John killed, but Herod protected him. Herod had a personal fascination and liking for John (see Mark 6:20), and at the same time feared the impact on the people if he were to have him destroyed. He compromised between his wife's demands and his own better judgement by having John put in prison where he would not be able to influence the people, but kept alive so his followers would not have sufficient grounds to rebel. However the opportunity came for Herodias to have John destroyed when her daughter danced for Herod at his birthday party, held for his high officials and military commanders. She so pleased them, he offered her anything she wanted, up to half his kingdom. The girl went to her mother for advice and came back to request the head of John the Baptist on a platter. Mark's record tells us the king was greatly distressed by this request, but because he had made his oath before his dinner guests and could not refuse her without great embarrassment, he sent an executioner to the prison who returned with John's head and presented it to the girl, who took it to her mother.

When a person's conscience is aroused by the accusation of guilt, they have two options before them. Either deal with the sin of which they are guilty, or remove the accuser. Herod's choice was ultimately the latter option. As is so often true, the accuser becomes the condemned, and the one who stands for truth becomes maligned. It was John and not Herod who suffered the immediate consequence of John's faithful declaration of truth, but it did not resolve Herod's guilt, ease his conscience or remove its consequences to him. Sin will always pay its own wages. However, a terrifying prospect haunted Herod at this stage, that John the Baptist had risen from the dead and was back in business. Something in Herod's own conscience permitted him to believe Jesus was John the Baptist risen from the dead and in so doing recognised the righteousness of John's case and a vindication of his stand against Herod's sin.

However, in his battle with his own conscience and with the conviction of his own sin, Herod eventually won! He never met Jesus personally until he visited Jerusalem at the time of Jesus' trial. When Pilate realised Herod happened to be in Jerusalem at the time, and that as a Galilean Jesus was under his jurisdiction, he sent Jesus to be interviewed by him. In the brief interview, all association of Jesus with John the Baptist has gone from Herod's mind, and instead he tried to persuade him to perform some miracle like a visiting court jester. When he refused Herod dressed Jesus in an elegant robe, mocked him and ridiculed him as a king, and sent him back to Pilate (see Luke 23:7-12). A conscience is a gift of God. Paul warns Timothy of the importance of '... holding on to faith and a good conscience', and warns, 'Some have rejected these and so have shipwrecked their faith' (1 Tim. 1:19-20). Herod did not shipwreck his faith for he was not a man of faith, but he shipwrecked his life.

It was when Jesus heard of Herod's thoughts that he was John the Baptist risen from the dead, that '... he withdrew by boat privately to a solitary place' (14:13). This statement does not follow verse 12, the account of John's burial which is told in parenthesis, but it follows verse 2, Herod's statement Jesus was John risen from the dead.

Herod is described as a 'tetrarch' (14:1). The term *tetrarch* literally means *the ruler of a fourth part*, though generally it came to be used of any subordinate ruler of a section of a country. This Herod was Antipas, the youngest son of Herod the Great who had been given the title 'King of the Jews' by Julius Caesar, and who is notorious in Scripture for his attack on all the baby boys in Bethlehem after the visit from the Magi at the time of Jesus' birth. On his death he had bequeathed his kingdom to his three sons, Archelaus, Philip and Antipas, the latter having inherited Galilee as his portion of his father's kingdom.

The new curiosity aroused about Jesus caused him to slip away alone, possibly across the lake of Galilee to escape from Herod's territory. However the solitude he sought was not to be.

2. The people's enthusiasm (14:13-21)

The crowds that followed on foot were waiting for Jesus when he landed on the other side of the lake, and his response to this invasion of his privacy was that '... he had compassion on them and healed their sick' (14:14). As evening approached, the disciples proposed Jesus should send the people away, so that they could go to the villages and buy themselves some food. His response was, 'They do not need to go away. You give them something to eat' (14:16). These disciples had been with Jesus for some time now. They had seen him in action, they had listened to his teaching, they had themselves been sent out to preach, teach and heal, but now he threw them this challenge, 'You give them something to eat.' John's Gospel tells he singled out Philip in particular and asked him, 'Where shall we buy bread for these people to eat?' He did not ask this because he did not know what to do, for 'He asked this only to test him for he already knew what he was going to do' (John 6:5-6). Jesus was not looking for advice, he was testing Philip and the other disciples generally to see how much they were really learning. Philip came back and said they only had two hundred denarii between them (about eight months' wages), not enough, he said, for each one of the five thousand crowd to have a bite (John 6:7). Others said eight months' wages might be enough but it was extravagant to spend all of that on feeding the crowd just one meal (Mark 6:37). It was Andrew who came up with the boy who had just five loaves and two fishes, enough normally for his own needs, and he offered them to Jesus with the apology, '... but how far will they go amongst so many' (John 6:9).

It was at this point, having ordered the people to sit down in groups of fifty, Jesus took the five loaves and two fishes and 'gave thanks' (14:19). This does not mean he 'said grace' or 'asked the blessing'. His 'giving thanks' was the most significant thing he did in the whole incident. Each of the four gospels notes this point, and when referring back to it later, John's gospel speaks of it as 'the place where the people had eaten the bread after the Lord had *given thanks*'. They did not say 'after he had performed the miracle of the feeding of the five thousand'. It was the place where he '*gave thanks*'. That was the cause which lay behind the miracle. What preoccupied Jesus in the situation was not the hunger of the people, nor was it the inadequacy of the food, or the impossibility of the problem, but his act of *giving thanks* was acknowledgement of the complete sufficiency of his Father to meet the people's need in an impossible situation.

To give thanks is to express grateful confidence in someone else's ability and willingness to do something on our behalf. This is what the

Lord Jesus Christ is expressing to his Father. His confidence lies not in himself but in his Father. Jesus said, '... the Son can do nothing by himself; he can do only what he sees his Father doing, because whatever the Father does the Son also does' (John 5:19), and '... it is the Father living in me who is doing his work' (John 14:10). Jesus did not work in independence of his Father, he worked in complete dependence on his Father. Giving thanks was the expression of that dependence and the disposition towards his Father that enabled the Father to do his work. Having given thanks and expressed his dependency on his Father, his part was to act on the assumption the Father would work, so with that assumption he broke the loaves, handed them to his disciples who handed them to the people. Matthew simply records, 'They all ate and were satisfied' (14:20).

The miracles of Jesus were not evidences of what he could do for his Father, they were evidence of what the Father would do for the Son. Peter, on the Day of Pentecost, described the miracles of Jesus as being '... miracles, wonders and signs, which God did among you through him' (Acts 2:22). God did them through Jesus.

The act of 'giving thanks' is a crucial one in the New Testament. At the grave of Lazarus, as he was about to be raised from the dead, Jesus prayed, 'Father I thank you ...' (John 11:41). At the feeding of the four thousand with seven loaves and fishes, he 'gave thanks' (15:36). Perhaps most remarkable of all, 'The Lord Jesus, on the night he was betrayed, took bread, and when he had given thanks, he broke it ...' (1 Cor. 11:23-24). He did not give thanks for his betrayal or for his death, but for his Father's ability to accomplish that for which he had been sent into the world. His Father would accept his offering and raise him from the dead.

A key to growth and progress in the Christian life is described by Paul to the Colossians, 'And whatever you do, whether in word or deed, do it all in the name of the Lord Jesus, giving thanks to God the Father through him' (Col. 3:17). To the Thessalonians Paul said, 'Give thanks in all circumstances, for this is God's will for you in Christ Jesus' (1 Thess. 5:18). In every situation that is bigger than our ability and resources, we are to do as Jesus did, 'give thanks', and having adopted a disposition of trust in the Father, to then do what seems obvious, to 'break the loaves' and begin to pass them around. The 'breaking of the bread' is an important ingredient in this miracle, for the supernatural intervention of God in a situation is precipitated by risky obedience.

The human agent in incidents of miraculous intervention by God, whether in the experience of the Lord Jesus Christ himself, or whether in Peter or Paul in the book of Acts, Moses or Joshua, Elijah or Elisha in the Old Testament, is never passive but always active. Trust *in God* is effective when accompanied by obedience *to God*.

Jesus had withdrawn earlier in the day to be alone in a solitary place. That opportunity had been denied him by the crowd, so after the feeding of the five thousand, he made his disciples go back into a boat to cross the lake of Galilee whilst he dismissed the crowd and went up on a mountainside alone to pray. Matthew tells us that Jesus '*made* the disciples get into the boat'. There seems a sense of compulsion about it, but he does not say why. John tells us that the crowd '... intended to come and make him king by force' (John 6:15). It was that which provoked Jesus to send the disciples away, whilst he too withdrew to a mountain by himself.

3. The disciples' stubbornness (14:22-35)

Having been sent by Jesus across Galilee, the disciples had rowed three to three and a half miles out (see John 6:19) and were therefore somewhere near the middle of the lake (its longest points are about 13 miles from top to bottom and 7 miles wide). Evening had come and Jesus was now alone on the hillside in prayer, but down on the lake a storm blew up, the boat on the lake was buffeted by the waves with the wind against it, and Jesus, from his vantage point, '... saw the disciples straining at the oars' (Mark 6:48).

It was much later in the night, 'during the fourth watch of the night', between the hours of 3 am and 6 am, Jesus came to them, walking on the lake. The picture is a fascinating one. The disciples are in the boat, buffeted by strong waves, having been there for something like nine to twelve hours, prevented from getting into the shore. They have every reason to be afraid. Storms on Galilee were more dangerous than storms on the Mediterranean Sea. On another occasion when Jesus was asleep in a boat during a storm on Galilee, the '... waves swept over the boat' (8:24). This storm was evidently not as violent as that, but the prospect of it becoming increasingly so would bring fear to the disciples. Suddenly they look up and see Jesus walking on the water. They think it is a ghost until he calls out, 'Take courage! It is I. Don't be afraid' (14:27). Peter recognised him and called back, 'Lord, if it's you, tell me to come to you on the water.'

Peter had recognised a very important fact. The thing that
threatened to be *over his head* was *under the feet of Jesus*. Jesus did not do
these things to impress, but to teach. He was not only demonstrating
his power to the admiration and marvel of his disciples, he was
demonstrating what he wished to impart to them. There was no
reason for Jesus to say to the disciples, 'It is I. Don't be afraid', if the
power he was demonstrating over the elements was for his benefit
and his victory over the storm only. What he demonstrated in himself
he would impart to them. Peter evidently recognised this, so made
his request, 'Tell me to come to you on the water.' In recognising the
victory and power of the Lord Jesus Christ, he wanted to share it in
his own experience. Jesus replied, 'Come!'

As Peter obeyed that invitation, got down out of the boat and
stepped on to the water he discovered that obedience coupled with
trust results in divine action. He too walked on the water, and
experienced a miracle over the physical laws of nature that should
have plunged him into the water.

In the previous incident of feeding the five thousand, it was Jesus'
attitude of trust in his Father, evidenced by his *giving thanks* coupled with
his action of *breaking the bread* that resulted in his Father's intervention
and the miracle occurring. The same principle is now activated as Peter
adopted a disposition of complete trust in Christ, took the action of
stepping onto the water, and experienced the miracle. Trust that does
not express itself in obedience is mere sentiment. Action that does
not grow out of trust in God is arrogance.

Paul speaks of '... the obedience that comes from faith' (Rom.
1:5). The two ingredients of obedience and faith must be irrevocably
locked together.

We don't know how far Peter walked on the water, but in due
course something went wrong. 'When he saw the wind, he was afraid,
and beginning to sink, cried out, "Lord save me"' (14:30). To say 'he
saw the wind' does not mean he suddenly noticed a wind blowing!
He had been rowing against the wind for most of the night and was
fully aware of it. His attention went from Christ upon whom he was
depending, to the problem against which he was fighting. When his
attention so changed the inevitable happened, 'he was afraid'. Fear is
the emotion we experience when faced with something stronger than
we are, and more threatening than our resources. When he stepped
out of the boat the power of the Lord Jesus Christ was stronger to

193

Peter than the wind and waves. Now the wind and waves had become stronger to him than the Lord Jesus Christ, and not only did he become afraid but he began to sink. He cried out, 'Lord, save me!' Jesus reached out and caught him and said, 'You of little faith, why did you doubt?' The problem was not the impossibility of the situation or the strength of the wind, it was his lack of trust.

The abiding lesson of this incident lies in our understanding that anything which threatens to be over our head is under his feet. Paul writes that when Jesus rose again from the dead, the Father '... put everything under his feet' (1 Cor. 15:27). We will not experience the stability and security that may be derived from this until we acknowledge our utter dependence on him and obey him in what is right in the situation. It is this criteria that brings God into the circumstances, and gives him the freedom to act in our lives.

At the end of Mark's account of this incident, he writes intriguingly, 'Then he climbed into the boat with them, and the wind died down. They were completely amazed, *for they had not understood about the loaves*; their hearts were hardened' (Mark 6:51-52). What did their lack of understanding about the loaves have to do with his walking on the water? In what sense were their hearts hardened? The lesson the disciples should have learned with the loaves and fishes as Jesus 'gave thanks' and acknowledged his dependence on the Father, was lost on them in the storm. He had challenged them to, '... give them something to eat', and the disciples had abysmally failed to provide any idea of how the feeding might take place. Then Jesus performed the miracle. Afterwards he put them in the boat and sent them across the lake knowing they would encounter a storm, giving them another opportunity to learn what to do in a situation that was out of their depth. But they had learned nothing! Why were they terrified in the boat? Because they had not understood about the loaves, they gave themselves no opportunity to prove the sufficiency and utter dependency of God when in the storm. Their hearts were stubbornly hard.

23.

Contrasting Assumptions
(15:1–16:12)

This section of Matthew's gospel carries a series of four events where Jesus took the people with whom he was dealing somewhat by surprise and reversed their assumptions.

In the first instance, some Pharisees and Scribes came to Jesus, and asked him a question about the tradition of the ceremonial washing of hands before eating, accusing his disciples of breaking the tradition (15:1-20). Their question was not for the purpose of learning something from Jesus, but of exposing his violation of their traditions and thus having reason to criticise and condemn him. He turned the tables on them in discussing the nature of cleanliness. They came believing themselves clean and sufficient, and left having been exposed as unclean and insufficient! This teaches: *The Nature of True Cleanliness*.

In contrast, the second incident involves a Canaanite woman who came on behalf of her demon-possessed daughter, expressing her unworthiness as a Gentile and pleading that as crumbs fall from a master's table to be eaten by dogs, she too might receive mercy (15:21-28). Jesus commended her for her great faith and her daughter was delivered. She came believing herself poor and insufficient, and left having discovered herself rich in faith. This teaches: *The Nature of True Godliness*.

The third incident is reminiscent of the miraculous feeding of the five thousand in the previous chapter. On this occasion, at the end of a three day gathering of four thousand men besides women and children, the crowd had nothing to eat. His disciples came to Jesus bemoaning the fact that in the remoteness of the place there was no means of getting enough bread to feed such a crowd. They had only seven loaves of bread and a few fish. As in the earlier miracle, these were multiplied, so Jesus broke the bread and fish, gave them to the disciples and they in turn fed them to the people. Afterwards they collected seven basketfuls of broken pieces that were left over (15:29-39). The disciples came to Jesus aware of their lack of resources and discovered everything they needed was available. This teaches: *The Nature of True Effectiveness*.

The fourth event is a coalition of Pharisees and Sadducees who come to Jesus to test him by asking for a sign from heaven. He told them the desire for miraculous signs was not an evidence of godliness but of wickedness (16:1-12). They came to test him by asking Jesus for a miracle to prove himself, and left with the corruptness of their own attitudes exposed. This teaches: *The Nature of True Evidences*.

1. The nature of true cleanliness: where apparent cleanliness is dirty (15:1-20)

This incident may initially not seem particularly significant. It is a discussion about why the disciples do not wash their hands before eating, not in the sense of washing for hygienic reasons, but in following the fairly elaborate ritual of ceremonial washing which took place after any dirt had been removed. However, trivial as the detail may seem, the event is far more significant than it at first appears. It represents the direct clash between Jesus and orthodox Judaism as it had developed. Encased in this confrontation are the key issues that separate Jesus from Judaism, and crystallise the principles of the New Covenant over the assumptions of the Old Covenant.

The Pharisees and teachers of the law who come to Jesus have travelled to Galilee from Jerusalem, no doubt specifically to investigate him and try to stop his ministry and prevent the growth of his influence. They latch on to this incident of the disciples not washing their hands before they eat, because it is a direct challenge to the authority of the traditions of their elders.

The issue at stake was the ceremonial cleansing. Uncleanness was contracted by touching or eating what was regarded as unclean. For instance, a woman was unclean during her monthly period, and after any time she had given birth to a baby. A dead body was unclean. A Gentile was unclean. Certain animals were unclean. This uncleanness was contagious. If a man touched something unclean, he became unclean. If someone touched him, they became unclean, and so it would spread. This meant that one might unwittingly become unclean by touching someone on the street who was unclean without being aware of it. To combat this possibility, an elaborate system of washings had been worked out and become mandatory. William Barclay in his Daily Study Bible quotes Edersheim's *The Life and Times of Jesus the Messiah* in describing some of these washings.

> The water was first poured on both hands, held with the fingers pointed upwards, and must run up the arm as far as the wrist. It must drop off from the wrist, for the water was now itself unclean, having touched the unclean hands, and if it ran down the finger again, it would again render the fingers unclean. The process was repeated with the hands held in the opposite direction, with the fingers pointed down; and then finally each hand was cleansed by being rubbed with the fist of the other. A really strict Jew would do this, not only before a meal, but also between each of the courses [1]

The question asked Jesus is why his disciples break with this tradition of the elders and do not wash their hands in this way before eating. Jesus' reply is to speak about the nature of true cleanliness. It is not what goes into a man that makes him unclean, but what comes out of him. What goes into a man's mouth, Jesus said, will go to the stomach and eventually pass out of the body. But the things which come out of the mouth come from the heart and it is this that makes a man 'unclean'. True cleanliness does not work its way from the outside of a person into their hearts, it works its way from the heart to the outside. Good behaviour does not make a person good. Good behaviour can be externally imposed by a set of laws that demand and reward right behaviour, but punish bad behaviour. This however does not produce true goodness. True goodness derives from a cleansed and changed heart, which is then able to express itself in right behaviour. However, the clean heart comes only from a work of God within the person. Good behaviour is a symptom of true goodness, not a cause of it. If a system of rewards and punishment for behaviour is strong enough it will induce conformity to the expected behaviour pattern, and the behaviour will appear good enough, but it is not true goodness. As Jesus elsewhere declared, 'No one is good but God alone' (Mark 10:18). True goodness derives from God alone. All the ceremonial

---

[1] William Barclay, *The Daily Study Bible*, Matthew, Vol. 2, The Saint Andrew Press, Edinburgh.

washing of the Jews was a futile activity as far as true cleanliness and goodness was concerned.

The Pharisees, not surprisingly, '... were offended when they heard this' (15:12), for a straightforward reason. The whole concern of Pharisaism was with external behaviour and external activity. Jesus quotes Isaiah as describing the Pharisees when he wrote, 'These people honour me with their lips, but their hearts are far from me' (15:8). Their language and terminology was a substitute for spiritual reality. Rabbi Taanith said, 'Whoever has his abode in the land of Israel and eats his common food with washed hands, and speaks the holy language, and recites his phylacteries morning and evening, he may rest assured he shall obtain eternal life.'[2] This assumption of the religious leaders was the opposite of Jesus' message. The line of demarcation between Jesus and the religious hierarchy was whether cleanliness worked its way from the outside of a person to the inside, or from the inside to the outside.

2. The nature of true godliness: where apparent poverty is rich (15:21-28)

Leaving his encounter with the Pharisees and teachers of the law, Jesus withdrew to the region of Tyre and Sidon. This is the third time in the last two chapters Jesus has withdrawn to be alone (see 14:13; 14:23) and each time he has been interrupted. This time he leaves Jewish territory altogether, taking his disciples with him, and going to Tyre and Sidon. Here at least he may be away from the crowds who demanded his attention and the religious leaders bent on discrediting him. Mark's gospel tells us that when he got to Tyre, 'He entered a house and did not want anyone to know it' (Mark 7:24). However, his peace and solitude was not to be, for a Canaanite woman knew who he was and that he was in the house.

She came to him and fell at his feet crying, 'Lord, Son of David, have mercy on me! My daughter is suffering terribly from demon-possession.' Jesus did not answer her straight away, and she kept crying out to him. Eventually his disciples urged him to send her away, considering her to be a nuisance. Jesus then spoke and said, 'I was sent only to the lost sheep of Israel. It is not right to take the children's bread and toss it to their dogs.'

---

[2] See G. Campbell Morgan, *The Gospel According to Matthew.*

This woman was not a Jew, and was not simply any Gentile. She was a Canaanite. The Canaanites had been the occupants of the land of Israel when Joshua had conquered it and driven them out. Through succeeding generations some had kept their identity and remained in or close to the land of Israel, but it was an identity that stood in contrast to the Jews and their status. She was outside the covenant, and outside the scope of Jesus' ministry to the lost sheep of Israel.

Her response was to kneel before him and say, 'Lord, help me! Yes Lord, but even the dogs eat the crumbs that fall from their masters' table.' Jesus replied, 'Woman you have great faith! Your request is granted.' What was the nature of this woman's faith? She recognised his identity ('Son of David'), his position, ('Lord'), her own undeserving nature, ('have mercy on me'), her dependency on him ('Lord help me') and his ability to give to whom he willed ('even dogs eat the crumbs that fall from their masters' table'). Recognising who Jesus is, what he does, and our utter dependency on him, are the essential components of faith. It was this faith that provoked the response in Jesus, and her daughter was healed at that very hour.

This example of great faith is reminiscent of the Roman centurion, another Gentile, who astonished Jesus by the greatness of his faith when he asked Jesus to simply '... say the word' and his sick servant would be healed (8:5-13). As in the case of the Canaanite woman, these two Gentile examples of faith were not expressed in requesting something for themselves but for another – the centurion's servant and the Canaanite woman's daughter.

This is in such contrast to the pathetic attitude to Jesus of the Jewish leaders, the favoured people of God. It is they who place obstacles, distractions and diversions in front of him at every turn. Here lies such a warning. The more familiar we are with the things of God, the more casual we may become in relation to them. The business of the Jewish leaders was to study, expound and live the written revelation of God in their Scriptures, but familiarity had bred contempt. Those of us who may have long familiarity with the things of God need to check we do not become casual in our attitude, for that casualness may lead to antagonism to the implications of his word, and rejection of obedience to his instructions. We need to remain fresh, new and real in our walk with God.

3. The nature of true effectiveness: where apparent insufficiency is enough (15:29-39)

Jesus returned to Galilee from Tyre and Sidon, and great crowds followed him up a mountain side, where he healed many of their sick. He stayed there three days, and at the end of it the crowd had nothing to eat. We then have the miracle of the feeding of the four thousand with seven loaves and a few fish. This event is reminiscent of the earlier feeding of the five thousand, and the location, whilst still 'along the Sea of Galilee' (cf. 14:14 and 15:29), is evidently a different one. This occasion was in a 'remote place', probably the uninhabited desert region to the south or southeast of the lake. The crowds on this occasion may have been Gentile, Jesus having come directly from the region of Tyre and Sidon where the Canaanite woman had requested mercy for her demon possessed daughter. The word translated 'baskets' is a different word to that used in the earlier incident. It means a general purpose flexible basket, more suitable to a Gentile context, rather than the wicker baskets used in the feeding of the five thousand, which are more associated with the Jews.[3]

Jesus told his disciples he did not want to send the people away hungry or they may collapse on the way, and so they needed to feed them. To this challenge the disciples replied, 'Where could we get enough bread in this remote place to feed such a crowd?' This situation is reminiscent of the earlier occasion when Jesus put a similar proposition to them before he himself fed the five thousand. On that occasion he said, 'You give them something to eat' (14:13-21). They had been unable to appropriate the sufficiency of God then in the situation, and they were unable to appropriate the sufficiency of God now. In the intervening period between the feeding of the five thousand and the feeding of the four thousand it would seem they have learned very little! They resort to the same tactic of counting their physical resources and concluding they do not have enough.

When Jesus asked them how many loaves they have, they respond rather meekly, 'Seven, and a few small fish.' He told the people to sit down, took the seven loaves and fishes, gave thanks, broke them, gave them to the disciples who in turn gave them to the people. To their amazement once again, 'They all ate and were satisfied.' The procedure of Jesus was once again to 'Give thanks', in acknowledgement of his

---

3. R. T. France, *Matthew*, Tyndale New Testament Commentaries.

dependency upon his Father, and the complete sufficiency of the Father, and then to act on the assumption his Father was in business, break and distribute the bread (see earlier comments on 14:13-21). The loaves and fish did not multiply in a huge pile in front of him, and then he began to distribute it. It was in the act of stepping out in the assurance of his Father's working, and distributing the food that the multiplication process took place.

There is an important principle of spiritual life involved here. We do not prove the working and sufficiency of God outside of '... the obedience that comes from faith' (Rom. 1:5). We might agree with the theory of God's willingness and sufficiency to interfere in our affairs and circumstances, but we will not know the reality of it without going out on the limb of obedience. That obedience must derive from belief to be effective. This is demonstrated by Jesus himself as a demonstration to his disciples of the principles by which they are to live, but they are slow to learn!

After this event, Jesus sent the crowd away and got into the boat once again, and travelled to the vicinity of Magadan.

4. The nature of true evidences: where apparent miracles corrupt (16:1-12)

The Pharisees and Sadducees are a strange coalition of antagonists to come to Jesus to test him by asking for a sign from heaven. The Pharisees and Sadducees were at the opposite poles of the Jewish religious spectrum. The Pharisees were the fundamentalists of their day. Everything was literal, and they lived by the minutest detail of law. To protect them from breaking the real law, they built protective fences around it to prevent them coming close. If they had lived in a day when a speed limit on the road was seventy miles an hour, they would have made it mandatory to not exceed sixty miles an hour to prevent themselves coming close to breaking the real law. They were legalists par excellence!

The Sadducees on the other hand were the liberals of their day. We do not have as much information about them as we do the Pharisees, but they prided themselves on independent thought and saw it as a virtue to dispute with their teachers. They accepted the written law of Moses, but rejected the scribal and traditional laws that had grown around them and which gave so much substance to the Pharisees' position. The Pharisees believed in angels, demons, the resurrection of the body, the supernatural and the after life. The Sadducees believed in none of this. They saw themselves as rational sceptics about such things.

This was a point of dispute well exploited by Paul after his arrest in Jerusalem following his third missionary journey. When brought before the Sanhedrin Council, and knowing some of them were Pharisees and some Sadducees, he said, 'I stand on trial because of my hope in the resurrection of the dead.' When he said this, a dispute broke out between the Pharisees and Sadducees and the assembly was divided. Luke in his account explains, 'The Sadducees say that there is no resurrection, and that there are neither angels nor spirits, but the Pharisees acknowledge them all' (see Acts 23:6-8).

These are the strange bed-fellows that came together in common opposition to Christ. As has been said, two dogs will fight each other until a rabbit runs by. Then they will both chase the rabbit. Jesus was the rabbit! Hostilities towards each other were suspended in their shared hostility to Jesus.

They asked Jesus for a sign from heaven. His response was consistent with his response to all demands for signs and miracles on tap. He told them they know how to interpret the appearance of the sky, red sky at night will be a good next day, and red sky in the morning is the warning of storms, but they do not know how to interpret the signs of the times. The only sign given them, he says, is the sign of Jonah. We have already seen what the sign of Jonah is (see 12:38-40). There Jesus likened Jonah's three days and nights in the belly of the fish to the Son of Man being three days and nights in the heart of the earth. The sign of Jonah was pointing to his own death, burial and resurrection from the dead. We can never make sense of Christ without understanding the cross, and a preoccupation with Christ on any other ground is to become aligned with '... a wicked and adulterous generation' (16:4).

There are many other facets to the life and ministry of Jesus Christ, but to make them the basis of our interest in him, or the message we declare about him is to have not only missed the main point but to have distorted his message. That is why the church is not called upon to preach signs and wonders, a social and political agenda, or a certain lifestyle. All of these may be legitimate issues and an outworking of the gospel once it has been appropriated, but these things are not in themselves our message, for they were not his message. We are called to preach Jesus Christ, crucified, buried and risen again. It is easy to become seduced by these secondary issues. For one thing they are legitimate issues, and for another, they are much more palatable to the world around us than is the preaching of the cross. It makes us appear 'relevant' when we are taken up with an agenda already set by our culture, but this is not our message. Our true message by its very nature marginalises us, but when embraced it transforms people's lives. As believers, our lives must have their social, political and supernatural dimension, as did Jesus and the early church, but these were not the issues at the heart of his ministry.

Leaving the Pharisees and Sadducees, Jesus crossed the lake once again. The disciples forgot to take bread. On the way Jesus warned them, 'Be on your guard against the yeast of the Pharisees and Sadducees' (16:6). This puzzled them. They discussed amongst themselves whether he had said this because they had not brought any bread with them, when Jesus asked them, 'You of little faith, why are you talking about having no bread? Do you remember the five loaves for the five thousand, and how many basketfuls you gathered? Or the seven loaves for the four thousand, and how many basketfuls you gathered? How is it you don't understand that I was not talking to you about bread? Be on your guard against the yeast of the Pharisees and Sadducees' (16:8-11). What then is this, 'yeast of the Pharisees and Sadducees'?

Jesus contrasts this 'yeast' with the experience the disciples had recently witnessed of his feeding the five thousand and his feeding the four thousand. In both of those events they had seen Jesus take the bread, give thanks, break it and pass it to the disciples who passed it to the crowd, and in the end had lots left over. In that act of trust in the Father, and the action that derived from that trust, they had seen the Father work miraculously, and above the needs of the hour. This was the real thing, the genuine expression of God's activity.

The Pharisees and Sadducees however had robbed their religion of its true power and its true expression of God. It was a system of rules and regulations that could be carried out without the active participation of God himself. It may have had a true origin in that it derived from the Mosaic law given on Mount Sinai by God, but in becoming detached from God was now just dead form. As yeast spreads all through the dough, and is in Scripture a consistent picture of evil, so the 'yeast' of the Pharisees and Sadducees if absorbed by the disciples would infiltrate and nullify every part of their experience of God. The yeast is not their hypocrisy, though there was much of that in the Pharisees in particular, it was their 'teaching' (16:12). It was their rationalism (on the part of the Sadducees) and their legalism (on the part of the Pharisees) that substituted God and robbed him of his role in them. If God were to withdraw from his people, Pharisaism and Sadduceeism would continue without any negative consequence, for God has already ceased to be the source of their strength. Legalism and rationalism had replaced God.

The feeding of the five thousand and the feeding of the four thousand with all the abundance left over, is set up by Jesus in this conversation with his disciples as the antithesis of the teaching of the Pharisees and Sadducees. Live in dependency upon God and they will always have enough and to spare. Reduce their spiritual life to the fulfilment of rules and rituals and they will destroy it. This remains as Jesus' warning to his people through all time.

24.

The church
(16:13-20)

One of the remarkable things about the ministry of Jesus is that he hardly ever spoke about the church! The New Testament makes very clear, particularly in the writings of Paul, that we are not simply brought into a private, individual relationship with Christ, exclusive of other people, but at the point at which we are indwelt individually by the Holy Spirit we are incorporated into a body of believers, of which Christ is the head, and every true believer is a member. As Paul writes, 'And in him you too are being built together to become a dwelling in which God lives by his Spirit' (e.g. see Eph. 2:22). This is the church and is of central importance to the New Testament.

However, the word 'church' left the lips of the Lord Jesus Christ himself on only two occasions in all four gospels, and both are only recorded in Matthew. In Chapter 16 he spoke about the universal church which comprises all believers at all times in all circumstances, when he said to Peter, '... you are Peter and on this rock I will build my church' (16:18). On the second occasion, in Chapter 18, he spoke of the local church in the context of speaking about the way to deal with a brother who has sinned against another. The offended person having spoken to him alone and not rectified it, should then take it to one or two others, but, 'If he refuses to listen to them, tell it to the church ...' (18:17). This refers to the local congregation in any one geographical location.

However, all that Jesus said about the universal church is contained in this passage in Chapter 16 and therefore must include the fundamental purpose of Jesus for his church.

Jesus talked about two things:

1. The foundation of the church (16:13-18a),
2. The function of the church (16:18b-19).

1. The foundation of the church (16:13-18a)

The key to this passage is the statement, 'I tell you that you are Peter and on this rock I will build my church.' The context was this occasion when Jesus took his disciples to Caesarea Philippi, some 25 miles (40 km) north of Galilee, and asked them the question, 'Who do people say the Son of Man is?' They gave him some interesting answers, reflecting different contemporary views, 'Some say John the Baptist; others say Elijah; and still others, Jeremiah or one of the prophets'. Having heard this Jesus asked, 'But what about you? Who do you say I am?', to which Simon Peter answered, 'You are the Christ, the Son of the Living God.'

It is in response to that confession Jesus replied, 'Blessed are you Simon son of Jonah, for this was not revealed to you by man, but by my Father in heaven. And I tell you that you are Peter, and on this rock I will build my church, and the gates of Hades will not overcome it.'

The big question is, 'What did he mean?' Is it a reference to *Peter himself?* If it is, does this give particular authority to Peter in the church, and should his successors be recognised as bishops and popes to whom the same authority is conferred (as in Roman Catholic teaching), or to his personal role as a leader of the early group of disciples? Is it a reference to *Peter's statement*, 'You are the Christ', and this acknowledgement is the foundation of the church? Grammatically that would be difficult.

My own understanding is that this statement sets up a contrast between Peter and Christ. There is an obvious play on words here. The name Peter literally means rock (the feminine word for rock 'petra' gives way to the masculine name for Peter, 'petros' in Greek, with the same relationship in Aramaic, the language in which this conversation takes place, 'kepha' and 'kephas'). The subject of the conversation has been Christ, 'Who do you say that I am?', and Jesus' reply includes the pun, 'You are Peter' (i.e. rock) 'and on this rock' (i.e. *this* referring to Christ himself) 'I will build my church'. The rock is not Peter, but Christ, and the contrast is made between them.

This idea of Christ as the rock is entirely consistent with other statements of the New Testament, in a way that the idea of Peter as the rock is not. Paul wrote, 'For no one can lay any foundation other than the one already laid, which is Jesus Christ' (1 Cor. 3:11), and he speaks of the church of both Jew and Gentile 'built on the foundation of the apostles and prophets, with Christ Jesus himself as the chief cornerstone. In him the whole building is joined together and rises to become a holy temple in the Lord' (Eph. 2:20-21). Peter is one of the apostles who together with prophets form foundation stones, but the chief cornerstone from whom the whole building derives its security is Christ.

Interestingly it is Peter himself who writes about Christ as *the stone* in contrast with believers generally as *stones* when he states, 'As you come to him, the living Stone – rejected by men but chosen by God and precious to him – you also, like living stones are being built into a spiritual house ... For in Scripture it states, "See I lay a stone in Zion, a chosen and precious cornerstone, and the one who trusts in him will never be put to shame". Now to you who believe, this stone is precious ...' (1 Pet. 2:4-7). Peter explains the uniqueness of Christ as the cornerstone, as though he may be wanting to clear up any misunderstanding about himself as more than just one of many, classified together as, 'like living stones'.

In the Old Testament, the word 'rock' is often used as a metaphor for God, but never for man: e.g. 'The LORD has become my fortress and my God, the rock in whom I take refuge' (Ps. 94:22); 'Let us shout aloud to the rock of our salvation' (Ps. 95:1). It therefore seems to be consistent with both Old and New Testament Scriptures to understand the statement of Jesus as referring to himself as 'the rock' and not to Peter.

It is the essential uniqueness of Christianity that has as its foundation not a doctrine, or body of truth, but a person. We cannot detach the teaching of Jesus from the person of Jesus, for his teaching derives from who he is, and in fact, Christian doctrine is the exegesis of his person and character. This sets Jesus Christ apart from every other religious leader in history. Others have come onto the scene and announced, 'I will show you the way', Jesus said, 'I AM the way'. Others have said, 'I will teach you truth', Jesus said, 'I AM the truth'. Others have offered to give life, Jesus said, 'I AM the life'. Others have promised to open a door, Jesus said, 'I AM the door'. Others claim to know where to find bread, Jesus said, 'I AM the bread of life'. Others promise to switch on the light, Jesus said, 'I AM the light'. All that Jesus taught derives from who Jesus is. This is one reason why Paul wrote, 'And if Christ has not been raised, our preaching is useless and so is your faith ... And if Christ has not been raised your faith is futile; you are still in your sins' (1 Cor. 15:14, 17). It is not because the resurrection is a final proof of Christ's authenticity, but rather because without a Living Christ, Christianity is a dead religion, for true Christianity is the outworking of Jesus Christ living his life in the Christian.

2. The function of the church (16:18b-19)

'And I tell you that you are Peter and on this rock I will build my church and the gates of Hades will not overcome it.' This picture of the 'gates of Hades' (literally, the place of departed spirits) not overcoming the church is a very interesting one. Before I thought more deeply about this, I assumed it meant the church will always withstand the attack of Hades, death and evil. No matter what onslaught the church of Jesus Christ faced it would always be able to stand its ground. Then I realised this is probably not what is meant. To talk about the 'gates of Hades' is not to talk of attack made on the church, for gates are not attacking weapons. In going to war, armies do not fight each other with gates! Gates are *defensive* rather than *offensive*. This is rather a picture of the church of Jesus Christ on the offensive, driving back the gates of Hades, which are unable to resist.

This should alter some of our understanding of spiritual warfare. There is a tendency to think of spiritual warfare as the devil attacking us, and therefore victory in the Christian life is measured in terms of our ability to resist his attack. So if we don't steal, don't lie, don't commit adultery and generally avoid doing what is wrong, we call that victory and regard it as successful living. The fact is, all of this may be true in our experience whilst we remain spiritually barren. It is not the ability to not do wrong that constitutes effective Christian living, it is the ability to do right! It is not a strong defence against evil, important as that may be, but a strong offence against evil, that drives back the gates of Hades.

This raises the question, How is the church to be on the attack? The following verse gives a clue. 'I will give you the keys of the kingdom of heaven; whatever you bind on earth will be bound in heaven, and whatever you loose on earth will be loosed in heaven' (16:19).

Whatever Jesus is talking about here, we may deduce two things. Firstly, he is talking about the 'keys of the kingdom of heaven'. In so doing he was evidently not talking about something incidental, but something vital and central that unlocks the activity of the kingdom of heaven on earth. Secondly, whatever he is referring to, the church appears to take the initiative, with heaven following through, 'whatever you bind on earth will be bound in heaven'. We might have expected him to say, 'whatever is bound in heaven will become bound on earth', with the initiative taking place in heaven and earth following, but he doesn't. Similarly he states, 'whatever you loose on earth will be loosed in heaven'. What is it that may be described as a key to the activity of the kingdom of heaven on earth, where the agenda of heaven is expressed and made possible through the activity of the church?

It is interesting that on the only other occasion Jesus spoke of the church (Matt. 18) he makes a very similar statement, 'I tell you the truth, whatever you bind on earth will be bound in heaven, and whatever you loose on earth will be loosed in heaven. Again, I tell you that if two of you on earth agree about anything you ask for, it will be done for you by my Father in heaven' (18:18-19). On this occasion he repeats 'binding and loosing' on earth and in heaven, but extends it to 'asking on earth' and being 'given from heaven'. The latter addition gives a clear reference to prayer, where 'asking' on earth and 'giving from heaven' is on a par with 'binding' and 'loosing' on earth and in heaven.

Prayer is a mystery for many of us. We reason this way: If God knows everything, what is the point of trying to tell him anything? If God is sovereign, as he is, and has good plans, as he does, what is the point of making suggestions as to what ought to be done? His own plans can not be improved on! Why don't we just pray, 'Your will be done' and leave the details to him? Clearly, that is inadequate, for scripture encourages us to pray. But why?

This was unclear to me until I began to study some while ago, why it was God had created human beings. When God created man he said, '"Let us make man in our image, in our likeness, and let them rule over the fish of the sea and the birds of the air, over the livestock, over all the earth, and over all the creatures that move along the ground." God blessed them and said to them, "Be fruitful and increase in number; fill the earth and subdue it. Rule over the fish of the sea and the birds of the air and over every living creature that moves on the ground"' (Gen. 1:26, 28). His intention was that man would rule the earth, not in independence of God but in dependence on God. However, Adam and Eve together acted in independence and in consequence became 'separated from the life of God' (Eph. 4:18), and a spiritual declension took place that is inherited by every human being born since then, for 'In Adam all die' (1 Cor. 15:22). Now separate from God, mankind ceases to possess the resources designed to enable them to function as intended, and the downward spiral of decay, sin and death that began in the Garden of Eden has continued to this day.

God has not lost control for he is sovereign and always will be, but he gave to man the responsibility to rule on the earth. As Job's friend Bildad said, 'Dominion and awe belong to God; he establishes order in the heights of heaven' (Job 25:2), and in his establishing of order he gave dominion to man on the earth. As David wrote, 'You made him ruler over the works of your hands; you put everything under his feet' (Ps. 8:6). This responsibility was not withdrawn from man the day he fell in sin. It is the reason life on earth is the mess it is, with so much confusion and disarray. God has not failed. Man has failed. Satan is described by Jesus as 'prince of this world' (John 12:31), not because at any time he has defeated God, for he never has, never can and never will, but because he has defeated man to whom God gave dominion over this world.

This is why prayer is so important. We do not by our praying hold a pistol to God's head, or twist his arm into some action about which he is reluctant. We cannot make God do what he does not wish to do, but we can prevent him doing what he might wish to do. In exercising the dominion God gave mankind over the earth, we may keep God out, or we may bring God in. God is not reluctant to give, but he has set his structures, and consequently James writes, 'You do not have, because you do not ask God' (Jas. 4:2). Prayer is bringing God into the situation, not to get him to serve us, but that his will may be done, and his agenda fulfilled.

However, if this statement of Jesus has a specific application to prayer, it has a more general application too. The principle contained here is that all God plans from heaven in terms of his working amongst people, he implements through his church. As the church binds and looses, heaven binds and looses. It is the activity of the church that is the vehicle for, and makes possible, the activity of heaven on earth. The construction of this statement in Greek is in the future perfect tense, that is, literally, 'whatever you bind on earth will *have been bound* in heaven and whatever you loose on earth will *have been loosed* in heaven'. It is not that the church dictates to heaven, or creates the agenda for heaven, but that the intentions and purposes of heaven are fulfilled in the world through the church.

The church of Jesus Christ cannot make God do what he does not want to do. The very thought is blasphemous, for God answers to no one in his creation. However the church can prevent God doing what he otherwise would do. We can never force the Holy Spirit to do anything beyond his will, but Scripture speaks of 'grieving the Holy Spirit' (Eph. 4:30) and thereby preventing what he would otherwise do. We cannot make God do anything, but Scripture speaks of people who 'limited the Holy One of Israel' (Ps. 78:41, AV). God's working in the world through his church may be inhibited and restricted by disobedience and non co-operation.

In this situation of a fallen world, God's strategy is to work through his church. In creation God gave to human beings 'dominion' over the earth. His purpose was that this dominion should be exercised in submission to God, but when in his foolishness, man went his own way, God did not withdraw the dominion over the earth he had entrusted to the human race. That responsibility still stands. As a result of human rebellion, instead of the will of God being done in the world, there is chaos and spiritual anarchy! If the will of God is being done in the world (as some believe), then it would make nonsense of the instruction of Jesus to pray, 'Your will be done on earth as it is in heaven'. It would credit God with at least some responsibility for the state of our fallen world, and destroy any moral ground for the Judgement Day yet to come. The corrupt condition of our world is not the responsibility of God who created it, but of man to whom he gave dominion over it.

This does not in any way undermine the absolute sovereignty of God, for it is his sovereign and exclusive choice that human beings should be entrusted with this responsibility, fully knowing the consequences! In consistency with the responsibility God has given human beings, he now works in the world through his people, and where they act in obedience to him and dependency on him, he acts. Where they refuse to do so, in that measure God is limited in his working and his Holy Spirit is grieved.

For example, God draws people to himself through human agency. Paul wrote, "'Everyone who calls on the name of the Lord will be saved." How, then, can they call on the one they have not believed in? And how can they believe in the one of whom they have not heard? And how can they hear without someone preaching to them? And how can they preach unless they are sent?' (Rom. 10:13-15). It is God alone who saves people, and it is God who sends people to preach, but the weakest link in the chain between the two is surely the obedience of the preacher. The response of 'believing' the message on the part of those to whom he is sent, is a result of divine activity in the heart of the person as a result of the preaching, but without the communication of the gospel in obedience to God, there is not a back up plan. God does not send angels to evangelise – he sends people! It is as the church acts in obedience to God in dependency upon his Spirit, that God works through the church.

There is a negative aspect ('binding') and a positive aspect ('loosing'). To bind is to forbid, and to loose is to permit. God's means in human affairs of both restricting what is wrong and in releasing what is right is to work through his church. The church is to be both salt (negatively) and light (positively) in society (see Matt. 5:13-14).

Having drawn from his disciples an acknowledgement of his true identity, 'You are the Christ, the Son of the living God', and then spoken to them for the first time about the church and its purpose and potential, it comes as something of a surprise to read Jesus then 'warned his disciples not to tell anyone that he was the Christ'. Our normal expectancy might be that having discovered something new about the Lord Jesus Christ we should pass it on. Why does he tell the disciples to keep quiet? Why this prohibition? We will explore the answer to that question in the next chapter!

25.

The nature of true discipleship
(16:21-28)

Why did Jesus forbid his disciples to 'tell anyone that he was the Christ'? (16:20). It comes as something of a surprise and seems rather strange! Peter had just acknowledged Jesus to be 'the Christ the Son of the Living God'. He had learned this not by human reason but by divine revelation, 'this was not revealed to you by man but by my Father in heaven'. Jesus had then spoken for the first time of plans for his church, the foundation on which it would be built, and the function it would fulfil. The disciples may have been filled with a growing sense of excitement as they listened to everything he was saying, only to be suddenly hit with the prohibition, 'Don't tell anyone!'

This was not the first or only time Jesus forbade people to speak about him (see 8:4; 9:29; 12:16; 17:9, and other occasions in Mark). It is not necessary to suppose the reasons for this are uniform, as each occasion may present its own reasons for a similar prohibition. The reasons on this occasion seems evident from its context in the following verses.

The issue on this occasion focuses on Peter, as does the whole of this conversation at Caesarea Philippi. Matthew writes, 'From that time on Jesus began to explain to his disciples that he must go to Jerusalem and suffer many things at the hands of the elders, chief priests and teachers of the law, and that he must be killed and on the third day be raised to life.' This was the first time Jesus spoke of his impending crucifixion.

The first acknowledgement of his true identity by the disciples led to the first explanation of his true mission, the cross. The language 'From that time on ...' indicates this was to become the recurring theme of Jesus speaking from now on, though remarkably, right up to the moment of the crucifixion itself, the disciples did not grasp this really was what lay in front of him.

It is to the statement about going to Jerusalem to be killed at the hands of the religious leaders there that Peter responds indignantly and significantly, 'Peter took him aside and began to rebuke him. "Never, Lord!" he said. "This shall never happen to you!"' (16:22). The two words 'Never, Lord' are a key to what happens next, for they are a contradiction in terms. To say 'Lord' is to rule out the freedom to say 'Never', and to say 'Never' is to overrule his position as 'Lord'. Peter evidently has a problem! In his earlier statement, 'You are the Christ the Son of the living God' (16:16) Peter correctly acknowledged Jesus as the Son of God and Jesus congratulated him, 'Blessed are you, Simon son of Jonah, for this was not revealed to you by man, but by my Father in heaven' (16:17). Doctrinally, Peter is absolutely correct. However, doctrinal accuracy is of no virtue unless that doctrine translates into personal experience, which is exactly Peter's situation at this point. The implications of Jesus Christ being the Son of God have not filtered through Peter's understanding to a disposition that rules out any right to say, 'Never, Lord'. In the space of six verses the statement of Jesus to Peter, 'Blessed are you Simon son of Jonah ...', has turned to, 'Get behind me, Satan! You are a stumbling-block to me; you do not have in mind the things of God, but the things of men' (16:23). In the earlier statement Jesus is speaking of Peter's comprehension of Christ, of his doctrinal understanding, of his theological position – and he is correct. But in the later statement Jesus is speaking of Peter's life, of his disposition towards Christ, of the extent to which his understanding has become experiential – and he is described as 'Satanic', a stumbling block and as operating in the opposing camp, 'you do not have in mind the things of God but the things of men'!

These are very strong words of Jesus. We might have expected them to have been spoken of the religious leaders of the day who were characterised by hypocrisy and resistance to Christ and might deserve the accolade, 'Get behind me, Satan.' But this was a disciple, and he was acting as a stumbling block to Christ.

There is little that is more dangerous to the work of Jesus Christ than someone whose doctrine is correct, but for whom doctrine has not become life. Their creed is right but their character is not. They are theologically correct but theocratically indifferent! They affirm Christ as Lord on a pedestal, but not in their heart. This may not be due to any lack of enthusiasm for Christ, which was certainly not lacking in Peter, but to misunderstanding his role and the principles that must govern true discipleship. This is perhaps why Jesus forbade them to tell anyone that he was the Christ. If the language of their lips does not find expression in the realities of their life, then their language lacks credibility. Correct doctrine does not in itself instil correct living. Something has to happen to Peter in order for his doctrine to become life. 'Then Jesus said to his disciples, "If anyone would come after me, he must deny himself and take up his cross and follow me. For whoever wants to save his life will lose it, but whoever loses his life for me will find it.' This is what it takes to turn truth into experience.

1. Deny self

We tend to think of 'denying self' as engaging in little heroic acts like not taking sugar in coffee, or going without chocolate for the forty days of Lent! Churches arrange 'self denial' lunches where instead of the normal Sunday roast they eat cheese and apples and donate the cost of the roast to people in need. This is all good and valuable, but is not what Jesus had in mind when he told his disciples to deny themselves.

The statement must be interpreted in its context. To 'deny self' was the exact opposite of what Peter was telling Jesus to do. Regarding the cross he had said, 'This shall never happen to you', not because he was being unkind or trying to be unhelpful! He was saying in effect, 'You are too good to die in this way, we will not allow it to happen.' His motivation was admirable for he was being protective of Jesus.

However the essence of discipleship requires the abandonment of self preservation. To have to 'deny himself' was to come to the place where what happens to the individual in fulfilment of the will of God becomes an almost irrelevant issue. For Jesus Christ to accomplish the will of his Father, he was to die on a Roman cross, with all the injustice and agony that would entail, but if that fulfilled the will of his Father then die on a Roman cross he must and would. Self preservation was not the issue. The will of God, however difficult it would be, was not up for negotiation or amendment, much less for correction and revision as Peter had suggested.

If this was true for Jesus himself, it was equally to be true of 'anyone who would come after me'. This is a fundamental ingredient in true, biblical discipleship. To 'deny self' is to come to the point of saying, 'What happens to me in the fulfilment of the will of God is not the important issue to me.' If to fulfil his will we are to leave the security of home and go to some far flung mission field of the world with all the difficulties that may entail, then that is what it takes. If to fulfil the will of God we stay around home with family and friends in a culture with which we are familiar, then that is fine. To live in relative poverty or wealth is an immaterial detail to the real issue that governs our lives. To remain single or to marry and have children is neither the goal nor the phobia of life. The goal is that at all times, in all circumstances, and at any cost we become the means by which God is able to do his work and fulfil his purpose, irrespective of personal implications to ourselves.

This sounds tough, demanding, and unreasonable, but it is in fact the gateway to true liberty. At the base of so many personal problems we face is a faulty attitude to oneself. If we fail to settle this fundamental issue of 'self denial' we will have to face and battle a thousand lesser issues which would otherwise be encompassed in settling this central and greater issue. There is no virtue in sacrifice for its own sake. There is virtue only in settling the issue of the Lordship of Christ, and everything else falls into place as a consequence of that. This is not to suggest everything else is easy, for the cross was not easy for Christ, but the issue of the cross was settled when the Son said to his Father before his incarnation at Bethlehem, 'I have come to do your will, O God' (see Heb. 10.5-7). To have faced that issue and submit unreservedly to God will have fundamental influence on every other issue. Every other dilemma and every other decision will find its response in relation to this one key issue.

2. Take up the cross

Not only must a disciple 'deny himself', but he must 'take up his cross and follow me' (16:24). If to 'deny self' is a more negative response, to 'take up the cross' is a more positive. This again, in the context of this passage, was exactly what Peter was telling Jesus not to do. Peter told Jesus that the cross 'shall never happen to you'. However, Jesus not only says he is to go to the cross and die, but that in order to be a disciple, every man, woman, boy or girl who would want to identify themselves with him must also 'take up his cross'.

Once again there are perhaps some widespread misunderstandings about what this entails. We tend to think that taking up the cross has to do with putting up with unavoidable problems in life! We talk about our aches and pains, our difficult circumstances and conclude, 'I suppose it is my cross.' One man told me he only had one cross to bear in life – his arthritis. I assured him it was not his cross, it was his arthritis! The cross is something far more than coping bravely with difficult problems!

To understand what it means for a disciple to 'take up his cross and follow me', we need to understand what it meant for Jesus to take up his cross. It was not a demonstration of how to act under extreme pressure (though it happens to be true that we will not find a better example of that). The cross to Jesus Christ was the ultimate expression of his obedience to the will of his Father.

In the Garden of Gethsemane, immediately prior to his arrest and crucifixion, Jesus prayed to his Father: "'My Father, if it is possible, may this cup be taken from me. Yet not as I will, but as you will." ... He went away a second time and prayed, "My Father, if it is not possible for this cup to be taken away unless I drink it, may your will be done'" (26:39, 42). There is no question that Jesus went willingly to the cross, but he did not go waltzing to the cross, whistling a tune on the way, shrugging his shoulders as though it was easy! He went in great anguish. He said to Peter, James and John, 'My soul is overwhelmed with sorrow' (26:38). In the garden he perspired as though he was bleeding, and an angel strengthened him (Luke 22:43-44). The hours of approaching the cross were a time of great anguish and torment to Jesus Christ. His prayer in Gethsemane was '... if it is possible, may this cup be taken from me'. In other words, 'If there is any other way that the salvation of humankind can be accomplished, any other way people may be reconciled to God and equipped to live as human beings were created to live, then please let that be the way.' This was in full realisation of all that lay ahead, yet his prayer was qualified with, 'Yet not as I will, but as you will.' The cross in the experience of the Lord Jesus Christ was the ultimate in his obedience to his Father. Paul later wrote of Jesus, '... he humbled himself and became obedient to death – even death on a cross!' (Phil. 2:8). To take up the cross is to live in utter obedience to the Father, irrespective of the consequences.

The disciples did not understand this at the time. Living under Roman rule however, every once in a while they might see a man carrying a cross down the road, hounded by soldiers and a mocking crowd. They knew one thing about that man, if nothing else. He would never come back along that road. He would die on the cross he was carrying.

To take up the cross as a disciple of Jesus Christ is not a commitment of convenience. There is a danger of seeing Christian living as little more than the means of furthering our own self interests in finding purpose and fulfilment, rather than as an abandonment of our plans and resources for his plans and resources. True discipleship is to be a one way road. Jesus said, 'No-one who puts his hand to the plough and looks back is fit for service in the kingdom of God' (Luke 9:62).

3. Follow me

To deny self, to take up the cross, is to 'follow me' (16:24). The earlier rebuke to Peter had been 'Get behind me, Satan.' Rather than allow the Lord Jesus Christ to set the direction and pace, Peter had tried to direct Jesus, to get in front of him and divert him from his stated end in Jerusalem. In so doing he became a 'stumbling block to me'. To obstruct his purposes, no matter how noble our aspirations, is to be a stumbling block to Christ.

The invitation to Peter is therefore a logical one: 'Follow me.' We are not left with decisions to make, so much as with orders to obey. It is his prerogative to 'direct our paths' (Prov. 3:6), and ours to 'walk in them' (Isa. 30:21). We should not conclude from this that life is simplistic, for it is not, but it is so very much more simple when we learn, 'We live by faith not by sight' (2 Cor. 5.7). If it is our responsibility to 'follow', then it is his responsibility to lead, and for that we must trust him to be totally competent!

4. Losing life is finding life

Jesus sums up this series of instructions by saying, 'For whoever wants to save his life will lose it, but whoever loses his life for me will find it' (16:25). This is not an invitation to literal martyrdom, but a statement that the only way to find life in its fulness is to lose it and give it away to God. The principle is that as we give our lives away to Jesus Christ, he gives his life away to us. Paul wrote, 'We always carry around in our body the death of Jesus, so that the life of Jesus may also be revealed in our body. For we who are alive are always being given over to death for Jesus' sake, so that his life may be revealed in our mortal body' (2 Cor. 4:10-11). It is our willingness to die that gives place to real life. Until we have learned to die we do not have the resources to live. The phrase has been coined, 'The secret of a changed life is in discovering it is an *exchanged* life.' The Christian life is something far more profound than Jesus Christ changing us, it is Jesus Christ *replacing* us with himself, so that, 'I no longer live, but Christ lives in me' (Gal. 2:20). We can never know the fulness of his life in us without the corresponding losing of our own lives to him.

Jim Eliot, martyred in his late twenties with four colleagues as they attempted contact with a remote tribe in the Ecuadorian jungle, wrote in his diary, 'He is no fool who gives what he cannot keep to gain what he cannot lose.' We cannot keep our lives anyway. Jesus went on to say, 'What good will it be for a man if he gains the whole world, yet forfeits his life? Or what can a man give in exchange for his life?' (16:26). Our inability to keep and control our lives is one of the indisputable facts of life, and there is therefore little more sensible and sane than to recognise this fact, deny ourselves, take up our cross, follow him, and lose the life we can never keep, in an unqualified surrender to Christ. The great thing is that in reality this is not losing life at all, it is finding life. When we are fully available to him, he is fully available to us, and we are equipped to live in the strength of his indwelling fulness.

If Peter was to go on living his life, his way, with his agenda, he was free to do so. God would not twist his arm, hold a gun to his head and force true discipleship. The Lord Jesus Christ is a shepherd not a sheep dog. We are not hemmed in and driven, but follow out of love and implicit trust in him. If Peter chose to go down his own path there may be all kinds of measured successes as far as he is concerned, but he would end with empty hands. Having kept his life he would lose it, and everything else with it. But if he would lose his life, jettison his own agenda and give himself away to Jesus Christ, this life might deal him some rough blows, he might even die on a Roman cross as is traditionally believed, but he will have found life in its true fulness, not only filled with God himself, but one that will never end. This is some exchange! It is the terms of true discipleship, and the grounds on which all that is truly of value is determined.

5. Awaiting the day

In the last two verses of this section, Jesus talks about two future comings. Firstly, 'For the Son of Man is going to come in his Father's glory with his angels, and then he will reward each person according to what he has done' (16:27). This is looking ahead to his return as judge. The value of our works assessed that day will not be found in the work itself as in the source from which that work derives. This is the point of the earlier verses, for in *losing* our lives we *find* life as he exchanges our resources for himself, and lives his productive and fruitful life in us. It is the fruit of that relationship, the fact of our being 'God's workmanship, created in Christ Jesus to do good works which God prepared in advance for us to do' (Eph. 2:10), that makes these works possible. As *God's workmanship*, he is the origin of the good works, and as *in Christ Jesus*, he is the means of those good works. The day of reckoning is yet to come.

However, he speaks of another coming when he concludes the statement, 'I tell you the truth, some who are standing here will not taste death before they see the Son of Man coming in his kingdom' (16:28). This is his coming as King in his kingdom, and will take place before some standing with him will taste death. It is a reference to the Day of Pentecost. The kingdom of God does not have geographical borders, but exists in the lives of those who submit to his kingship. Jesus said, 'The kingdom of God does not come with your careful observation, nor will people say, "Here it is," or "There it is," because the kingdom of God is within you' (Luke 17:20-21). This is not a reference to the Second Coming of Christ when he will set up a kingdom on earth, as is evident from Jesus' statement about that event when he said, 'No-one knows about that day or hour, not even the angels in heaven, nor the Son, but only the Father' (Matt. 24:36). This event however is known and will take place in the lifetime of many of those listening. Through the events of his death and resurrection in Jerusalem, he will ascend to his Father and return at Pentecost to make his home in those who will receive him. Then the terms of true discipleship, so specifically laid out in this section, will be implemented and experienced in his waiting disciples.

26.

The glory and the power
(17:1-27)

The remarkable transfiguration of Jesus takes place in the first part of Chapter 17. His face shone like the sun, his clothes became a dazzling white and there appeared with him Moses and Elijah (17:1-13). The inner core of his disciples, Peter, James and John, were with him on the mountain, but the story comes down to earth immediately when they descend the mountain and rejoin a crowd of people around an epileptic boy the other disciples had been unable to heal (17:14-23). Jesus healed the boy, and then went on with his disciples to Capernaum where he arranged the payment of the temple tax (17:24-26). These three events have to do with the issues of, *transfiguration* of Jesus, *transformation* of an epileptic boy and the *taxation* of Jesus and his disciples.

1. The transfiguration (17:1-13)
The transfiguration took place six days after the events at Caesarea Philippi when Jesus had asked his disciples whom people said he was, then drew from Peter his confession, 'You are the Christ, the Son of the living God.' Following that confession Matthew records, 'From that time on Jesus began to explain to his disciples that he must go to Jerusalem and suffer many things at the hands of the elders, chief priests and teachers of the law and that he must be killed and on the third day be raised to life' (16:21). This was the first time he had declared this purpose to his disciples, and from then on his direction is set for Jerusalem and the cross.

Now, six days later, this remarkable event took place, when Jesus took his inner core of disciples, Peter, James and John, up a high mountain and 'was transfigured before them'. The location of this mountain is not specified in the Gospels. It may have been on the Hermon range in the general region of Caesarea Philippi where

Jesus was located six days previously. Traditionally, however, it is regarded as Mt. Tabor in Galilee. If there is not a precise location of the event, neither is there an explanation of the meaning of the event in the text. Perhaps there is the contrast of his revelation to them at Caesarea Philippi of his humiliation and death, and this revelation of his exaltation and glory. His face shone like the sun, his clothes became as white as the light, and there appeared with him two of the aristocracy of the Old Testament, Moses and Elijah, representing it could be said two of the major themes of the Old Testament, the law and the prophets. These initial details of this event were staggering enough to these three apostles who witnessed it all.

Moses had in his day gone up Mount Sinai to meet with God, also taking three men with him, Aaron, Nadab and Abihu (Exod. 24:1). Whilst there, his face too had shone, '... his face was radiant because he had spoken with the LORD. When Aaron and all the Israelites saw Moses, his face was radiant, and they were afraid to come near him' (Exod. 34:29-30). However there was a difference in the shine seen in Moses' face on that occasion, and that seen in Christ's face on this occasion. The glory in Moses' face was a reflected glory (see 2 Cor. 3:7-18), it did not originate in himself but in God, and it faded with the passing of time. His light was like the light of the moon which shines only as a reflection of the sun. Of Jesus Matthew writes, 'His face shone like the sun' (17:2). This was the real, original, genuine light, for the life of God in Christ, 'was the light of men' (John 1:4) and showed itself in a visible way on this occasion.

The death of Moses some fifteen hundred years before was shrouded in mystery. He died alone in Moab on the threshold of Canaan at the age of one hundred and twenty. God buried him, and 'to this day no one knows where his grave is' (Deut. 34:6). The fact he died is not in question, for there is another intriguing reference to Moses' body in the book of Jude where it speaks of '... the archangel Michael ... disputing with the devil over the body of Moses' (Jude v. 9). What the dispute was about, or why Michael and the devil should be interested in the body of Moses, we may only speculate, but could it have had to do with the fact God had a future role for the body of Moses here at the transfiguration? The transfiguration was the only time Moses actually set foot in the Promised Land, something denied him after his forty years in the wilderness, and he did so in the company of the Lord Jesus Christ, whose company and presence had been foreshadowed in the promises made concerning the Promised Land.

Elijah was the prophet who did not die. He had been taken up to heaven in a chariot of fire in a whirlwind (2 Kgs. 2:11), but his return in some form or other was anticipated in the Old Testament. The book of Malachi concludes with the promise, 'See, I will send you the prophet Elijah before that great and dreadful day of the LORD comes' (Mal. 4:5). It was on the Mount of Transfiguration that Jesus explained this to be John the Baptist. 'The disciples asked him, "Why then do the teachers of the law say that Elijah must come first?" Jesus replied, "To be sure, Elijah comes and will restore all things. But I tell you Elijah has already come, but they did not recognise him.... Then the disciples understood he was talking to them about John the Baptist' (17:10-13). John was not a reincarnation of Elijah of course, but was very much in the style and image of Elijah (see earlier comments on Matthew 3).

The revival of the ministry of Elijah was a popular theme amongst the Jews, some seeing him returning as a kind of saviour. When Jesus cried from the cross, 'My God, my God, why have you forsaken me', some said, 'He's calling Elijah.... Let's see if Elijah comes to save him' (27:46-49).

Moses and Elijah represent the two main components of the Old Testament revelation, the law and the prophets, both of which are incomplete without Christ. The law of Moses revealed the demands of God, but whose effect was only to leave people helpless to implement them, until Christ brought the possibility of their fulfilment (see comments on 5:17ff). Elijah stands in the tradition of the ecstatic prophets (which began in the days of Samuel) but is at the same time the forerunner of the written prophets. As the bridge between them he stands in the Old Testament as the pinnacle of the prophetic ministry, whose ultimate focus and interest was the coming of the Messiah, the Lord Jesus Christ, to implement God's programme for mankind. Without Christ therefore, both Moses' and Elijah's ministries are purposeless cul-de-sacs.

In addition to their relationship to Christ, there are many intriguing similarities between Moses and Elijah. Both met with God at Horeb (see Exodus 3, Moses' encounter with God at the Burning Bush where God spoke out of the fire, and 1 Kings 19, Elijah met God at Horeb, but in this incident God did not speak in the fire, but after the fire in 'a gentle whisper'). Both men were in Horeb having run for their lives, Moses from Pharaoh, and Elijah from Jezebel. Both were sent back from where they had come (Exod. 4:19 'Go back to Egypt'; 1 Kgs. 19:15 'Go back the way you came...'). Both experienced a miraculous river crossing: Moses at the Red Sea (Exod. 14:21-22), Elijah in the Jordan River (2 Kgs. 2:8). God spoke to both men by fire twice. To Moses at the Burning Bush (Exod. 3) and on Mount Sinai (Exod. 20); and to Elijah on Mount Carmel (1 Kgs. 18) and when facing the army of the King of Samaria (2 Kgs. 1). They are the last mentioned men of the Old Testament (see Mal. 4:4-6). Both men were accompanied and succeeded by men whose own ministry was significant, Moses by Joshua and Elijah by Elisha.

In the New Testament they appear together on the Mount of Transfiguration but additionally are sometimes identified as the two men at the empty tomb of Jesus (Luke 24:4; John 20:12); the two men at the ascension of Jesus (Acts 1:10) and as the two witnesses on the streets in Jerusalem at a future time (Rev. 11:3). It is interesting that Luke's record says 'they spoke about his departure which he was about to bring to fulfilment at Jerusalem' (Luke 9:31) which perhaps further identifies them with the two men at the empty tomb and at the ascension. Whatever else may be true, the appearance of Moses and Elijah with Jesus establishes the link between the old and new covenants, that link being Christ himself.

What actually happened to Jesus at this point is something of a mystery to us. Clearly something objective happened. It was not an altered state of mind in Peter, James and John that gave them the appearance of this phenomena. Something actually happened. Some have suggested a metamorphosis, as a tadpole might turn into a frog or a caterpillar into a butterfly, and where here the man Jesus is transformed into deity, and the shining of his face like the sun, his clothes becoming as white as light, are expressions of deity. Perhaps it is best to let Peter be the explainer of this event when he wrote years later: ['we were eye-witnesses of his majesty. For he received honour and glory from God the Father when the voice came to him from the Majestic Glory, saying, "This is my Son, whom I love; with him I am well pleased." We ourselves heard this voice that came from heaven when we were with him on the sacred mountain. And we have the word of the prophets made more certain, and you will do well to pay attention to it, as to a light shining in a dark place, until the day dawns and the morning star rises in your hearts' (2 Pet. 1:16-19).] He doesn't claim, 'We were eyewitnesses of his deity', but 'of his majesty'. As God, no one can see him. Paul describes him as living 'in unapproachable light, whom no-one has seen or can see' (1 Tim. 6:16). This light on the Mount of Transfiguration, bright and dazzling as the sun though it was, was not 'unapproachable' and therefore not a full revelation of his deity. It was, says Peter, a revelation of the majesty of Jesus, and 'you will do well to pay attention to it, as to a light shining in a dark place'. The majesty of Jesus anticipates a day that is going to dawn when we shall live in the full light of God. That day is not yet, and in the meantime, Jesus Christ is the light in the darkness of the night, the morning star announcing the dawn, preparing us for the sunrise of the new day.

Whilst Moses and Elijah appeared and were talking with Jesus, Peter, taken aback by the occasion, quite typically, said to Jesus, 'Lord, it is good for us to be here. If you wish, I will put up three shelters – one for you, one for Moses and one for Elijah' (17:4). It is probably a very human reaction to respond to some great revelation of God by wanting to do something, and demonstrate a response by action. Being is ultimately more important than doing. Here the Lord Jesus was simply being. Peter wanted to be doing.

While he was still speaking a cloud enveloped them. The presence of God is often indicated in Scripture by the presence of a cloud (e.g. Exod. 13:21; Exod. 19:16; Exod. 24:18; 1 Kings 8:10-11; Isa. 19:1; Luke 21:27; Rev. 14:14-16). As Peter talked and the other two disciples watched, the Father spoke from the cloud and said, 'This is my Son, whom I love; with him I am well pleased. Listen to him!' (17:5). In other words, 'Peter, keep quiet! Don't take your own initiatives, listen to him!' These words of the Father are clearly reminiscent of his speaking at the baptism of Jesus, the only previous time the Father has spoken audibly to the Son from heaven. The cloud and voice terrified the three disciples, they fell face down on the ground in fear. Jesus touched them and told them to not be afraid. They looked up and there was no one there but Jesus. The cloud, the light, the voice and the companions were gone, they were left only with Jesus. But it was to him that all the other players and phenomena had pointed during this remarkable event.

Coming down the mountain Jesus again instructed them to tell no one what they had seen. If at Caesarea Philippi the disciples had learned that truth in itself does not make a person spiritual (see notes on 16:21-28), in this incident they learn that experience in itself does not make a person spiritual. They had witnessed the most amazing portrayal of the glory of God in Christ that would be witnessed during his earthly ministry, but they were not entrusted to tell others of its significance.

There is sometimes a polarisation in the church of Jesus Christ in these two areas. There are those who care most about having doctrine right and less about personal experience of God and there are those who care most about experience and less about doctrine. Both are missing the point. Doctrine and experience are equally necessary, but neither is in itself the criteria for spiritual reality and effectiveness. That criteria is the indwelling life of Christ himself, which would become available to these disciples at Pentecost. In the meantime, 'Don't tell anyone!'

These disciples had so much to unlearn about the Messiah, and unlearning is usually a harder process than learning. The first time Peter speaks with true understanding of Christ is on the Day of Pentecost: 'Men of Israel, listen to this: Jesus of Nazareth was a man accredited by God to you by miracles, wonders and signs, which God did among you through him, as you yourselves know' (Acts 2:22). This is someone so very much more than one in whose honour shelters should be built, as Peter had suggested on the mountain. He lived on earth every bit as a true man, but as a man through whom God worked. Peter gives his own testimony in his second epistle when he says: 'His divine power has given us everything we need for life and godliness through our knowledge of him who called us by his own glory and goodness' (2 Pet. 1:3). He called us by his own glory, the glory Peter had seen so visibly displayed on the Mount of Transfiguration and which as a magnet draws iron filings, so Peter had been drawn.

2. A transformation (17:14-23)

On reaching the foot of the mountain, they were approached by a man whose son suffered greatly from seizures, whom the other disciples had been unable to heal. Jesus rebuked and drove out the demon and the boy was healed. The main point of this story is the particular rebuke Jesus gave the disciples. When they asked why they couldn't drive out the demon he replied, 'Because you have so little faith' (17:20), having first given a general diagnosis of his times, 'O unbelieving and perverse generation' (17:17).

The disciples had earlier been given power to drive out demons and heal the sick (see 10:1), but in this case had failed to dislodge the problem, despite their apparent attempts. What was it then at fault? Evidently it was their lack of faith. Faith is a disposition of trust in God, that looks to him to intervene and work. Perhaps the disciples had reduced exorcism to a technique, to a method, to a ritual or to a series of actions which had become detached from God himself. Whatever else faith in God is, it is an exclusive trust in his ability. It is not 'bigger' or 'greater' faith that is needed, for Jesus explicitly says to them, 'I tell you the truth, if you have faith as small as a mustard seed, you can say to this mountain, "Move from here to there" and it will move. Nothing will be impossible for you' (17:21). Mustard seed was the smallest known seed in the Middle East. It is not the substance of the faith that is at stake, but its object. The object is God himself. Our faith does not dictate to God what he must do, it allows him to do what he wills to do in our circumstances and situation. To place faith in an aircraft does not predetermine the direction of the aircraft. To place faith in an aircraft is to trust it to fly you to wherever it is going. To place faith in God is to be caught up with what God is doing, not getting God involved in what we are doing. When Jesus said, 'My Father is always at his work to this very day, and I, too, am working' (John 5:17), he was identifying his own work as a consequence of his Father's work. This is the result of living by faith. God's activity becomes our activity. Whatever other details may have been involved in the failure of the disciples to drive out the demon, at its root lay their dependency on something other than the Father, and it was this for which they were rebuked.

3. Taxation (17:24-27)

Following the event of exorcising the demon from the troubled boy, Jesus came with his disciples back to Galilee from which they had been absent for some time. They had been in Tyre and Sidon (15:21); Caesarea Philippi (16:13); and the Mount of Transfiguration (17:1). On the journey home, he told them again of his impending betrayal, arrest, crucifixion and resurrection on the third day. This was the second time he had told them this. After the first at Caesarea Philippi, Peter had rebuked him. This time, 'the disciples were filled with grief' (17:23), still not understanding what he was really telling them.

On arriving in Capernaum, collectors of the two-drachma tax, which paid for the upkeep of the temple (based on Exod. 30:11-16), asked Peter, 'Doesn't your teacher pay the temple tax?' This tax had nothing to do with Rome and was not collected by the notorious tax collectors. This was a domestic tax which every Israelite over twenty was ordered to pay for the maintenance of the temple and its ministry. It is described in Exodus as a payment of 'a ransom for his life', designed to 'atone for your life' (Exod. 30:12, 15). It represented a commitment to the function and ministry of the temple as a means of communion with God. The temple was not cheap to run and every Israelite adult was to contribute his share. There was some controversy over this tax. Some paid it annually, some paid it once for a lifetime and others, such as the Sadducees, refused to pay it at all.

Peter replied in the affirmative to the question about Jesus' payment of the tax, 'Yes he does.' When Peter came into the house Jesus discussed this with his disciples, and indicated they actually had no obligation to pay at all, for kings do not collect taxes from their own sons. The temple had become little more than a commercial operation to some, and not the base of vibrant spiritual life and activity. Money is necessary to the ongoing of God's work, and in the New Testament it is to be voluntarily given. 'Each man should give what he has decided in his heart to give, not reluctantly or under compulsion, for God loves a cheerful giver' (2 Cor. 9:7), and this would be the normal arrangement.

However, there are those who only work in a legalistic mind set, so in order to avoid offending others and create an unnecessary barrier between them, they should pay the tax as required. If they do not pay it, some may interpret it as lack of regard for the temple itself, and that should be avoided. Small actions may cause large problems to others, and in those cases our sensitivity to others and our love for them means we may need to sometimes do things we would not consider essential, but send valuable signals to other people.

Jesus chose which battles to fight and which to ignore. To fight every battle is to raise the level of things of lesser importance to a greater significance than they deserve and this inevitably sends confusing signals. To fight the big battles often establishes principles that solve the lesser battles at the same time. It takes wisdom to discern which is which and to act accordingly.

It was not a big issue, but so as not to offend others, Peter was sent to throw his line into a lake, catch a fish and in it he would find a four-drachma coin. With that he was to pay the tax of both Jesus and Peter.

27.

Greatness and growth in the kingdom
(18:1-35)

Chapter eighteen begins the fourth main teaching section of Matthew's gospel, in which, in response to four questions put to him, Jesus speaks of the governing principles of the Kingdom of heaven. The first question is asked by the disciples together, 'Who is the greatest in the kingdom of heaven?' (18:1-14), the second by Peter, 'Lord, how many times shall I forgive my brother?' (18:15-35), the third by the Pharisees, 'Is it lawful for a man to divorce his wife for any and every reason?' (19:1-12) and the fourth by a rich young man, 'What good thing must I do to inherit eternal life?' (19:16-30).

1. Greatness in kingdom terms (18:1-14)

The question 'Who is the greatest in the kingdom of heaven?' was not an idle question asked by the disciples. It appears to have been a preoccupation to them! Mark's account tells us it was this issue that provoked Jesus to ask them, 'What were you arguing about on the road?' (Mark 9:33). Luke also records this incident as arising when Jesus had just said to them, 'Listen carefully to what I am about to tell you: The Son of Man is going to be betrayed into the hands of men.' As Luke pitifully adds, '... they did not understand what this meant' (Luke 9:44-45). In their ignorance of anything more important to discuss, they turned their attention to which of them was the greatest.

On a later occasion in the Upper Room, immediately after Jesus had told the disciples at the Last Supper of his impending death, 'a dispute arose among them as to which of them was considered to be greatest' (Luke 22:24). We may be fairly sure the nature of the dispute was not Peter nominating John as the greatest, and John bashfully thanking Peter but nominating Andrew, and Andrew nominating Philip, and

Philip suggesting Matthew, with each nominating another! Almost certainly they were nominating themselves with Peter assuming there need be little dispute about the matter – it was him! John probably got a little heated by that, accused Peter of being on an ego trip, and nominated himself, to the disquiet of the rest who were equally keen to nominate themselves!

Jesus' response amounts to a complete reversal of human values. He called a little child and had him stand among them. Then he said to the disciples, 'I tell you the truth, unless you change and become like little children, you will never enter the kingdom of heaven' (18:2, 3). The key is 'change'. Four are suggested by the passage.

(a) There has to be a change of attitude to self (18:3-4)

'Whoever humbles himself like this child is the greatest in the kingdom of heaven' (18:4). The very question asked by the disciples revealed their kingdom interests as preoccupied with status and position, indicating they actually had no clue about the real nature of the kingdom at all. Greatness in the kingdom is characterised by humility and dependency.

The humility of children is expressed in awareness of a lack of self sufficiency, and their complete dependency on others. A little child is incapable of supplying his own food, clothing, shelter and warmth, yet he never doubts these things. A young child may wake up in the morning with no means of putting food on the table, of clothing himself, of deciding the events of the day, or knowing when to go to bed again at night, yet it never enters his head to doubt the ability of his parents to provide all he needs. Dependence on resources outside of themselves is very natural for children, and is the first principle of growth and greatness in the kingdom.

To become great in the kingdom of heaven involves a jettison of our own plans and a humble dependency on God. It has been said before that in Christian living, 'the way up is down, and the way down is up'. James wrote, 'Humble yourselves before the Lord, and he will lift you up' (Jas. 4:10), and Peter wrote, 'Humble yourselves, therefore, under God's mighty hand, that he may lift you up in due time' (1 Pet. 5:6). Conversely, Jesus later said, 'Whoever exalts himself will be humbled' (23:12). The first ingredient in true greatness is to be completely disinterested in greatness, and to humbly live in dependency on God and in the service of others.

(b) There has to be a change of attitude to society (18:5)

'Whoever welcomes a little child like this in my name welcomes me' (18:5). To welcome a child is to serve the child. Children need to be served. True greatness in the kingdom of God is not found in measuring people by what we get from them. The value of true friendship must consist of what we may do for them. Self-interest is too often the bottom line of our involvement with other people, but this has to change, and change radically, if we are to know anything of true greatness.

I remember once hearing someone criticise a church that seemed to attract a number of social misfits and other 'odd' people. He felt this was something of an embarrassment and a hindrance to the effectiveness of that church in its appeal and evangelistic potential. Some would look at them and not want to be associated. The fact is, the reverse is true. The measure of greatness in the kingdom will be evident in how people who often experience rejection find themselves welcomed, loved and made part of the people of God.

True greatness in the kingdom comes from the attitude to others that does not measure others by their social or economic standing, the colour of their skin, the clothes they wear, or the skills they have, but loves and cares for them because they exist.

(c) There has to be a change of attitude to sin (18:6-9)

Temptation in this life is unavoidable, but said Jesus, 'Woe to the man through whom they come.' To do that which stimulates others to sin is a horrendous thing, so much so, 'If anyone causes one of these little ones who believe in me to sin, it would be better for him to have a large millstone hung around his neck and to be drowned in the depths of the sea.' A new attitude to sin is part of growth in the kingdom, not just in a personal self interest in avoiding sin, but in concern about those features of our behaviour and society that become the cause of others to sin.

He then makes it personal, 'If your hand or your foot causes you to sin, cut it off and throw it away ... And if your eye causes you to sin, gouge it out and throw it away.' This is reminiscent of a statement of Jesus in the Sermon on the Mount (5:29-30), though this time in addition to the eye and the hand he speaks of the foot leading into sin. This is radical discipline of the body he is speaking about. We are not to literally mutilate the body but bring it under control.

(d) There has to be a change of attitude to service (18:10-14)
Here Jesus tells the story of the lost sheep, and how the shepherd left the ninety-nine safe sheep to search for the lost one until he found it. 'In the same way your Father in heaven is not willing that any of these little ones should be lost.' This is an attitude to service that knows no perimeters. It is not engaged in for the fulfilment and satisfaction of the servant but the benefit of those served.

The disciples were in great danger of a self-interest in Jesus Christ, where being associated with them was a means to greatness. The Lord Jesus cut to the core of that attitude, and taught them true greatness is characterised by genuine humility, by a concern to provide for those in need, by a ruthless discipline with regard to sin, and by an attitude of service that goes beyond what is humanly reasonable to reach and rescue just one.

2. Forgiving a brother (18:15-35)
The second question, 'Lord, how many times shall I forgive my brother when he sins against me?', was asked by Peter in the context of Jesus explaining the procedure to follow if 'your brother sins against you' (18:15). On three previous occasions in Matthew, Jesus speaks about this issue (see earlier comments on 5:23-24; 6:14-15; 7:1-5). In each case Jesus speaks of sin concerning a 'brother', someone with whom we have a relationship, and in particular in this passage, a brother who 'sins against you' (though it should be acknowledged that these words are missing from several important manuscripts and there is therefore some uncertainty whether they are part of the original text). What is clear however is that this is not an invitation to go probing into the sins of others that are outside the terms of a personal relationship I may have with the person concerned, but to deal with wrong in a brother as it has its effects on me, for the purpose of winning our brother over, and bringing forgiveness and restoration to him. To speak of 'winning' your brother suggests gain to both parties, and that gain is the object of the exercise.

There are three aspects taught in this section, all to do with our relationship to sin in others.

1. Deal with sin effectively	18:15-20
2. Forgive sin completely	18:21-22
3. Treat others appropriately	18:23-35

1. Deal with sin effectively (18:15-20)

There are four stages outlined in responding to the brother who sins against you, with the option of each stage resolving the problem, eliminating the need to go further.

(a) Go and show him his fault, just between the two of you

This is the simplest but probably the most difficult instruction. Few of us enjoy confrontation of any kind, especially when it involves challenging someone else about their faults and failings. But this is kindness. The motivation is not to win a superior position over an issue, but out of love for the brother to restore him to a right place with God.

Notice the issue at this stage is 'just between the two of you'. Do not involve others even in praying about it, much less seek to gain support and backing for your case. In many instances this private challenge will resolve the issue, and the guilty person may be grateful for the kindness shown him in not letting it be swept under the carpet.

(b) If he will not listen, take one or two others along

However, if the first approach does not work, then in accordance with the instruction given in the law of Moses, take one or two others along 'so that every matter may be established by the testimony of two or three witnesses' (see Num. 35:30; Deut. 17:6; Deut. 19:15. See also in the New Testament, John 8:17; 2 Cor. 13:1; 1 Tim. 5:19; Heb. 10:28). The importance of this stage is self evident. If the accused person resists the accusation, it may be because he stubbornly refuses to acknowledge his guilt or because the accusation is in fact unfounded, misinterpreted or distorted. In either case, bringing in one or two others establishes the likelihood of a more impartial understanding of the case and a means of coming to a resolution.

(c) If he refuses to listen, tell it to the church

If the problem is not resolved by the first two stages, the case should be taken to the local church, to which the person concerned has an accountability. This gives some indication of how important it is to the Lord Jesus that sin is faced as sin, and it is dealt with fully. The issue is larger than simply a personal one between two people, it affects the interests and purposes of God and must be challenged on that level by the church.

This statement gives incidental insight into the importance of the church in the purposes of Christ. The church is not a building or a religious club held together by a set of rules. The constitution of any true church of Jesus Christ is given two verses later where Jesus states, 'where two or three come together in my name, there am I with them' (18:20). It is the corporate union of those indwelt by the Holy Spirit who in meeting 'in my name' represent Jesus' interests and seek to fulfil his business. We must understand both the individual and the corporate indwelling of the Spirit. Paul writes, on the one hand, 'Do you not know that your body is a temple of the Holy Spirit, who is in you, whom you have received from God? You are not your own' (1 Cor. 6:19), stressing the individual indwelling of the Spirit, and on the other, 'And in him you too are being built together to become a dwelling in which God lives by his Spirit' (Eph. 2:22), stressing the corporate nature of his indwelling. It is not possible to live the Christian life for the purpose for which we have been saved, outside of the fellowship of other believers for whom we share responsibility and to whom we have accountability. In our day of stressing the rights and freedoms of the individual we are in danger of losing a true and biblical understanding of the church. Fellow Christians have a God-given participation in our lives, and not least is that evident in the disciplinary role given to the church in this passage.

(d) If he refuses to listen to the church, treat him as a pagan or tax collector
This is the final level to which this process may go. By their refusing to listen to the church the accused person is to be treated as someone outside of Christ, in need of being brought to repentance. To 'treat him as a pagan or tax collector' is not to have nothing to do with him, for that is not how we are to treat pagans! We are to win pagans to Christ, not reject them. Whereas this person has retained his salvation, he has lost his conscious fellowship with God and is in need of repentance and restoration both to God and to the fellowship of his church. There was an incident in the church in Corinth in which this very thing took place. Paul writes of the man who was guilty of sin he refused to put right: 'hand this man over to Satan, so that the sinful nature may be destroyed and his spirit saved on the day of the Lord' (1 Cor. 5:5). His body will be of no use to Jesus Christ here on earth in his present condition, but his spirit will be saved. Salvation is not at stake, but usefulness to God is.

These are not a series of gentle suggestions to deal with sin, they are definite instructions. Campbell Morgan wrote some time ago, 'Any church of Jesus Christ is weak in the proportion in which its members allow false pity or sentiment to prevent their being faithful to this great work of attempting to show an erring brother his fault, in order that they may be restored.'[1]

2. Forgive sin completely (18:21-22)

Following this instruction by Jesus, Peter raises the question, 'Lord, how many times shall I forgive my brother when he sins against me? Up to seven times?' Peter probably thought that was a generous number of times, especially as the Rabbis recommended a person should not be forgiven more than three times, but Jesus replied, 'I tell you, not seven times, but seventy-seven times.' This statement of Jesus may well allude back to Lamech's vindictiveness in Genesis 4:24, 'If Cain is avenged seven times, then Lamech seventy-seven times', but instead of seeking vengeance for what is intended to mean an unlimited number of times, forgiveness is to be given on an unlimited number of occasions. Some translations suggest Jesus said, 'Seventy times seven' though 'Seventy-seven' is more likely, but the very argument as to whether seventy-seven or four hundred and ninety is the issue runs counter to the very point Jesus makes in response to Peter's suggestion of seven times. Forgiveness is to be ongoing where there is repentance.

Clearly from the context of this passage, where the sinner does not recognise or repent of his sin, forgiveness is not available at that point, hence the instruction to 'treat him as a pagan or tax collector'. But where there is repentance, forgiveness is always to be available (cf. Luke 17:3: 'If your brother sins, rebuke him, and if he repents forgive him').

3. Treat others appropriately (18:23-35)

Jesus concludes this section with a story of the man who owed his master 'ten thousand talents', and since he was not able to pay he begged his master to forgive him to avoid himself, his wife, children and possessions being sold to repay the debt. His master took pity and cancelled the debt. Leaving his master's presence, the servant found a fellow servant who owed him 'one hundred denarii', a pittance in

---

[1] G. Campbell Morgan, *The Gospel According to Matthew*, Oliphants, p. 232.

comparison to the debt the first servant had been forgiven. He grabbed him, began to choke him, demanding the repayment of his debt. When he realised the man couldn't do so, he had him thrown into prison until he could pay it back. When the master who had forgiven the large debt heard of this, he called his servant back to him, ascertained the truth of what had happened and said, '"You wicked servant, I cancelled all that debt of yours because you begged me to. Shouldn't you have had mercy on your fellow-servant just as I had on you?" In anger his master turned him over to the jailers to be tortured, until he should pay back all he owed' (18:32-34). If this is not a horrific enough story, Jesus adds to Peter and the rest the very sobering words, 'This is how my heavenly Father will treat each of you unless you forgive your brother from your heart' (18:35).

To refuse forgiveness of others is to close off the forgiveness of God towards us. This is not because we earn God's forgiveness by forgiving others, but that our forgiveness of others is a natural consequence to his forgiveness of us. Paul wrote, 'Be kind and compassionate to one another, forgiving each other just as in Christ God forgave you' (Eph. 4:32); and 'Bear with one another and forgive whatever grievances you may have against one another. Forgive as the Lord forgave you' (Col. 3:13). A true sense of the undeserved forgiveness we enjoy in Christ will stimulate us to forgive others. If we have a problem with the latter it is because we have a problem with the former – we do not appreciate the nature or extent of our own sin!

If greatness in the kingdom derives from my sense of humility and utter dependence as a child on God (18:1-14), growth in the kingdom derives from my sense of humility and utter gratitude for his cleansing, which permeates all my dealings with other equally fallen people (18:15-35).

28.

Divorce and discipleship
(19:1-30)

Two more questions are asked of Jesus in Chapter 19, following the two question he answered in Chapter 18. Firstly the Pharisees ask, 'Is it lawful for a man to divorce his wife for any and every reason?' (19:1-12) and secondly, a rich young man asks, 'What good thing must I do to inherit eternal life' (19:16-30). Sandwiched between these two questions is the briefly recorded incident of the disciples' attempt to protect Jesus from children, brought to him that he might pray for them. Jesus rebuked the disciples and said the kingdom of heaven belonged to such as they (19:13-15).

1. Marriage and divorce (19:1-12)
The question asked by some Pharisees, 'Is it lawful for a man to divorce his wife for any and every reason?' seems a strange one to have asked, particularly as the Pharisees themselves had their own strong opinions on the subject. The question was obviously not a genuine one, but a not-so-subtle attempt to push Jesus into one of two camps regarding views of divorce. Two leading Rabbis who lived a generation or so before Christ had given contrasting interpretations of Moses' statement about divorce in Deuteronomy 24 when he spoke of a man finding 'something indecent' about his wife and writing her a certificate of divorce as a result. Shemmai interpreted it very narrowly and taught that the 'something indecent' was adultery alone, and there were no other grounds on which a man could legitimately divorce his wife. The school of Hillel however gave the widest possible interpretation to this, and taught that 'something indecent' could apply to almost anything a husband found distasteful in his wife. If a husband decided he did not wish to live anymore with his

wife because she had some habit which he did not like, or he didn't like the way she cooked his food, or was simply growing old and wrinkly, he could give her a certificate of divorce and find himself a more attractive alternative. Needles to say, the latter idea tended to dominate, for it made least demands, and marriage in consequence was treated very lightly by many of the population. Some husbands treated their wives as a personal possession, almost as one might treat his cattle. He would marry and divorce to suit his own whim. Divorce was so common place that religious leaders had given up resisting it, and instead only insisted on giving a certificate of divorce so that the arrangement was legal (see Matt. 5:31).

It is against this background that Jesus was asked, 'Is it lawful for a man to divorce his wife for any and every reason? In other words they were asking, 'Are you on the side of Hillel or Shemmai?' Notice that their questions was not about the legitimacy of divorce but about the reasons for divorce, for they assumed its legitimacy.

Jesus' reply was not to talk in the first place about divorce, but to talk about marriage. A proper understanding of divorce cannot exist outside a proper understanding of marriage. If a couple begin to consider divorce, their primary need is probably not to understand the legalities and intricacies of divorce, but to understand the purpose and function of marriage. Jesus speaks about four things:

Sexuality is God's creation v. 4
Marriage is a commitment v. 5-6
Divorce is a concession v. 7-9
Celibacy is a calling v. 10-12

Sexuality of God's creation (v. 4)
Jesus commences his answer with 'Have you not read ...' and quotes from the Old Testament scriptures. Jesus Christ expressed no opinions where the revealed will of God in Scripture had already spoken. The appeal to precedence or tradition held no place in Jesus' teaching when the Scriptures already addressed the issue. The pressure of changing times, fluctuating morality, majority opinions, relevance to culture, or political correctness, did not influence his understanding or adjust his insistence on truth as it had been already revealed by God in Scripture.

Sexuality is created by God as heterosexuality: '... the creator made them male and female'. Firstly, *he made them different.* This is not a statement about the status of men and women, but about their function. Men and women are equal in dignity and status, but different in function. Any society which seeks to blur the distinction between male and female is violating God's purpose in creation.

Secondly, *he made them dependent.* Before the fall took place, God said, 'It is not good for man to be alone' (Gen. 2:18). Everything else in creation God declared to be 'good' and 'very good', but man alone is 'not good'. The sex drive and sexual dependency of male and female in marriage is not a consequence of the fall, but a part of the perfection with which God first created humanity. Sexuality has often been something of an embarrassment in the history of the church, with celibacy being seen as a higher and better way, and abstinence a virtue. Jesus speaks about celibacy later in the chapter, but then as only acceptable to some. The normal law of life is for marriage, not celibacy, and this is God's design.

Marriage is a commitment (vv. 5-6)

'For this reason a man will leave his father and mother and be united to his wife, and the two will become one flesh.' The fundamental building block of society is the family. A man is to leave his father and mother, cleave to his wife and form a new family unit. In the normal course of things the new marriage will result in children, who in turn will eventually leave their parents, cleave to their partner in marriage and form their family.

The instruction to a man to 'leave his father and mother' goes back to the Garden of Eden before fatherhood and motherhood had taken place! Marriage predates the teaching of Christ and the law of Moses and is the most primitive instruction about life. A high view of marriage is not an ordinance of Christianity but of creation. It is not given as the order for redeemed humanity, but for created humanity, and for that reason we must affirm marriage in society at large and not just within Christendom.

The result of marriage is described as 'they are no longer two but one'. This is more than the physical oneness of sexual union, but the deeper oneness of soul and spirit as well as body. That union is described as a divine act fulfilling a divine purpose, 'What God has joined together let man not separate.' The description of marriage as the union of two people 'God has joined together' does not refer only to marriage between two people who have concluded this to be God's specific will for them, but to marriage itself. It cannot be argued that a marriage is invalid because God had not joined the two together! The institute of marriage itself is by God's decree and in accordance with his will, and in that sense all marriage is a joining together by God. Therefore, as marriage is ordained by God, he says, 'let man not separate'.

Divorce is a concession (vv. 7-9)

We must begin by acknowledging divorce is never right, and Jesus affirms that by the statement, 'What God has joined together let man not separate.' God says in the Old Testament 'I hate divorce' (Mal. 2:16). Whenever divorce takes place and for whatever reason it is always a consequence of something wrong.

The full teaching of Jesus on divorce is confined to four passages in the gospels: Matthew 5:31-32; 19:3-9; Mark 10:2-12 and Luke 16:18. These four passages give duplicate records of two occasions in which Jesus spoke about this (e.g. Matt. 5 and Matt. 19 cover both occasions). In the two Matthew occasions Jesus granted that 'marital unfaithfulness' becomes a ground for divorce, but both Mark and Luke omit that detail. Here in Matthew 19 he states, 'I tell you that anyone who divorces his wife except for marital unfaithfulness, and marries another woman commits adultery.' The word translated in the NIV as 'marital unfaithfulness' is *pornea*, which is often translated as 'fornication' (e.g. see AV) as distinct from the word *moicheia* which means adultery. The distinction is sometimes made that *fornication* refers to premarital sexual intercourse and *adultery* to extra-marital sexual intercourse. If these definitions stand, then the exception clause of Jesus does not relate to adultery during the marriage, but to sexual activity before the marriage as ground for divorce. However, although it is true that these two words are distinguished from one another (e.g. Matt. 15:19 'For out of the heart come evil thoughts, murder, adultery [moicheiai], fornication [porneiai], theft, false testimony ...' etc.), we should understand adultery to be an exclusive word, with one strict definition as extra-marital sex, whereas 'pornea' is a more inclusive word that can apply to a range of illicit sexual activity. In the New Testament it is used of prostitution (21:32-33), incest (1 Cor. 5:1) and sexual immorality in general (Mark 7:21-22), whilst in the Septuagint (the Greek version of the Old testament) it is also used of adultery

(Jer. 3:9). Comparing its use in the Scriptures generally, this word should be understood as an inclusive reference to any illicit sexual relationship outside of the marriage. It is perhaps not so much that this is a reason for divorce as it is itself a violation of the exclusive commitment of each partner to the other that is the substance of marriage, and to engage in sexual activity with someone other than the marriage partner is itself a breaking of the marriage.

Jesus then states that to remarry after divorce is to commit adultery. This is a hard saying, particularly in our own day of easy divorce and general lax morality. We cannot escape the implications, however, that remarriage in such circumstances, involving a substitute sexual union for that indissoluble union which God has created, though legal in the eyes of the law, remains adultery (though legalised adultery) in the eyes of God. In Jesus' earlier statement in Chapter 5:32 it is the remarriage of the divorced wife which is labelled adultery, but here it is the remarriage of the divorced husband. Remarriage itself is presupposed by Christ when he states, 'Anyone who divorces his wife, except for marital unfaithfulness, causes her to become an adulteress ...' (5:32). The only ground on which this may be said is on the assumption that the divorced person will remarry. The issue addressed by Jesus then is not remarriage which is assumed by his statement as inevitable, but divorce.

There is another ground given by Paul on which a marriage may be permitted to dissolve. To the Corinthians he wrote, 'If any brother has a wife who is not a believer and she is willing to live with him, he must not divorce her. And if a woman has a husband who is not a believer and he is willing to live with her, she must not divorce him.... But if the unbeliever leaves, let him do so. A believing man or woman is not bound in such circumstances; God has called us to live in peace' (1 Cor. 7:12-15). This relates to someone who is converted to Christ whilst already married to an unbeliever. The separation in this case is not initiated by the believer, but the unbeliever, who now finds their spouse a difference person to the one they married before becoming a Christian, and does not wish to remain in the marriage. In this case he says the Christian is permitted to let them go, but themselves remain unmarried (1 Cor. 7:10).

The appeal to Moses' statement in Deuteronomy 24 by the Pharisees did not make divorce legitimate, for Jesus answered them, 'Moses permitted you to divorce your wives because your hearts were hard.' They had changed the whole meaning of Moses' rules for divorce by their question, 'Why did Moses command that a man give his wife a certificate of divorce and send her away?' Jesus corrected them, saying that Moses did not command any such thing! He permitted them to divorce but did not command them to. He permitted them, not because it was ever right, but because their hearts were hard. Divorce took place because of their stubbornness of heart, and Moses made arrangements for it to happen properly, not because it was right but because it had become necessary.

All of this presents God's blueprint for marriage, a high ideal intended to be the experience of mankind from the time of God's first declaration about it in the Garden of Eden. However, despite God's clear purpose in marriage, the reality of human sinfulness is never more evident than in its closest relationships. Such is human failure to live as we should – 'Moses permitted you to divorce your wives because your hearts were hard.' Moses did not 'command' divorce as the Pharisees said to Jesus, but he 'permitted' it on the grounds that where hearts were so hard it might become the only realistic option. Divorce was, and is, never the will of God. When walking with God, incompatibility of temperament, conflicting interests or other dissimilarities can never be a legitimate ground for divorce. It may mean a hard and difficult relationship, but in dependency on Jesus Christ there is always hope. Where a marriage irretrievably breaks down it is due to hardness of heart and a refusal to seek humbly the grace of God in rebuilding what 'God has joined together'. There clearly are occasions when that takes place, as in the days of Moses which gave rise to his permitting people to divorce. Even God declares himself to have divorced Israel in the days of Jeremiah: 'I gave faithless Israel her certificate of divorce and sent her away because of all her adulteries' (Jer. 3:8). Israel, the Northern kingdom with its capital Samaria, in contrast to Judah the Southern kingdom with its capital Jerusalem, was taken into exile by the Assyrians in 722 BC and their identity lost. The Jews of Jesus' day and beyond are all descendents of the kingdom of Judah. The north ceased to be God's channel through whom he would fulfil his purposes, for he declares himself to have divorced them. Ezra on return to Jerusalem after the exile commanded the people who had married foreign wives to 'separate yourselves ... from your foreign wives' (Ezra 10:11). These situations were never right ones, and were always a result of something wrong.

At the heart of this statement of Jesus is an unswerving loyalty in marriage that is at the heart of both our loyalty to Christ and our integrity of life. This may not be a high quality in our general culture today, but we dare not respond to Jesus' teaching with the idea that things are somehow different today, for his teaching was equally at variance with the culture of his own day as it may be with ours. His disciples (not the Pharisees who asked the question) respond by saying, 'If this is the situation between a husband and a wife, it is better not to marry' (19:10). The standard set by Jesus was so high they conclude that in their day and in their culture it was probably better not to marry.

Celibacy is a calling (vv. 10-12)

When the disciples concluded it was perhaps 'better not to marry', Jesus agreed with them to a certain extent! 'He replied, "Not everyone can accept this word, but only those to whom it has been given. For some are eunuchs because they were born that way; others were made that way by men; and others have renounced marriage because of the kingdom of heaven. The one who can accept this should accept it."'

Marriage is the norm, but celibacy is an option. Jesus says there are three reasons why a person may remain single. Firstly he says some are 'born that way'. For some it may be quite natural and preferable to remain unmarried. Others are 'made that way by men'. This could refer to literal castration (not uncommon in Jesus day) or to other factors that have taken place that may prevent a person from marrying. Thirdly, 'others have renounced marriage because of the kingdom of heaven'. There has been through history those who have renounced marriage in order to be free to serve God in some particular way that would be inhibited by marriage. There is no special virtue in this, nor is it a higher way than marriage, but the contribution of single people to the work of God is immeasurable and has involved in many cases a deliberate renunciation of marriage.

What about a fourth group? They have not married for the sole reason they have never met anyone with whom they have established a relationship that has led to marriage. They would ideally like to marry, and should the opportunity arise they will, for none of the three reasons above seem to apply. Statistics indicate there are just slightly more boys born than girls in the world. If every girl married there would be some men left who would not marry for the simple logistical reason of the lack of available members of the opposite sex. In the church however the ratio is reversed, for there are considerably more Christian women than men. If every Christian man married a Christian woman, there would be some women who would not marry, for no good reason other than the lack of available men. This is not a choice but may be a heavy burden to carry in life. Paul implies in his teaching on marriage that celibacy, along with marriage, is a 'gift from God' (1 Cor. 7:7). This does not necessarily mean that celibacy is itself a gift, but that the ability to live a full and satisfying life outside of marriage is a gift for which God may be trusted. Fulfilment and completion may be found in the depth of a satisfying relationship with him, which does not detract from the sense of need for human and physical relationships, but which provides deep nourishment of the soul and may be enjoyed as a gift from God. It must be said in any case that non marriage is preferable to a wrong marriage.

2. Children and the kingdom of heaven (19:13-15)

Having recorded Jesus' attitude to marriage and divorce, Matthew immediately records something of Jesus' attitude to children. Little children were brought to him that he might place his hands on them and pray for them, 'But the disciples rebuked those who brought them' (19:13). In the previous chapter Jesus had taken a child and used his humility and simplicity as an example to the disciples of the nature of true greatness. Children loved Jesus and he loved them. How we treat children and how they respond to us says a great deal about us.

The disciples presumably thought Jesus was concerned with more important things than children, so they rebuked those who brought them. But there are no more important things than children. The man is in the boy and the woman is in the girl. Even if it was reasoned by the disciples that the concentration of Jesus' ministry should be on the mature, society influencing adults it was a mistake to assume the influence could begin when they were adult. The kind of person a man is depends very much on the kind of boy he was. What he does as a man may be traced to what he experienced as a boy. The quality of the next generation of adults is determined by what we do with this generation of children. It is an entirely false view of life to see children as irrelevant and of no great significance until they reach maturity. For some it is sadly too late by then. It has been said, 'Give me a child until he is seven and I will give you the man.' The story is told of the American evangelist D. L. Moody who returned home from preaching one night. His wife asked him how he got on and he reported there had been 'two and a half converts'. She assumed two adults and one child, but Moody corrected her. It was two children and one adult. One life was probably half over, two had almost their whole lives ahead of them. It is stated that something like eighty percent of all Christians are converted by the age of twenty. The greatest investment of time is that invested in children, and we parents had better believe it.

The disciples did not understand this, but Jesus did. He rebuked the disciples for hindering them, 'for the kingdom of heaven belongs to such as these'. He placed his hands on them and prayed for them before moving on from there.

3. The terms of eternal life (19:16-30)

The fourth question in this section is asked by an anonymous young man who approached Jesus and asked 'Teacher, what good thing must I do to get eternal life?' There was an assumption in his question that eternal life was related to something good that would win the favour of God. We might want to rebuke him for this, but we would be wrong to do so, for he identified something crucial. It is something good which wins the favour of God, but what? Jesus responded in reply, 'Why do you ask me about what is good? There is only One who is good.' What defines goodness? It is not some arbitrary standard, defined by its consequences or by a general consensus. Goodness is defined by the character of God. That which is good, is good because it is consistent with what God is. Equally that which is bad, is bad because it is inconsistent with what God is. God's moral character is the absolute by which everything else is measured.

This raises the question, how do we know the nature of God's character? The answer to that is the ten commandments. Jesus said to the man, 'If you want to enter life, obey the commandments.' He associated the 'only One who is good' with the 'commandments'. The ten commandments were not given as an arbitrary set of rules for the people of Israel to follow, they were given to reveal the moral character of God.[1] The commandments teach us what God is like, and

---

1. See my book, *Alive in Christ* published by Kregel Publications, Grand Rapids, Michigan 49501 in which I explore more fully the Ten Commandments as an expression of the character of God, and how Christ fulfills the demands of the law in human experience by restoring the character of God that has been lost through sin.

therefore what human beings are to be like having been created 'in his image'. The goodness that qualifies us for eternal life must derive from God. It is his righteousness, imparted to us, that qualifies us to share in his eternal life.

The initial function of the law, however, whilst revealing God's character, is to expose our failure and our inherent inability to conform to his character. The man asked Jesus which of the commandments he should obey, and Jesus replied, 'Do not murder, do not commit adultery, do not steal, do not give false testimony, honour your father and mother, and love your neighbour as yourself.' These seemed reasonable to the young man and he confidently replied, 'All these I have kept.' It is amazing how we can deceive ourselves about our goodness. Jesus then said an obvious thing to him, 'If you want to be perfect, go, sell your possessions and give to the poor, and you will have treasure in heaven.' This was quite a logical response to a man who claimed to love his neighbour as himself. But, 'when the young man heard this, he went away sad, because he had great wealth'. His bluff was called!

To be a true disciple of Jesus is not only to recognise our need for the life of God to be imparted to us so as to be our source of goodness, but to surrender unreservedly to the Lordship of Christ in our lives. Jesus said, 'No-one can serve two masters. Either he will hate the one and love the other, or he will be devoted to the one and despise the other. You cannot serve both God and Money' (6:24). The young man's response not only indicated his failure to depend on God for his righteousness, but it exposed the existence of another master in his life – his money. To enjoy eternal life on Jesus Christ's terms involves surrender to his Lordship. This is a fundamental ingredient of genuine Christian experience.

The disciples were astonished! Here was a young rich man, a man of influence, described in Luke's record as a ruler, who had come asking a good question, but who had left empty handed and sad. Jesus did not run after him and reduce the demands he had made, or allow him to pick and choose his own preferred ingredients in discipleship. He let him go his own way and turned to say to the disciples, 'it is hard for a rich man to enter the kingdom of heaven.'

So high were the demands of Jesus in this chapter that after talking about marriage the disciples responded, 'If this is the situation between a husband and wife, it is better not to marry' (19:10), and then after his treatment of the rich young man they respond, 'Who then can be saved?' (19:25). We only begin to understand the teaching of Jesus when we understand the impossibility of it. To every human being, the demands of Jesus Christ are impossible, but to God, they are not only possible but reasonable. Jesus replied to the disciples. 'With man this is impossible, but with God all things are possible' (19:26). The presence and activity of God is the indispensable ingredient in Christian living. The essence of Christian living is not found in what we do for him, but in what he does for us, and this principle stands true in this chapter for marriage as well as for discipleship.

Peter responds to this by saying the disciples had left everything to follow Christ, to which Jesus assures them that God will give you everything needed to those who have left everything to follow him! 'Everyone who has left houses or brothers or sisters or father or mother or children or fields for my sake will receive a hundred times as much' (19:29). Surrender of our lives to Jesus Christ is not loss but gain. We lose our lives in order that we find his life, to be lived in us to the full (see 16:25), and it is his presence within that is the source of all God demands us to be.

29.

Getting priorities right
(20:1-31)

Three events occupy Chapter 20. The parable of the workers in the vineyard who were employed at different times in the day yet paid an equal pay at the end of it (20:1-16), the request of the mother of James and John that her sons sit on the right and left of Jesus in his kingdom (20:20-28), and the healing of two blind men in Jericho who cried out for mercy and were healed of their blindness (20:29-34). In each of these events a key statement is made by Jesus that provides a clue to a uniform theme running through. To those complaining about the inequality of paying a full wage to a man who worked part of the day as well as to the one who worked all day Jesus said, 'So the last will be first and the first last' (20:16). To the mother of James and John wanting top places in the kingdom he said, 'Whoever wants to be great among you must be your servant' (20:26). To the blind men crying for mercy Jesus asked a profound question which at first may have seemed an unnecessary question, 'What do you want me to do for you?' The consistent quality of these statements is their challenge of basic assumptions and their turning around of the logical sense of priorities.

The parable of the workers in the vineyard (20:1-16)
The story is simple: a landowner hired men early in the morning to work in his vineyard for a denarius a day. Around nine o'clock that morning, at twelve noon, and at five in the afternoon he each time found some men standing around with nothing to do and hired them. At six o'clock that evening the work day was over. The owner told the foreman to call the workers and pay them their wages beginning with the last ones hired and going to the first. Having paid those hired

in the late afternoon a denarius for the one hour they had worked, the rest expected more, those having worked the longest getting the most. However, he paid the same to each, and to understate the case, those who had worked through the heat of the day 'began to grumble against the landowner'. His response was to say he had paid each of them what he had agreed to pay them, and that he had the right to do what he wanted with his own money. The point was not that those who had laboured all day had been underpaid, for a denarius was a normal day's wage, but those who had worked less had been overpaid, the recipients of the landowner's generosity. Jesus' comment on the end of the story is, 'So the last will be first and the first last' (20:16).

What then is the point of this parable? It has all the appearance of being unfair, and our natural sense of justice sides with the complaints of the men who had worked all day only to feel cheated of an appropriate reward at the end of the day. At the beginning of the day, one denarius had seemed fair enough to them, but not when at the end of the day the same amount was being paid for one hour's work as for twelve hours' work. It was not the rate for a day's work that provoked them, as it was the fairness of the system that paid the same for only one hour of work as for twelve hours that caused them to grumble.

This parable can only be adequately understood in the light of the preceding chapter where Peter had asked the question, 'We have left everything to follow you! What then will there be for us?' (19:27). This itself had followed Jesus' response to the rich young man who had asked what he must do to receive eternal life and, despite his claim to have kept the commandments, was told he still lacked one thing, 'If you want to be perfect, go, sell your possessions and give to the poor, and you will have treasure in heaven. Then come, follow me.' The disciples were astonished by this and asked, 'Who then can be saved,' to which Jesus replied, 'With man this is impossible, but with God all things are possible.'

It was at that point Peter said, 'We have left everything to follow you! What then will there be for us?' Jesus' reply is to acknowledge there will be reward a hundred times anything anyone has given up and lost, but with the proviso, 'Many who are first will be last, and many who are last will be first.' Then follows the parable, which concludes with the same statement, 'So the last will be first, and the first will be last.' It is this which the parable is clearly designed to illustrate. This parable does not have relation to social or economic order, where an employer may treat his employees at whim (see the parable of the talents [25:14-30] for a different picture of just rewards for enterprising work done), but to spiritual order, to the economics of the kingdom of heaven to which Jesus likens this parable.

It is in the first instance a rebuke to Peter's implied superiority in contrasting himself with the rich young man, and the idea he had earned a right to privilege and that on the basis of his own sacrificial living ('We have left everything to follow you'), he is now in line for some great reward proportionate to this. It is true that there will be reward, says Jesus, but the economics of the kingdom of heaven are radically different to expectancies on earth. In fact they appear unjust and unfair by the expectations of this world.

It is never the length of our service, the profile of our ministry, the notoriety of our accomplishments, or the recognition of our standing that has anything to do with kingdom rewards. It is the faithfulness of our obedience to God and our dependence on God that is the true measure of our lives.

There is an obvious application of this principle to the failure of some Jewish believers to accept the reception of Gentiles in the early days of the church. Jesus Christ was the fulfilment of what had been promised to Abraham and his descendants. It had taken centuries of covenants, laws and ceremonies to arrive at this moment when the Messiah came. Now these Gentile 'outsiders', who had been 'separate from Christ, excluded from citizenship in Israel and foreigners to the covenants of the promise, without hope and without God in the world' (see Eph. 2:11-13) were wanting to participate in a full share of the blessing. This was not fair! The Jews had been in this for centuries, and now the Gentiles were coming in and expecting a full share of the benefits. This lay at the root of an insistence on circumcision, the mark of God's covenant with Abraham, that plagued the spread of the gospel in its early years. At least circumcision was an acknowledgement of a need to start at the beginning! But these are not the economics of the kingdom of heaven! It is something more than equality, it appears as inequality, 'the last will be first, and the first will be last'! This point was made by Jesus at the time of the healing of the centurion's servant. Here was a man, a Gentile, whose faith in Christ exceeded anything Jesus had found in Israel, so much so, the record tells us, Jesus 'was astonished' and said to those following him, 'I say to you that many will come from the east and the west, and will take their places at the feast with Abraham, Isaac and Jacob in the kingdom of heaven. But the subjects of the kingdom will be thrown outside, into the darkness, where there will be weeping and gnashing of teeth' (8:11-12). The first will be last and the last first.

The principle of the parable has wider application than to the relationship of Jew to Gentile, for it is teaching truth about general values in the kingdom of heaven. There is no 'pecking order' in the kingdom, where some have higher status than others. We may even say that those who presume higher status for themselves, on grounds of their longevity of service or the notoriety of their lives will by that very assumption be last rather than first. There is a wonderful unconsciousness of true spirituality. Those who are preoccupied with their own holiness and spirituality are literally that – preoccupied with themselves! Genuinely holy people are preoccupied with God rather than themselves, and in fact are generally less conscious of themselves, other than of their innate inability! Their dependence on God is *because* of their consciousness of weakness, and therefore it follows that the more aware we are of their own natural failure (about which Scripture is very clear), the more dependent we become on God, therefore the more God works and the more effective we become. However the more conscious we are of our effectiveness, the less dependent on God we are in danger of becoming!

The story of the Prodigal Son illustrates this point where the older son, conscious of his own loyalty to his father found himself 'last' in his own sense of joy and fulfilment, whereas the younger son who had messed his life up, was now so full of gratitude to the mercy, patience and goodness of his father and is 'first' in his sense of fulfilment. We are rarely more vulnerable than when we feel ourselves strong, or stronger than when we feel ourselves weak and are thrown in dependency on God. This is why Paul wrote, 'That is why, for Christ's sake, I delight in weaknesses, in insults, in hardships, in persecutions, in difficulties. For when I am weak, then I am strong' (2 Cor. 12:10).

Many of God's people can see evidence of his working in them and through them, and for that they may legitimately rejoice in gratitude to God. But some of his choicest people see very little of that. Jeremiah in the Old Testament preached for forty years with no response to his ministry except persecution, ridicule, abuse and subsequent abduction from Judah. We could write 'failure' across his life and ministry, and the people of his day would have to agree it was an apt summary. Isaiah was called to a non-productive ministry by being told to preach a message that no one would understand, 'Be ever hearing, but never understanding; be ever seeing, but never perceiving. Make the heart of this people calloused; make their ears dull and close their eyes. Otherwise they might see with their eyes, hear with their ears, understand with their hearts, and turn and be healed.' When Isaiah cried out, 'For how long, O LORD?', God answered: 'Until the cities lie ruined and without inhabitant, until the houses are left deserted and the fields ruined and ravaged, until the LORD has sent everyone far away and the land is utterly forsaken' (Isa. 6:9-12). He was commissioned to a ministry of failure from which there would be no let up! These men struggled deeply with their own roles and with understanding what God was doing, especially Jeremiah about whose personal struggles we know more than any other character in the Bible. Yet through it all God was accomplishing lasting purpose, not least in their legacy of two of the longest books in our Bible.

The request of the mother of James and John (20:17-28)

This event follows immediately on Jesus' parable of the workers in the vineyard, and illustrates the slowness with which the disciples understood what Jesus was saying to them! His statement, 'How foolish you are and how slow of heart to believe' (Luke 24:25), does not only apply to the two on the road to Emmaus to whom he addressed it, but could be an equally accurate diagnosis of the general state of the disciples at this stage!

Jesus took the twelve disciples aside as they headed towards Jerusalem and told them, '... the Son of Man will be betrayed ... will be ... mocked and flogged and crucified. On the third day he will be raised to life' (20:18-19). This is the third announcement of his death and resurrection that Jesus is recorded as giving his disciples in Matthew's gospel (see 16:21 and 17:22-23). For the first time he specifies the mode of his death ('crucified') and speaks of the involvement of Gentiles ('turn him over to the Gentiles'). This moment is now drawing closer, they are already on their way to Jerusalem, and only days separate them from this climactic event.

It is however at this point that the mother of James and John burst on to the scene. Kneeling down in front of Jesus she asked him to grant her a favour, that 'one of these two sons of mine may sit at your right and the other at your left in your kingdom' (20:21). Mark's gospel gives the account as James and John making the request (see Mark 10:35-45). Almost certainly it was the same occasion, but the focus of the request is of course the position to be occupied by James and John. Their mother was a frequent companion of Jesus and his disciples, being one of those women who 'followed Jesus from Galilee to care for his needs' (see 27:55-56). However she clearly had ambitions for her sons too and planned to see them occupying important positions in the kingdom whenever it might be established.

This request comes in stark contrast to the statements just made by Jesus, 'the last will be first, and the first last' (20:16). Jesus' reply was to say she did not know what she was asking. 'Can you drink the cup I am going to drink?' he asked the two sons. 'We can,' they answered! That they would indeed drink from his cup Jesus granted, though they had no idea what he was talking about. The word 'cup' is often a metaphor for suffering as when Jesus prayed in Gethsemane, 'may this cup be taken from me' (26:39), and in the Upper Room with his disciples, 'This cup is the new covenant in my blood, which is poured out for you' (Luke 22:20). (See examples elsewhere: Isa. 51:17; Jer. 25:15-17; Ezek. 23:32; Zech. 12:2; and Rev. 14:10).

The logic of James' and John's request seems to be this: We can pay the price, we can drink the cup, so we should reap the reward! This is of course in complete conflict with what Jesus has just taught them about the economics of the kingdom of heaven, in response to Peter's similar assumption, 'We have left everything to follow you! What then will there be for us?' (19:27). 'God owes me something here' is the assumption!

When the other ten disciples heard about it they were unimpressed and indignant (20:24). Why? They too wanted positions of prestige in the kingdom. Their understanding of the kingdom was physical and geographical, as remained evident after the resurrection when the disciples asked Jesus, 'Lord, are you at this time going to restore the kingdom to Israel?' (Acts 1:6). Apart from their misunderstanding of the kingdom, they have more importantly misunderstood the nature of greatness. The Gentiles lord it over people, Jesus reminded them, but, 'Not so with you. Instead, whoever wants to become great among you must be your servant, and whoever wants to be first must be your slave' (20:26-27). The nature of true greatness in the kingdom is to serve. Jesus had already spoken to them about this when he said, 'whoever humbles himself like this child is the greatest in the kingdom of heaven' (see notes on 18:4). This is again the principle of the last being first and the first last! To be great is to be the servant. 'Whoever wants to be first must be your slave'. This is another reason why the truly great person in the kingdom is the least conscious of it. To have a consciousness of being 'great' is evidence of our not being so. The concern of the great person in the kingdom is their role as a servant of Jesus Christ and consequently, as a servant of his fellows, with desires to serve their interests and build them up. This is exactly, said Jesus, the role he came to play as a man, for the disciples were to act in a way that is '... just as the Son of Man did not come to be served, but to serve and to give his life as a ransom for many' (20:28).

The healing of two blind men (20:29-34)

Leaving Jericho, on their way to Jerusalem, Jesus and his disciples, followed by a large crowd, passed two blind men on the road side. Mark's account of this event records only one man, whom he identifies as Bartimaeus. Perhaps Bartimaeus went on to become a disciple of Christ, known to readers of Mark's account, and so Mark omits any mention of his companion so as to concentrate on the experience of the familiar Bartimaeus, whereas Matthew tells the story of both men, neither of whom he names. These two men cried out to Jesus for mercy.

The crowd rebuked them for their impertinence, but they shouted all the louder, 'Lord, Son of David, have mercy on us.' Jesus stopped and asked them a question that sounds a little strange, 'What do you want me to do for you?' One might have thought that an unnecessary question, for the answer should be obvious. But it is of course a good question. It is possible to be wanting Jesus to do far less than his purpose would be. These blind men had asked for mercy many times from many people. If asked, 'What do you want me to do for you?' they might reply, 'I want some bread', 'Give me a blanket to keep myself warm at night', 'May I have a cushion to make my begging more comfortable', 'I need some cold water to quench my thirst', and all of those things may be legitimate. It is possible to ask God for lots of legitimate things which never deal with the fundamental need of our lives, that we might be whole again!

Jesus Christ did not come into the world to deal with the symptoms of people's alienation from God, merely to cleanse them of their guilt, be on hand to answer their prayers for help in times of difficulty, or even to provide security for their future. He came to make people complete, as God intended them to be when he first created them. He came to reconcile us to God, to restore his life into human experience. At the source of all else that may be wrong in the human condition is our alienation from God, 'separated from the life of God' (Eph. 4:18). Whatever other pressing needs appear in our lives, this is their source, and to be reconciled to God is what it takes to be complete again. The two blind men answered the question, 'What do you want me to do for you?' by saying, 'We want our sight.' We want the fundamental problem that has made our begging necessary to be dealt with, so Jesus touched their eyes, and 'immediately they received their sight and followed him'.

This is getting priorities right, the theme of Chapter 20! The economics of the kingdom have to do with faithfulness to God, not external profile (20:1-16). Greatness in the kingdom is found through servanthood not status (20:17-28). Satisfaction in the kingdom is found by allowing God to deal with the fundamental needs in our lives, not just their symptoms (20:29-34).

30.

Entry into Jerusalem
(21:1–22:14)

It was the Sunday of the week in which Jesus was subsequently crucified that he arrived in Jerusalem to such wide acclaim. Chapter 21 recounts his arrival on the back of a borrowed donkey (21:1-11). This is followed by his denouncing of those who had made the temple a den of robbers (21:12-17), his cursing of the fig tree (21:18-22) the questioning of his authority by the elders and priests (21:23-27), and a series of three parables denouncing the religious leaders of Israel (21:28–22:14).

The triumphal entry into Jerusalem (21:1-11)

During Passover time, Jerusalem was crowded with visitors. Every Jewish adult from a twenty mile radius was obligated to attend the celebrations, and this number was added to by many, many more who would crowd in from further afield for the occasion. William Barclay tells us that as many as two and a half million might have been in Jerusalem for the Passover celebrations. Three decades later, the Roman governor took a census that indicated nearly a quarter of a million lambs were slain in Jerusalem at the Passover that particular year. According to Barclay, Passover regulations required that there be a minimum of ten people to participate in each lamb, thus giving his estimated figure of those present in Jerusalem for the festival.[1] Smaller estimates have been given of the crowd. Myron Augsburger quotes Joachim Jeremias as stating the population of Jerusalem was 30,000 with around 125,000 pilgrims for the Passover, making a total of around 150,000.[2] Whatever the exact figure, it was a large crowd, the

---

[1] William Barclay, *The Gospel of Matthew*, Vol. 2, p. 262.

city was heaving with people. Jesus' dramatic and triumphal arrival in the city coincided with this gathering.

All four gospels record the arrival of Jesus in Jerusalem on this occasion, though this is the first time Matthew records Jesus entering Jerusalem at all. He earlier speaks of large crowds from Jerusalem following him in Galilee (see 4:25), and of Pharisees coming from Jerusalem to question him (15:1), but although he speaks of going to Jerusalem for the purpose of being crucified (16:21; 20:18), the narrative only brings him here in this last week before his crucifixion. (John's gospel records at least three previous visits.) It is evident in Matthew that Jesus was familiar with Jerusalem, for on his arrival he wept over the city saying, 'O Jerusalem, Jerusalem, you who kill the prophets and stone those sent to you, how often I have longed to gather your children together, as a hen gathers her chicks under her wings, but you were not willing' (23:37).

However, for Matthew's gospel, coming into Jerusalem is something of a climax for which anticipation has been building. Ever since the disciples had identified Jesus as 'the Christ, the Son of the living God' at Caesarea Philippi (16:16), the narrative states, 'he must go to Jerusalem' (16:21). Now he arrives. Not only is the place itself significant, but his arrival at the time of the Passover festival is significant, for the Passover was itself a clear foreshadowing of his own death. John the Baptist introduced Jesus to the world as, 'the Lamb of God, who takes away the sin of the world' (John 1:29). The significance of the relationship between Jesus Christ and the Passover Lamb had not been lost on John the Baptist.

He approached Jerusalem from the Mount of Olives, having spent the previous night in Bethany (see John 12:1). Before entering he sent two disciples to find the colt of a donkey and take it for his use. On all other occasions of which we have record, Jesus went on foot. He had walked from Galilee, but for the last mile or two he travels into Jerusalem mounted on a donkey. To the onlooker he may have appeared a few days later as a helpless victim in the hands of the Jewish Sanhedrin Council and the Roman governor. But he wasn't. Riding into the city he demonstrated his control of his situation. He requisitioned the animal, a right which belonged to royalty and

---

[2] Myron Ausburger, *Matthew*, The Communicator's Commentary (Word UK 1987).

claimed by the Rabbis. Mark makes the point even more forcibly by stating the colt on which he rode had never been ridden before. Instead of bucking and kicking, it was subdued, fulfilling the prophecy of Zechariah, 'See your king comes to you, gentle and riding on a donkey, on a colt, the foal of a donkey' (21:5 quoting Zech. 9:9).

As Jesus began his journey towards Jerusalem, a very large crowd gathered and spread their cloaks before him, while some cut branches from the trees and spread them on the road, and shouted 'Hosanna to the Son of David', identifying him as of the royal line, and 'Blessed is he who comes in the name of the Lord', quoting Psalm 118:26, a Psalm chanted at all the main festivals and carrying an implicit identification of him as Messiah. The whole city was stirred, resident and visitor alike. 'Who is this?' asked some, 'This is Jesus the prophet from Nazareth in Galilee' answered others. At the time of his birth when the Magi came to Herod asking for the whereabouts of the 'one who has been born king of the Jews', the whole city was disturbed (2:3). Now, he is welcomed as the King of the Jews and the whole city is stirred. Campbell Morgan says the Greek word translated 'stirred' has connotations of an earthquake![3] His coming shook the city mentally and morally as an earthquake might shake a city physically. This was a very delicate moment. As the city builds to its great celebration of Passover, here to the authorities is an unwelcome diversion, '... the chief priests and teachers of the law ... were indignant' (21:15).

Denouncing the temple traders (21:12-17)
On entering the city he went to the temple. Acknowledged by the crowd as Messiah and King on his journey into Jerusalem, he demonstrates the implications of this by entering the temple and driving out the traders who had turned the house of prayer into a den of robbers. The term 'house of prayer' is one used by Isaiah when he writes of, '... foreigners who bind themselves to the LORD to serve him, to love the name of the LORD, and to worship him ... these I will bring to ... my house of prayer. Their burnt offerings and sacrifices will be accepted on my altar; for my house will be called a house of prayer for all nations' (Isa. 56:6-7). This is a widespread invitation to foreigners to come and participate in the covenant God made with Israel, but here exploited by the locals who inflated their prices with excessive rates of exchange

---

[3] G. Campbell Morgan, *The Gospel According To Matthew*, p. 262.

and high cost of animals necessary for sacrifice.

The term 'den of thieves' is also a description given of the temple by Jeremiah quoting the words of the Lord, 'Has this house which bears my Name, become a den of robbers to you?' (Jer. 7:11). This statement by Jeremiah precipitated the destruction of the temple by Nebuchadnezzar soon afterwards, as this statement of Jesus precipitates the destruction of the temple which he speaks specifically about in the next day or two (see 24:1-2).

Jesus overturned the tables of the money changers, released the doves sold for sacrifice, and drove out all who were buying or selling. One brief sentence follows this action to indicate the temple functioning as God's house, 'The blind and the lame came to him at the temple, and he healed them' (21:14), and the children excitedly shouting, 'Hosanna to the Son of David.' This brief moment of joy provoked swift reaction. The scribes and priests, indignant at the evidence of true godliness in the temple, rebuked him for accepting the affirmation of the children. Children often recognise spiritual truth and realities which the more sophisticated have distorted and hidden. Jesus quotes to the priests the words of the Psalmist, 'From the lips of children and infants you have ordained praise' (Ps. 8:2).

Cursing the fig tree (21:18-22)

Early next morning having spent the night in Bethany, Jesus came back to the city, and being hungry, went to a fig tree but found nothing but leaves. He cursed it saying, 'May you never bear fruit again', and the fig tree withered. His disciples were dumbfounded.

This story, which on first reading seems extravagant and vindictive, is clearly a parable of events going on in Jerusalem at the time, particularly in the temple. The prophet Micah likens the barrenness of Israel to finding 'none of the early figs that I crave' (Mic. 7:1). Mark explicitly states in his account of the incident that 'it was not the season for figs' (Mark 11:13), but around six weeks before the main crop, small edible knobs appear, as a forerunner of the real fruit. It was the absence of these that provoked Jesus to curse the tree.

The allusion to the temple seems obvious. The worship and disciplines of the temple were given by God as forerunners of Christ, 'one greater than the temple' (see 12:6). But this fore-fruit, designed to anticipate the true fruit was absent. The significance of the temple rituals, foreshadowing the work of Jesus Christ, had been so eroded in their meaning that instead of Jesus being seen as the fulfilment of the temple activity, he was seen as its antagonist. It is a sober truth that what God will bless as an expression of his purpose, he will curse if it becomes a substitute for his purposes. To promote spiritual truth necessarily involves a clearing away of the debris of pseudo spiritual activity which has grown up and surrounded that truth. In reply to the disciples' amazement at his cursing the fig tree, Jesus tells them not to doubt but have faith and they will not only see unproductive fig trees wither, but mountains thrown into the sea!

Matthew's record of this event is dramatic and instantaneous, 'Immediately the tree withered'. Mark records the same event taking place over twenty four hours. He cursed the tree one day, and the disciples saw it withered at its roots the next (Mark 11:12-14, 20). Luke records a parable in which a man went to look for fruit on his fig tree for three years, but did not find any, so asked his servant to cut it down, at which the servant asked for one more year in which he would dig around and fertilise it, and if there was no fruit then he would cut it down (Luke 13:6-8). God is patient and long-suffering with his people, but the time comes when his wrath is held back no more. As Paul wrote of the Jews, '... who killed the Lord Jesus ... They displease God and are hostile to all men ... The wrath of God has come upon them at last' (1 Thess. 2:15-16).

Key questions (21:23-46)

Returning to the temple in Jerusalem, the scene of the previous day's disruption, the chief priests and elders seek to antagonise Jesus and his response to them illustrates and explains his cursing of the fig tree. They first ask him a question, 'By what authority are you doing these things? And who gave you this authority?' This was no casual question. This was asked by men whose own authority had probably never been challenged. These were the religious leaders, priests, scribes and Pharisees, members of the Sanhedrin Council whose authority amongst the Jews was supreme. Their antagonism to Christ had been building for some time and was now approaching its climax. They had seen him cleanse the temple on the previous day and now he had returned to the same spot with the audacity to teach the people. This was their patch! It was their authority being undermined by his actions. Their coming to Jesus was no doubt something of an official visit, representing the authorities in Jerusalem, disturbed by his actions and the popular response to him of the people (see 21:46).

He answered their question about his authority with a question of his own, followed by two parables, so pointed in their meaning that 'When the chief priests and the Pharisees heard Jesus' parables, they knew he was talking about them' (21:45). In responding to their questions about him, he exposed them as those from whom the kingdom of God was to be taken away – cursed like the fig tree which did not bear fruit.

Jesus responded to their question about his authority by asking them a clever question about the origin of John the Baptist's ministry, 'Was it from heaven or from men?' This placed his inquisitors in a dilemma. John had been executed some time before, and as is so often the case, his death had enhanced his reputation. If they said John's ministry was not from God they would provoke the anger of the people. If they said John's ministry was of God they would have to logically accept the ministry of Jesus to whom John pointed and for whom he claimed only to be a forerunner, 'He came as a witness to testify concerning that light, so that through him all men might believe. He himself was not the light; he came only as a witness to the light' (John 1:7-8). Having discussed it amongst themselves and realised the dilemma into which Jesus had led them, the priests and elders replied rather pathetically, 'We don't know.' Then he said, 'Neither will I tell you by what authority I am doing these things.'

Life takes precedence over language (21:28-32)

Jesus followed this up by two parables, each of which involved a question to the Pharisees and priests, by which once more they incriminated themselves. The first is a parable of a father and his two sons (23:28-32). The first of these two sons was sent by his father to work in his vineyard. He initially refused, then changed his mind and went. The second son was also sent to the vineyard. He at first said he would go, but changed his mind, and did not go. Jesus asked the question, 'Which of the two did what the father wanted?' The answer was obvious, and the religious leaders fell into the trap! The one who did what the father wanted was the first son. To agree to go yet not go, is to not go! To not agree to go, but then go is to go! The language used and the reality experienced were in conflict in both cases, but the actual experience of either going or not going took precedence over the promises made by each son and represented the reality of their obedience or disobedience. The pointed application of this to the Pharisees and priests was that although tax collectors and prostitutes made no claim to any favoured relationship with God as the religious hierarchy did, they believed John the Baptist, repented of their sin, and, 'are entering the kingdom of God ahead of you' (21:31). However, the priests and Pharisees, who gave all outward appearance of allegiance to God, did not repent and believe the preaching of John the Baptist.

The behaviour of neither son in the story is ideal of course, for one would prefer sons who did what they said they would! But the point is that it is not rhetoric but actual response that counts. It is not right belief that measures our response to God, but right behaviour. Like these priests and Pharisees, it is possible to reduce Christianity to little more than the correct usage of theological language and concepts, so deceiving ourselves that because we speak the language we experience the life. Old Testament prophets warn of this. Jeremiah speaks of 'trusting in deceptive words that are worthless' (Jer. 7.8). Micah writes of judges who bribe and of prophets who tell fortunes for money, 'Yet they lean upon the LORD and say, "Is not the LORD among us? No disaster will come upon us"' (Mic. 3.11). God says to Amos, 'I hate, I despise your religious feasts ... Away with the noise of your songs ... But let justice roll on like a river, righteousness like a never-failing stream' (Amos 5:21-24). In the New Testament John warns, 'If we claim ...', by right sounding language, which does not represent the reality of our lives, '... we lie and do not live by the truth' (see 1 John 1:6, 8; 10; 2:4, 9; 4:20). The religious leaders of Jesus' day were those who said 'I will' but didn't, and their use of correct language deceived them into a false security.

The kingdom will be taken away (21:33-46)

The second parable contained another question. A landowner planted a vineyard and rented it to some farmers. When harvest time approached he sent his servants to the tenants to collect the fruit. The tenants seized his servants, beat one, killed another and stoned a third. He sent more servants and they treated them the same way. Finally he sent his son, but the tenants killed him too. Then came the question, 'When the owner of the vineyard comes, what will he do to those tenants?'

The people correctly replied, 'He will bring those wretches to a wretched end, and he will rent the vineyard to other tenants, who will give him his share of the crop at harvest time.' They had unwittingly given Jesus the explanation of their own situation. The vineyard is a familiar picture of the Jewish nation (e.g. see Isa. 5:7, 'The vineyard of the LORD Almighty is the house of Israel and the men of Judah'). They had rejected the servants sent from God, the prophets who demanded they give God his due, and finally he has sent his Son. He too is rejected. They vividly illustrate their own guilt by resolving immediately after the telling of this parable 'to arrest him' (21.46).

The fig tree Israel is cursed. The small edible knobs that appear early on the fig tree as a forerunner of the real fruit are absent. The acts of worship centred on the Jerusalem temple are not preparing people for Christ, and they are to be cursed. The condemnation of Israel's position is complete so 'the kingdom of God will be taken away from you and given to a people who will produce its fruit' (21:43). If the two parables at the end of Chapter 21 indicate the rejection of God by the Jewish people, then who are the people who will produce the fruit of the kingdom? It is this which Jesus addresses in his next parable.

To the street corners (22:1-14)

Jesus now told a parable about a wedding banquet planned by a king for his son. There are two aspects to the story. Firstly, the king issued invitations to those eligible to attend, but when the moment came, they refused to come, so he sent his servants to the streets to invite anyone who was available and willing to attend the banquet. That is the first aspect of the story. Secondly, when the king himself came to the banquet he found a guest not wearing wedding clothes, and he ordered him thrown out into the darkness. The first aspect refers to the refusal of the Jews to participate in the kingdom of God, consistent with the previous two parables, which climaxed in the statement 'the kingdom of God will be taken away from you' (21:43), and the subsequent invitation to any and everyone to come and participate. The second illustrates the fact that although the invitation is to all, attendance at the banquet requires being appropriately clothed. It will be helpful to us to look at these two aspects separately.

It was the custom of the day to issue an initial invitation to a banquet, which would have already been responded to by the invited guests. Then, when the meal was ready, a second invitation was delivered summoning the guests to attend. In this parable, the king sent his servants 'to those who had been invited to the banquet', and who presumably had already indicated their willingness to attend, but with the second invitation 'they refused to come'. This is a clear reference to the Jewish people, already in covenant with God. But, like the parables of chapter 21 where in the first, one son turned back on his promise to go to the vineyard, and in the second, the tenants of the vineyard refused to pay the agreed rent to its owner, instead killing the owner's servants and son, so now, those who have initially covenanted to attend the banquet refuse to do so when the final invitation is issued. The invitation to participate in the kingdom of God is not sudden. There have been earlier invitations and announcements through the law, the covenants and the prophets, but now Christ comes with the final invitation and with it an ultimatum, to come now, or be shut out for ever.

This parable is not to be confused with a similar one in Luke 14 in which a man prepares a great banquet, invites many guests who all make excuses when the meal is ready. The invitation is then extended to the highways and byways where 'the poor, the crippled, the blind and the lame' are welcomed (Luke 14:15-24). That story was told by Jesus at a meal in the house of a prominent Pharisee, this one in the temple courts. That one emphasises the open invitation to those outside, this one emphasises the rejection of those who refused to come, 'The king was enraged. He sent his army and destroyed those murderers and burned their city' (22:7). In Luke's parable, it is a generous man who issues the invitation, but in Matthew's parable it is a king, and to refuse to attend is tantamount to insubordination, for which severe punishment awaits the guilty.

The response to the invitation by the invited guests was not uniform. Some responded with indifference, 'they paid no attention and went off – one to his field, another to his business' (22:5). These activities were not bad in themselves, just more interesting to these people. Believing they had better things to do, they would not be bothered by this invitation. They would just ignore it! It is often not bad things which take us from Christ, it is the arrangement of values that allows other legitimate things to become more important to us and more demanding of us, than the summons, the invitations and the interests of Jesus Christ. This first group missed the feast through indifference.

Others missed the feast through sheer rejection, 'The rest seized his servants, mistreated them and killed them' (22:6). They actively opposed the summons and flatly rejected the invitation by killing the messengers. It is a myth to assume that to destroy the messenger is to destroy the message, yet not only is that the response of those in this parable, but Jesus stated it to have been the response of the forefathers of the Pharisees through their history, '... you are the descendants of those who murdered the prophets' (23:31). To violently reject or to indifferently neglect is ultimately the same – they did not participate in the banquet. Both categories of neglection and rejection were present amongst the Jewish people, though it was the Pharisees and religious leaders in particular who were guilty of rejection. As Jesus spoke to them, they were already looking for a way to arrest him and destroy him (21.46). In the parable, the king burned the city of those who killed the servants, and Jesus is almost certainly referring to the destruction of Jerusalem which would take place in 70AD, and which the next chapters (23–24) speak so explicitly about.

The kingdom is being taken from those who had first right to it, the Jews, and is being opened to all on the highways and byways of life. It is not only the 'tax collectors and prostitutes' of the previous chapter (21:32) who enter the kingdom of God, but also the Gentiles who were not in the scope of the earlier invitation. The invitation however, although widely extended, is conditional on appropriate clothing! In this second aspect of the story, the king comes in to see his guests and notices a man not wearing wedding clothes. 'How did you get in here without wedding clothes?' the man was asked. For his neglect he was tied hand and foot and thrown outside into the darkness. The door of the banquet was open to anyone, 'both good and bad'. But whereas any ragamuffin could be invited, he could not remain a ragamuffin. He was to be clean and dressed. The 'wedding garment' was not a particular kind of garment so much as appropriate clean clothing, preferably white.[4] The scripture often speaks of being 'clothed' in such a way as to be acceptable to God. Paul writes, '... all of you who were baptised into Christ have clothed yourselves with Christ' (Gal. 3:27), and, 'When the perishable has been clothed with the imperishable (1 Cor. 15:54). The Psalmist writes of being 'clothed with joy' (Ps. 30:11) and 'clothed with righteousness' (Ps. 132:9). Isaiah writes, 'For he has clothed me with garments of salvation and arrayed

---

[4] See *Matthew* by R. T. France, p. 313 in Tyndale New Testament Commentaaries, Inter Varsity Press.

me in a robe of righteousness' (Isa. 61:10). There is that which covers us and gives us our new identity, 'salvation', 'joy', 'righteousness', 'the imperishable', and 'Christ' himself. There are no grounds on which a person may stand confidently before God other than as he is clothed with Christ and has become the beneficiary of all that Jesus Christ makes available. The invitation of God extends to the whole world, but we may only enjoy its benefits when made ready by Jesus Christ himself. To seek to participate in God's banquet on any ground other than God's terms will be to be thrown 'outside into the darkness', for as Jesus then said, 'many are invited but few are chosen'.

The invitation is universal, but to be amongst the chosen is to respond on God's terms. God does not tease us by inviting many and choosing few, for inherent within the invitation are the resources to fulfil the invitation. Paul wrote, 'The one who calls you is faithful and he will do it' (1 Thess. 5:24). With the invitation comes the garment, a response of dependency on the one who called, to do it. The reason many are called but few chosen is that many of those who are called do not allow the one who called them to do it. They rely on their own ability, their own righteousness, and their own resources, rather than on God and his working. When the king comes, they are rejected. They are in the banquet hall, they fellowship with those dressed in the genuine wedding garment, but they are exposed and cast out. The replacement of the Jews who remained out of the banquet is no more by any Gentile than inclusion could have been by any Jew, but by those who will wear the wedding garment, and be 'clothed with Christ' (Gal. 3:27).

The teaching of Jesus in these parables is about the rejection of the Jewish people from the focus of God's purpose in the world, and their replacement with a new order, those from the highways and byways who will identify with Christ and be brought into union with him. But the fig tree Israel is cursed. The small edible knobs that appear early on the fig tree as a forerunner of the real fruit are absent. The laws, the covenants and temple centred in Jerusalem, designed to anticipate the Messiah and prepare the people for Christ, are fruitless and barren. The condemnation of Israel's position is such that 'the kingdom of God will be taken away from you and given to a people who will produce its fruit' (21:43).

31.

All things new
(22:15-46)

Jesus is still in the temple courts. His teaching and actions have demonstrated the corruption of God's chosen people, their rejection of Christ and his consequent invitation to all and sundry to participate in his kingdom. In this Jesus has been on the attack. He has placed the Jewish hierarchy on the defensive, and has exposed them as excluded from the kingdom of God by their own rejection of the Messiah. The door to God's kingdom has now been opened to those who were previously on the outside.

This inevitably provoked the religious leaders, who took up the offensive, went out and laid plans to trap him with his own words. They plan a series of trick questions with which they hope to discredit him. There are three in this chapter. The first is from the Pharisees and Herodians and sounds straightforward enough, 'Is it right to pay taxes to Caesar or not?' (22:15-22). Secondly, the Sadducees come and ask him about the fate of a woman at the resurrection who was married successively to seven brothers, 'Will she be the wife of all seven?' (22:23-33). Thirdly, the Sadducees and Pharisees got together and asked him, 'Which is the greatest commandment in the law?' (22:34-40). Finally, Jesus himself asks them the question, 'What do you think about the Christ?' (22:41-46).

A new allegiance (22:15-22)
The question, 'Is it right to pay taxes to Caesar or not?' was not the straightforward question it might appear. Israel was an occupied country, subject to Rome, as was much of the Mediterranean world at that time. The imposition of Roman taxation was a sore point for the Jews. Tax collectors were themselves outcasts of society,

and there were many resistance movements collectively labelled as 'Zealots' who resented paying tax to Rome, regarding it as treason against God, Israel's true king. Israel was a theocracy, and their allegiance was to God not Rome. One of Jesus' own disciples was 'Simon the Zealot', who, when a Zealot, had nationalistic interests and ambitions, which included resistance of Rome. This question was designed as a 'trap' (22:15) and the trap is easy to see. If Jesus said it was right to pay the tax he would stand discredited in the eyes of many of the Jewish people. If Jesus said it was not right to pay taxes to Caesar, he would have laid himself open to a charge of sedition and provided the opportunity of a definite charge to be brought against him before the Roman authorities, and would inevitably lead to his arrest. As it happens, when he was later brought before Pilate, one of the trumped up charges brought against him was that 'He opposes payment of taxes to Caesar' (Luke 23:2), something of which Pilate found no evidence.

The fact that this question was jointly asked by Pharisees and Herodians is greatly significant. His questioners stood in two opposing camps on this matter. Whatever his answer he would offend and provoke one of them. The Pharisees were orthodox believers in the prime allegiance of Israel to God, and strictly speaking, the emperor who demanded tribute from the Jews was regarded as a blasphemer, for they recognised only one master – God. The Herodians were the party of Herod, the puppet king of Galilee who owed his position and power to the Romans, and worked in full unison with them and willingly bowed the knee to Caesar. This was a strange marriage, united only by their vested interest in the destruction of Jesus Christ.

Their approach to Jesus oozed with flattery, 'we know you are a man of integrity and that you teach the way of God in accordance with the truth. You aren't swayed by men, because you pay no attention to who they are', which in reality must have galled them. The Pharisees were constantly swayed by the opinions of others and paid much attention to who they were (e.g. 6:1-18), but they could afford the smooth talk and the generosity of their flattery for they would shortly trap him. Jesus saw right into their hearts and recognised their 'evil intent', and exposed them to themselves, 'You hypocrites, why are you trying to trap me?' They were not interested in a real answer to the question for their intent was simply to trap him, but the question itself is a serious and important one. How are we to reconcile our allegiance to governments and human authority with our allegiance to God, especially where the human authority is corrupt and engaged in activity directly in conflict with God?

Jesus did not participate in their game by giving them the luxury of his coming down on one side, so as to provoke and give ammunition to the other. He took a Roman coin to the value of the tax, and asked whose portrait and inscription was on it. They rightly answered 'Caesar's'. Then he said to them, 'Give to Caesar what is Caesar's, and to God what is God's.' This was not a clever evading of the issue. There is responsibility to God and there is responsibility to government, but our responsibility is to give what is their due, 'to Caesar what is Caesar's, and to God what is God's'. We are not to give to Caesar what is God's. There are legitimate demands a government makes upon its people, and that right is ordained by God. Paul wrote, 'Everyone must submit himself to the governing authorities, for there is no authority except that which God has established. The authorities that exist have been established by God' (Rom. 13:1). It is not that individual authorities are ordained by God, so that it should be believed the rule of Caesar was God's specific will for Rome at that time, but rather that the principle of government is God ordained, whoever may happen to be in office.

The mentality of the Pharisees in particular was a legalistic one. They wanted rules and laws about everything, and phrased their question in such a way as to expect a rule in reply, 'Is it lawful to give tribute unto Caesar, or not?' (AV). They wanted to know what was 'lawful'. They understood laws and preferred life to be ordered according to them. This mentality makes life very simple and straightforward, giving great power to the lawmaker and eliminating much need for those under authority to think for themselves. Jesus however did not give a law, he gave a principle, 'Give to Caesar what is Caesar's and to God what is God's'. If you teach a person a law you have addressed one single issue. If you teach a person a principle you may have addressed a thousand separate issues to which that one principle can be applied. It is not the detail of who, how and when they should pay taxes, but the principle of responsibility to both the law of the land and to God.

There has always been a tendency amongst Christian people to create a distinction between the spiritual and secular, between the heavenly and earthly, and to departmentalise life to such extent as to feel obligated to withdraw as much as is possible from that which is 'secular' and 'worldly'. Monasticism would be an extreme case of this, but many within Christendom who would not dream of entering a monastery have been as equally guilty of escaping from participation and responsibility in the political, economic and social structures of society. This mentality redefines worldliness as anything the people of the world like to do, rather than the attitude of heart described in Scripture as worldliness, 'the cravings of sinful man, the lust of his eyes and the boasting of what he has and does ... comes from the world' (1 John 2:16). Worldliness is not external to us, something outside our front doors waiting to seduce us, but it is within, an attitude waiting to corrupt the heart. We do have an obligation to take our place in the fallen society around us. To pay taxes to Caesar does not imply an endorsement of Roman Imperialism but an acknowledgement of the realities of life in Israel at that time. The people were not to give to God what is God's in isolation from responsibility to human government, but allegiance to God involves full allegiance to act responsibly towards the society of which we are a part. The fact a government may legislate laws that are un-Christian or even anti-Christian, e.g. the legalisation of abortion, does not invalidate our responsibility to that government. Christians have a double citizenship. They are citizens of the country in which they live, and they are citizens of heaven, but to be a citizen of heaven does not negate obligations as citizens on earth. To fail in their responsibilities to one is to fail in their responsibilities to the other. Some Christians have refused to vote in national elections on the grounds that their citizenship is in heaven and they therefore have no legitimate participation in political processes on earth! This is to deny the principle contained in Jesus' reply to this question. We have obligations to Caesar, and we are to meet them. We have obligations to God, and we are to meet them. So legalistic was the thinking framework of the Pharisees and Herodians that 'When they heard this they were amazed'. That Jesus should give them a principle rather than a rule amazed and confounded them! They would have to work out the details for themselves, something 'religious' people are very wary of.

They were amazed by his answer, but their amazement did not draw them to him, 'they left him and went away'. Intellectually he had confounded them, and the logic of their position would be to learn from him. But that was not their interest. They had not asked him a question in order to learn an answer. Their disposition was entrenched against him, thus his answer to the question, despite the fact it amazed them, did not help them or lead them forwards. It only humiliated them and they withdrew only to re-arm themselves and come back again (see v. 34). A person's disposition is more important than the expression of their curiosity.

A new position (22:23-33)

Next it was the turn of the Sadducees to question Jesus. They present a rather extreme situation. 'Teacher,' they said, 'Moses told us that if a man dies without having children, his brother must marry the widow and have children for him. Now there were seven brothers among us. The first one married and died, and since he had no children, he left his wife to his brother. The same thing happened to the second and third brother, right on down to the seventh. Finally, the woman died. Now then, at the resurrection, whose wife will she be of the seven, since all of them were married to her?' This was not a genuine question on the part of the Sadducees for they did not believe in the resurrection in the first place. They were the wealthy, aristocratic, governing class in Israel, much more willing to co-operate with the Romans than were the Pharisees. Theologically, they were liberal, rejecting much of the Old Testament scripture, though holding firmly to the books of Moses. Significantly, in view of their question, they did not believe in heaven, hell, angels, the spirit or in any after life, for they believed the soul perished with the body. They attempted to hold a 'religious' view of life that was totally rational and eliminated the supernatural. This question then was a further trap in which they hoped to provoke further opposition to Jesus, and probably to them was tinged with humour. Whose wife will this poor woman be at the resurrection when faced with all seven brothers?

Jesus' answer begins by exposing the fundamental flaw of their question. 'You are in error because you do not know the Scriptures or the power of God. At the resurrection people will neither marry nor be given in marriage; they will be like the angels in heaven' (22:29-30). Interestingly, their question had begun with a quotation from Scripture, 'Moses told us ...' (quoting from Deut. 25:5-6), but Jesus says, 'You do not know the Scripture...'. To be able to quote extracts from the Bible is not to know the Bible! We can construct all kinds of doctrines, and produce all kinds of red herrings, on a selected use of Scripture. The devil quoted Scripture in order to tempt Jesus in the wilderness (see 4:6), but he stopped quoting at a crucial point in the text! To know the Scriptures and the power of God is to interpret the details in the light of the general purpose and thrust of God in the world. We cannot detach the Scriptures from the 'power of God' and it still make sense, for it is supremely the revelation of his power in human affairs that is its message.

Their not knowing the Scriptures made their question invalid because it presupposed a set of circumstances that do not exist if there is no marriage in heaven. Because they did not know the Scriptures, they were ignorant of this. They were asking a question about heavenly issues with a completely earthly mentality, and it is not possible to understand eternal issues from a rational mindset or to interpret heavenly situations in human terms. For the rationalist who will only believe what he can touch, see, smell, feel, hear and thus prove by his rational senses, the supernatural God will always be an enigma. He will always be able to suggest hypothetical circumstances for which there is no non-supernatural answer.

Concerning the resurrection of the dead, Jesus said, 'But about the resurrection of the dead – have you not read what God said, "I am the God of Abraham, the God of Isaac, and the God of Jacob"? He is not the God of the dead but of the living.' This refers back to God's introduction of himself to Moses at the burning bush (Exod. 3.6). There he declares himself in the present tense to be the God of Abraham, Isaac and Jacob. It was not a past tense relationship with the patriarchs that Moses could read about in history, but a present tense relationship. From this Jesus makes clear the immortality of the soul. He is not the God of the dead! These people, though absent from earth at the time God spoke to Moses, are not dead! Abraham is spoken of in the present tense, Isaac is spoken of in the present tense, Jacob is spoken of in the present tense! To leave the body is not to be dead, but to be alive outside of the body. There will be a resurrection body to come one day, but these people are not in the meantime dead, or in some kind of 'soul sleep' awaiting resurrection. They remain alive, awaiting a resurrection of the body, but not a resurrection of life. If they knew the Scriptures (and so understood what God had said), and if they knew the power of God (and so understood what God can do), they would know this.

Jesus turned the conversation from the particular details of the question they raise to the reason why they raised it – their ignorance of the Scriptures and the power of God. 'When the crowds heard this, they were astonished at his teaching.' He silenced the Sadducees, who like the Pharisees in the previous encounter, 'left him and went away'.

A new commandment (22:34-40)

Hearing Jesus had silenced the Sadducees, some Pharisees got together, worked out a new approach and sent 'an expert in the law' to test him with a question. The question appeared simple, 'Teacher, which is the greatest commandment in the Law?'

Once again the Pharisaic obsession with law is evident. Apart from the actual ten commandments God gave Moses on tablets of stone, there were altogether 613 commandments given by God to Moses on Mount Sinai, 365 negative and 248 positive. The Pharisees were not content with that, so added their own laws around the given law to protect themselves from the real law. Their obsession then extended to trying to categorise the relative importance of each of the command-ments. For example, one school of thought favoured the commandment, 'You must not misuse the name of the Lord your God' and believed that all the rest of the law grew out of this one supreme command. They ask Jesus which commandment he favoured as the greatest.

The response of Jesus is not to choose a command and hold it above the others, but to give the supreme governing principle which makes any commandment great. That principle is love. He included all the commandments in his answer, ' "Love the Lord your God with all your heart and with all your soul and with all your mind." This is the first and greatest commandment. And the second is like it: "Love your neighbour as yourself." All the Law and the Prophets hang on these two commandments.' These two commandments are explicitly in the Old Testament: 'Love the LORD your God with all your heart and with all your soul and with all your strength' (Deut. 6:5), and 'Love your neighbour as yourself' (Lev. 19:18).

It is important in any discussion of the law to see they are not an arbitrary set of rules, but are supremely an expression of the moral character of God (see notes on 5:17ff). The moral character of God is ultimately expressed in the statement 'God is love' (1 John

4:8). Therefore, all true expression of the law of God must involve an expression of the love of God. What God demands can never be detached from what he is. Therefore, the principle by which the law of God is to function is the principle which expresses what God is, love. That love is firstly towards God and secondly towards people. To detach the law from love may be to remain legally correct, but it will cease to express the character of God.

To love God with '... all your heart and with all your soul and with all your mind' is an impossible and humanly unreasonable demand! It means that everything upon which our heart is set, everything with which our soul is preoccupied and everything that interests and captivates our mind will express love for God! The reality is that our hearts, souls and minds give more evidence of selfishness and indifference than love. As is often true in the teaching of Jesus, he presents the requirements of God in such a way as to expose the inevitable despair that must come to the conscientious heart of the person who would try to live this way. If the law is summed up in the word 'love' because God is love, then true righteousness is only possible by the expression of the life of God himself, lived miraculously within the Christian. True love is a fruit of the Spirit, not a fruit of the determined Christian. The Spirit of God is alone its source. Hence all the law and all the prophets hang on these two commands to love God and love our neighbour. Unless we are driven to an honest despair of our own ability, and learn to rest in the sufficiency of God alone, we can never fulfil the demands of the law.

A new Lord (22:41-46)

Finally, when the Pharisees were together Jesus asked them the question, 'What do you think about the Christ?' This of course is the ultimate issue. We may arrive at correct answers to peripheral questions, but it is this central question upon which everything else is built. It was this question Jesus asked the disciples at Caesarea Philippi, 'Who do you say I am?' (16:15), and on Peter's answer, 'You are the Christ the Son of the living God', Jesus began to speak about his purpose, 'From that time on Jesus began to explain to his disciples that he must go to Jerusalem and suffer many things ... that he must be killed and on the third day be raised to life.' He did not explain his purpose until they had understood his person. The teaching and work of Jesus Christ can never make sense without a knowledge of who he is. All earlier questions in this chapter were beating about the bush. They did not derive from knowledge but ignorance. The answers Jesus gave did not remove their ignorance, for this one central issue was not yet the guide of their thinking, 'Who is the Christ?'

The question Jesus asked about the Christ was specific. 'Whose son is he?' They replied, 'The son of David'. This was the standard reply. The Messiah was expected to restore the royal line of David to the throne of Israel. He would be a political and military leader who would throw off the subservience of Israel to Rome, and re-establish their dignity, their power and their glory, and more than that, be the conqueror of all nations. If their answer was correct, he is David's son, how is it that David himself called him 'Lord'? Jesus quotes David, 'The LORD said to my Lord: "Sit at my right hand until I put your enemies under your feet"' (Ps. 110:1). Jesus then asks, 'If then David calls him "Lord", how can he be his son?' A man does not call his own son 'Lord'. Jesus did not expect an answer to the question. Some questions are designed to provoke thought, not to produce answers. Answers to such questions have the effect of putting the question to bed so that we are no longer provoked by its implications.

It was this title the crowds had given Jesus when he had entered Jerusalem early that same week when they cried out, 'Hosanna to the Son of David!' (21:9 and 15). It was this that had made the leaders of the temple indignant (21:15), and almost certainly it was this that had provoked their offensive against him now. By clear implication, he was informing them of his Messiahship. The episode concludes, 'No one could say a word in reply, and from that day on no-one dared to ask him any more questions' (22:46).

32.

Distorted spirituality
(23:1-39)

Chapter 23 is probably the most devastating chapter in all four gospels. In it Jesus exposes and denounces the religious hierarchy of the day, the Scribes and the Pharisees, by pronouncing seven 'woes' on them, in some of the strongest language ever to leave his lips. The previous chapters have been building to this, and, humanly speaking, it was probably that last straw in provocation that led to his crucifixion so soon afterwards, which was orchestrated largely by the very people he here denounced.

This passage is not only valuable to us for its detail about the practices and attitudes of the Scribes and Pharisees, but as a general diagnosis of false righteousness and pseudo spirituality. The temptation to similar pseudo spirituality has never been far removed from any, even within genuine Christendom, though it is very difficult to recognise and acknowledge in ourselves, for, as with the Pharisees, its foundation may often be shown as having biblical ground. Yet the spirit of Pharisaism is very much alive. The roots of the teaching of the Scribes and Pharisees are in the divine revelation given to Moses, and as such Jesus said, 'You must obey them and do everything they tell you. But do not do what they do, for they do not practise what they preach' (23:3). The very fact their teaching has its origin in Moses gave their teaching its sense of authority, and justified their pronouncements, but at the same time it was this very thing which blinded them to their real position and remoteness from true godliness. To argue from the letter of the law can give a smug satisfaction about the legality of our position, yet be in fundamental conflict with the spirit and purpose of God's requirement.

Because Jesus endorsed the actual teaching of the Scribes and

Pharisees, 'The teachers of the law and the Pharisees sit in Moses' seat' (23:2), we cannot dismiss them simply as the propagators of false religion, for in its objective form they were not. Rather we should see this as a case of spiritual distortion and, to that extent, the principles of Jesus' teaching in the passage have their wider application to almost any case of spiritual distortion that claims its roots in biblical revelation.

We may divide the passage into two sections. Firstly, Jesus speaks about the *experience* of spiritual distortion, identifying its results, its motivation and its authority (23:1-12). Secondly, he speaks about the *effects* of spiritual distortion, making seven negative statements, all beginning with 'Woe to you ...', with each specifying the opposite consequences to the effects of genuine spirituality.

1. The experience of spiritual distortion (23:1-12)

Its results (vv. 1-4)

Jesus says of the Scribes and Pharisees, 'They tie up heavy loads and put them on men's shoulders' (v. 4). Any application of the word of God in the lives of the people of God that results in the imposition of a burden upon their shoulders is the complete opposite of the freedom and rest offered by Jesus. It was to the 'weary and burdened' that Jesus said, 'Come to me ... and I will give you rest' (11:28), but for the Scribes and Pharisees it had become a virtue to be 'weary and burdened'! The weight of the burden under which they lived was to them the evidence of their integrity and seriousness with which they took the commands of God. However, the very burden from which Jesus offered freedom was the burden the Pharisees and Scribes imposed on people, and they saw virtue in so doing.

Any understanding of the gospel of Jesus Christ that imposes a heavy burden on those it claims to liberate is clearly false. Its basis is the imposition of rules and regulations, and its responsibilities are found in the sheer hard work of fulfilling them to the best of our ability. Those may be the ingredients of religion, and some have found it possible with the imperatives of Scripture to argue them as Christian experience, but it is to miss the whole point. The demands of God are greater than our ability to perform them, which is blatantly obvious as we read and understand what he requires of us. Therefore it is not in implementing them by our own self effort but in abandoning any sense of human ability and resting in dependency on the power of the indwelling life of God that genuine Christianity functions.

The invitation of Jesus 'Come to me all you who are weary and burdened' should be coupled with a second invitation of Jesus to 'Abide in me ...' (John 15:4 AV). These two invitations encompass the whole of Christian experience. To *come to Christ* in an initial act of surrender that does not lead to the continuing process of *abiding in Christ* is to produce only a sense of frustration and failure. We cannot fulfil the requirements God demands of us alone, for as Jesus stated in the context of asking his disciples to abide in him, 'apart from me you can do nothing' (John 15:5).

The function of the law of God is not to provide a blueprint for us to fulfil on the basis of doing our best to obey them, but to serve as the means of exposing our inability to do so. Paul wrote, 'For what the law was powerless to do in that it was weakened by the sinful nature, God did by sending his own Son ... in order that the righteous requirements of the law might be fully met in us, who do not live according to the sinful nature but according to the Spirit' (Rom. 8:3-4). The requirements of the law still stand, for they represent the character of God (see earlier notes on Matt. 5:17-48), but the fulfilment of the law of God is only by the Spirit of God. The New Covenant promised by God to Israel through the prophets does not involve a *revision* of the law, but a *relocating* of the law from tablets of stone on which it was given to Moses, to the human heart on which it is to be written by the Holy Spirit (see Jer. 31:33 and Ezek. 36:27).

It might be argued that the Scribes and Pharisees were operating under the Old Covenant and this is of course true. But the imposition of the law externally applied should have led people to a sense of humility in acknowledging their inherent weakness, not a smugness in their own self-sufficiency. This was the purpose of the law, but instead it led on the part of the Scribes and Pharisees to a sense of self-righteousness and arrogance. They had built fences around the law in a supposed attempt to prevent themselves breaking the real law, and the effect was the opposite of true righteousness. They became preoccupied with trivialities and neglected the true purpose of the law. As Jesus said, 'You give a tenth of your spices – mint, dill and cummin. But you have neglected the more important matters of the law – justice, mercy and faithfulness' (23:23).

When keeping the law is our goal, guilt becomes our motivation.

We become characterised inevitably by either an unrelenting sense of despair and failure, or by a sense of self righteousness and pride. True godliness derives not from a sense of accomplishment, but from realism about our own intrinsic inability and our corresponding dependency on the Holy Spirit to produce God's character in our lives and accomplish his will. Consequently, when the Christian life is a heavy burden on our shoulders it is because we have assumed the responsibility of producing godliness by our own ability. We have rendered the indwelling life of the Holy Spirit as irrelevant to the task and have failed to grasp the real message in the gospel.

Its motivation (vv. 5-7)

Jesus said of the Pharisees, 'Everything they do is done for men to see' (23:5). Their motivation is the recognition and approval of people. This is a logical consequence, for if we are dealing with laws that are applied externally (rather than the Holy Spirit who operates internally) we inevitably become concerned with the approval of those who view the external – other people.

This is exactly how Jesus described the 'hypocrites' in the Sermon on the Mount. They announced their giving to the needy with trumpets, 'to be honoured by men' (6:2). They loved to pray on the street corners and synagogues 'to be seen by men' (6:5). They disfigured their faces and looked sombre 'to show men they are fasting' (6:16). The whole exercise has become oriented towards pleasing or impressing other people. Everything they did was with an eye over their shoulder to see who was watching. If no-one was watching there was little value in the act!

Status before other people had become everything. Jesus said of these Pharisees and Scribes, 'Everything they do is done for men to see: They make their phylacteries wide and the tassels on their garments long; they love the place of honour at banquets and the most important seats in the synagogues; they love to be greeted in the market-places and to have men call them "Rabbi"' (23:5-7). Phylacteries are small leather boxes strapped on the wrist and forehead containing quotations from Exodus and Deuteronomy, as a literal response to the instruction to take the law of God and 'Tie them as symbols on your hands and bind them on your foreheads' (Deut. 6:8. See also Exod. 13:16, Deut. 11:18). It is still practised by many orthodox Jews today. The Pharisees wore large ones to draw attention to themselves and their exemplary piety!

The long tassels they wore on their garments were in response to instructions, '... you are to make tassels on the corners of your garments, with a blue cord on each tassel. You will have these tassels to look at and so you will remember all the commands of the LORD, that you may obey them and not prostitute yourselves by going after the lusts of your own hearts and eyes' (Num. 15:38-39. See also Deut. 22:12). The whole point of course was that the law of God should characterise the people's thinking (the forehead), their actions (the hand), and their whole demeanour (the garments). These were external symbols, rituals given to the people as a reminder of the realities God required of the heart. All *rituals* were for the purpose of pointing to *realities* outside of the ritual itself. When the *reality* gets lost the *ritual*, instead of pointing to the reality, inevitably replaces the *reality*, and the symbol becomes of greater significance than the substance it was originally designed to portray. Hence the preoccupation with external symbols and external approval is an inevitable characteristic of this kind of pseudo spirituality, and had become the main characteristic of the Pharisees and the Scribes.

Even worse perhaps, 'they love the place of honour at banquets, and the most important seats in the synagogue' (23:6). Traditionally the seats on the left and right of the host at a banquet were the seats of the honoured guests. The most important seats in the synagogue were those of the elders who sat facing the congregation. They were on full display and no-one present would fail to see the pose and displays of piety this position offered the Pharisee. They loved it, they desired it, and they wallowed in the sense of spiritual snobbery it gave them.

The measure in which we need others to see and approve our walk with God is the measure of its unreality. When Jesus contrasted the hypocrites in the Sermon on the Mount with the genuine article he said, 'Your Father who sees in secret will reward you' (6.4, 6, 18). True spirituality is concerned with God and finds its security not in a display of piety for the benefit of other people's approval (which in any case is unlikely to impress them), but in an intimacy with God that requires no human approval to be valid.

Its authority (vv. 8-12)
In the light of the above, it is logical that they needed the titles that went with their status, 'Rabbi ... Father ... Teacher', and Jesus trod heavily on their sensitivities when he forbade them all.

Rabbi: 'But you are not to be called "Rabbi", for you have only one Master and you are all brothers.' There are those who love to master other people, and there are those who rather than take responsibility for their own lives, prefer to be mastered. But there is no master but Christ. Allegiance to other people must never be a substitute for allegiance to Christ, nor must allegiance to other people be made the test of our allegiance to Christ. We are described as 'all brothers'. We relate to one another as siblings in the Lord Jesus Christ, but he alone is Master, and our submission and allegiance to a Master is exclusively to Christ.

When it is true that 'everything they do is done to be seen by men' (23:5), then it becomes inevitable that a pecking order emerges as to whom we prefer to be 'seen' by. This gives great power to those we want to please, and great opportunity for the abuse of that power which we have granted to them. This is not to encourage individualism that has no regard for legitimate authority, but to identify the consequences of failing to see each other as 'brothers', and Christ as Master, and under whose authority all other legitimate authority must derive.

Father: 'And do not call anyone on earth "father", for you have one Father, and he is in heaven.' A father, by definition, is one who has imparted life. No one can impart spiritual life, but God. The new birth, regeneration, is a consequence of divine action where God gives spiritual life. As John writes, '... to all who received him, to those who believed in his name, he gave the right to become children of God – children born not of natural descent, nor of human decision or a husband's will, but *born of God*' (John 1:12-13). No priest, no pastor and no evangelist can ever impart life to another. That is the exclusive prerogative of God, so in spiritual terms, no one but God may be called 'father'.

Teacher: 'Nor are you to be called "teacher", for you have one Teacher, the Christ'. Teaching is one of the specified gifts of the Holy Spirit, yet no-one may claim to be an originator of truth. The source of truth is God, revealed in Scripture and ultimately in Christ who claimed, 'I am ... the truth'. The writer of Hebrews states, 'In the past God spoke to our forefathers through the prophets at many times and in various ways, but in these last days he has spoken to us by his Son ...'

(Heb. 1:1-2). God's final word to us is Christ, and we cannot add to that, amend that, nor improve on that. It is in this sense that no-one is to be called 'teacher'. There is now nothing original to add to the divine revelation already given to us. All true teaching of spiritual truth will have its source in Scripture, its focus on Christ and its effect in conforming us to his image. We are not at liberty to have our own angle, our own special emphasis, or our own interpretation and remain legitimate. True teaching leaves the teacher dispensable, but Christ indispensable.

The section ends with the antidote to Pharisaic spirituality, 'The greatest among you will be your servant. For whoever exalts himself will be humbled, and whoever humbles himself will be exalted' (23:11-12). In true spirituality, the way to fail is to push our way up, the way to grow up is to keep ourselves down in humble dependency and obedience. We must not strive to be masters but servants, not to be teachers so much as to be taught, not to impart life but to receive life. We stand on level ground as children of God with access to equal resources.

If this then is the experience of spiritual distortion, resulting in burdens being placed on people's shoulders, motivated by the approval and applause of others, and deriving authority from those who take upon themselves the prerogatives that belong to God, our only true master, father and teacher, then we must examine the effects this has on those who perpetrate this.

2. The effects of spiritual distortion (23:13-39)

Here Jesus gives seven denunciations which commence 'Woe to you ...'. Each of these statements is condemning in itself, with the culminative effect causing him to conclude, 'You snakes! You brood of vipers! How will you escape from being condemned to hell?' (23:33). This is extremely strong language, and frighteningly so, when we know it is addressed to those who 'sit in Moses' seat' (23:2) and see them-selves, not as the protectors of some human philosophy, but the proclaimers of God's revelation in the law. They would purport to be doing the will of God, yet they are, says Jesus, preparing themselves for hell!

'Woe to you, teachers of the law and Pharisees, you hypocrites! You shut the kingdom of heaven in men's faces. You yourselves do not enter, nor will you let those enter who are trying to' (23:13). The first denunciation refers to entering the kingdom. Far from being those who open its doors to people, they shut the kingdom in people's faces. Those who claim exclusive access to the kingdom along lines of certain disciplines and human requirements that qualify a person as a fit inheritor of the kingdom, have in fact lost the keys to the kingdom, and by their exclusiveness have the opposite effect to what they claim. They actually shut the kingdom in men's faces.

Several commentators have seen a reverse image in these statements to the beatitudes of Jesus in the Sermon on the Mount. There the first beatitude states, 'Blessed are the poor in spirit, for theirs is the kingdom of heaven' (5:3). Here, the arrogance of the Pharisaic pride of spirit, shuts the door to the kingdom in people's faces, and has the reverse effect of the humility of the poor in spirit which gives access to the kingdom of heaven.

'Woe to you, teachers of the law and Pharisees, you hypocrites! You travel over land and sea to win a single convert, and when he becomes one, you make him twice as much a son of hell as you are' (23:15). In their own blindness they zealously seek to win others to share their own doom. To seek converts is not wrong, for the disciples of the Lord Jesus are commissioned to do that, but we can never do more than reproduce in others what we have experienced for ourselves. In contrast with the second beatitude, 'Blessed are those who mourn, for they will be comforted', there is no comfort here. There is no true mourning of spiritual poverty, only a self righteousness grounded in self delusion, resulting not in comfort but condemnation.

'Woe to you, blind guides! You say, "If anyone swears by the temple, it means nothing; but if anyone swears by the gold of the temple, he is bound by his oath." You blind fools! Which is greater: the gold, or the temple that makes the gold sacred? You also say, "If anyone swears by the altar, it means nothing; but if anyone swears by the gift on it, he is bound by his oath." You blind men! Which is greater: the gift, or the altar that makes the gift sacred?' (23:16-19). These 'blind fools' and 'blind men' who arrogantly swear by the gold of the temple rather than the temple which makes the gold significant, and by the gift on the altar rather than by the altar which makes the gift significant, are demonstrating their own preoccupation with the secondary rather than the significant. The contrast Jesus makes does not justify swearing, for he has already addressed that in the Sermon on the Mount where he said, 'Do not swear at all ... Simply let your "Yes" be "Yes" and your "No" be "No"; anything beyond this comes from the evil one' (5:33-37). It is the distortion of values that is the point here, and significantly it is the human activity and responsibility rather than the divine initiative that is the focus of attention. The gold in the temple is moulded by man and becomes the focus, rather than the significance of the temple itself as the dwelling place of God. The gold would be of no significance were it not for the temple, yet the gold is the focus of their swearing. The gift on the altar, the expression of human response, rather than the altar itself which represented God's interests, has become the focal point. This confidence in things human contrasts markedly with the third beatitude, which emphasises meekness and humility, 'Blessed are the meek, for they will inherit the earth.'

'Woe to you, teachers of the law and Pharisees, you hypocrites! You give a tenth of your spices – mint, dill and cummin. But you have neglected the more important matters of the law – justice, mercy and faithfulness' (23:23). Once again, true values have been exchanged and distorted. If in the previous denouncement the attention was on the human response rather than divine initiative, in this one, they are preoccupied with outward conduct rather than inward character. A person may tithe and fulfil all the obligations the law puts on him, yet his heart be untouched. The more important matters are those of the heart, 'justice, mercy and faithfulness', out of which the more external ones will naturally grow. They are concerned with externals rather than internals. This again contrasts with the fourth beatitude, 'Blessed are those who hunger and thirst for righteousness, for they will be filled' (5:6). The internal thirst for righteousness is the source of true satisfaction for the soul.

'Woe to you, teachers of the law and Pharisees, you hypocrites! You clean the outside of the cup and dish, but inside they are full of greed and self-indulgence' (23:25). The external activities over against inner integrity is again the focus, and calls again for the denunciation, 'You blind Pharisees. First clean the inside of the cup and dish, and then the outside also will be clean.' When we are concerned with the means to cleanliness on the inside, cleanliness in our outer behaviour will look after itself. External goodness is a symptom of true godliness, not its cause. What we do is an expression of what we are, and what we are in our innermost being is the first concern in godly living. This fifth 'woe' contrasts again with the fifth beatitude. Here they are full of 'greed and self-indulgence' rather than an attitude of self-giving mercy, 'Blessed are the merciful for they will be shown mercy.'

'Woe to you, teachers of the law and Pharisees, you hypocrites! You are like whitewashed tombs, which look beautiful on the outside but on the inside are full of dead men's bones and everything unclean' (23:27). The outward appearance of whitewashed tombs gleaming in the light of the sunshine hides the fact of death and uncleanness on the inside. The Mosaic law stated that, 'Anyone who touches a human bone or grave will be unclean for seven days' (Num. 19:16), so with great effort they made the outside clean and white, disguising the truth of its uncleanness! The sixth beatitude speaks of, 'Blessed are the pure in heart for they will see God.' To the Pharisee the externals had become more important than the heart, rather than the heart being the source of the externals. They had failed to grasp the proverb in their scriptures, 'Keep your heart with all diligence; for out of it spring the issues of life' (Prov. 4:23 NKJV), and instead settled for externals.

'Woe to you, teachers of the law and Pharisees, you hypocrites! You build tombs for the prophets and decorate the graves of the righteous. And you say, "If we had lived in the days of our forefathers, we would not have taken part with them in shedding the blood of the prophets." So you testify against yourselves that you are the descendants of those who murdered the prophets' (23:29-31). With their self-righteous pomp and pride they affirm they would never have attacked the prophets of God, yet their spiritual genealogy goes right back to those who rejected and even murdered them. It is quite easy to rewrite history in our own image, to affirm our stand with the great and good, to appeal to those who cannot now object that we are of their kind. The Pharisees did this then, as Jesus Christ and Paul are acclaimed by advocates of all kinds of cults, sects and aberrations of the truth today. But in reality these Pharisees are the antagonists and murderers of those who stood as representatives of God. The seventh beatitude speaks of, 'Blessed are the peacemakers', in direct contrast to the diagnosis Jesus gave here of the Pharisees and Scribes as descendants of murderers.

These seven woes lead to a vitriolic summary of the accusation Jesus brings against these people when he declares, 'You snakes! You brood of vipers! How will you escape being condemned to hell? Therefore I am sending you prophets and wise men and teachers. Some of them you will kill and crucify; others you will flog in your synagogues and pursue from town to town' (23:33-34). This last statement stands in contrast to the last of the eight beatitudes,

'Blessed are those who are persecuted because of righteousness, for theirs is the kingdom of heaven.' The Pharisees and Scribes are not the *persecuted*, they are the *persecutors*. They are not the friends of God's people, but his enemies. They do not further the work of God, they fight it. All the righteous blood shed since the time of Abel, the first martyr of the Old Testament, killed in anger by his brother Cain as Abel's offering was accepted and Cain's was not (see Gen. 4:2-8) to Zechariah son of Berekiah, the writer of the Old Testament book that bears his name and would be the last martyr of the Old Testament (see Zech. 1:1). Some identify the Zechariah mentioned by Jesus here with 'Zechariah son of Jehoida' who was martyred at the end of the Old Testament era, and who said as he was dying, 'May the Lord see this and call you to account', suggesting the vengeance Jesus here speaks about (see 2 Chron. 24:21-22). To speak of the martyrs 'from Abel to Zechariah' is to cover the record of martyrdom in the Old Testament from its beginning to end, stating that the spirit and disposition of their murderers lives on in the religion of the Pharisees and Scribes.

But there is never condemnation from the lips of Jesus without also the possibility of hope and rescue. 'O Jerusalem, Jerusalem, you who kill the prophets and stone those sent to you, how often I have longed to gather your children together, as a hen gathers her chicks under her wings, but you were not willing' (23:37). I would rescue you, says Jesus and have longed to do so, but you were not willing. These were not the crocodile tears of one who planned their judgement as part of his own ultimate purpose. He longed to gather them to himself, and rescue them from their fate, but as 'blind fools' they were not willing, choosing instead to perpetuate the illusion of their own hearts.

We stand before God, every one of us, entirely responsible for our response to the revelation we have been given of Jesus Christ and the truth of God which centres in him. The judgement of God is a consequence of the stubbornness of man.

33.

The destruction of Jerusalem
and the second coming
(24:1-35)

The two chapters, 24 and 25, form one discourse in which Jesus addresses his disciples about future events. He has left the scene of his denouncement of the Pharisees and teachers of the law which took place in public (23:1), in the courts of the temple (24:1), and has crossed the Kidron Valley with his disciples, and climbed the Mount of Olives. As he walked from the temple he called the attention of his disciples to its buildings and said, '... not one stone will be left on another, every one will be thrown down'. Later, as Jesus sat on the Mount of Olives his disciples questioned him about this, 'Tell us when this will happen, and what will be the sign of your coming and of the end of the age' (24:3).

The question asks about two issues, the destruction of Jerusalem, and the signs surrounding the end of the age. Both are apparently connected in the disciples' minds, though how much they understood about the second coming of Christ at the end of the age we do not know, for at this stage they still rejected the notion that Christ would be crucified and, when he was, did not expect his resurrection! Perhaps they anticipated Jesus would disappear from the scene to escape the growing antagonism towards him, and then return to them when the danger was over, and they wondered when that might be. Perhaps as the focus of their anticipation of the Messiah's ministry was still related to his restoring the kingdom to Israel (see Acts 1:6), the end of Jerusalem was equated in their thinking with the end of the age.

Whether the disciples understood the significance of it or not, it is true that the destruction of Jerusalem would mark an end to one aspect of Jesus' ministry (events surrounding it forever separated

Christianity from Judaism), and would express God's judgement on Israel; as the coming of Jesus at the end of the age will mark the end to another aspect of his ministry (the church), and will express God's judgement on the world. Whatever the understanding of the disciples that lay behind their question, our concern is to understand the answer Jesus gave to the question.

Chapter 24 is not an easy chapter to interpret. It begins with Jesus elaborating on his initial statement about the destruction of the temple itself (which took place a generation later in AD 70) and moves on to talk about his own second coming at 'the end of the age', the second issue the disciples had introduced in their question. Although these two events are assumed by the disciples to be related, as they combine both events in one question, clearly they are distinct.

To distinguish where Jesus ceased talking about one and began talking about the other is a difficulty for the interpreter of this passage. It seems there is a combination of statements about the immediate and the long term future, with some detail applying to the destruction of Jerusalem, some to the second coming of Christ and some to both. The earlier judgement on Jerusalem being a foreshadowing and type of the final judgement to come.

Many Old Testament prophesies fit this pattern of an immediate sign foreshadowing a long term event. For example, Isaiah told King Ahaz of a sign God would give him, to reassure him that the king of Aram would not conquer Judah, 'The virgin will be with child and will give birth to a son and will call him Immanuel' (Isa. 7:14). This was immediately fulfilled in the birth of Maher-Shalal-Hash-Baz, born to King Ahaz and his wife, but is quoted again in Matthew 1:23 as a prophetic announcement of the birth of Christ. There were some details of that prophecy that applied to the birth of Ahaz's son, some details that applied to the birth of Christ, and some details that overlapped them both. With the benefit of hindsight it is quite easy to see which fits what, but it is not always easy in prospect. As the second coming of Christ has not yet taken place, determining how this chapter gives insights into that, rather than depicting some of the horrific details that surrounded the destruction of Jerusalem, is not as easy as dealing with fulfilled prophecy. Some see a telescoping of far and near events into one picture, so that 'the widely separated mountain peaks of historic events merge and are seen as one'[1], and this may well be so.

Despite the many and varied ways the text has been understood, I would suggest a division of this passage as follows. Firstly, after a description of the setting and the asking of the question (24:1-3) an overview of warnings is given that applies to both the destruction of Jerusalem and the end of the age (24:4-14). Then specific warnings are given about the destruction of Jerusalem. all of which are to take place in the lifetime of the generation of those to whom Jesus spoke (24:15-35), followed by statements about the uncertainty of the timing of Christ's coming (24:36-51), and parables about aspects of judgement at his coming (25:1-46).

1. The setting and the question (24:1-3)

Jesus has left the temple area where he brought the terrible denouncement of woes on the Pharisees and Scribes, when his disciples called his attention to its buildings. This may seem a strangely mundane thing to talk about after such a devastating series of pronouncements. But to assume that would be to miss the final words of that denunciation which include, 'Look, your house is left to you desolate' (23:38). The temple which to all appearance was still functioning, going through its rites and rituals, having its priests on duty to fulfil their various obligations, is actually devoid of any true spiritual content. Not only are the religious leaders of the nation spiritually bankrupt, which was the subject of his denunciations, but the temple, designed as God's dwelling place amongst his people, is spiritually desolate. They have detached the rituals from the realities they were designed to represent, making the rituals an end in themselves, and they have concerned themselves only with a whitewashed appearance that hid the corruption of the inside (23:27). This house then, says Jesus, is 'desolate'.

As they leave the area, the disciples call his attention to the building. Why would they do that? Quite possibly to point out the magnificence of the building, its grandeur, its large stones, its marvellous masonry, its beauty and artistry, as an astonished response to Jesus' description of it as 'desolate'. The temple was the glory of Jerusalem! Jesus' reply to this was, 'Do you see all these things? I tell you the truth not one stone here will be left on another, every one will be thrown down.' It may be a wonderful building, but when it ceases to fulfil the purpose

---

[1] See William Hendriksen, *The Gospel of Matthew*, p. 846.

for which God brought it into being, it is fit only for destruction. What God ordains and blesses as an expression of his purpose becomes redundant when it becomes a substitute for his purpose. This was now the state and predicament of the temple in Jerusalem.

This statement and its implications seemed to have stunned the disciples into silence. This conversation took place as they left the temple area. They then walked down the valley towards the Kidron brook, crossed over and climbed the Mount of Olives on the other side. As Jesus was sitting on the Mount of Olives the disciples came to him privately. Clearly they are troubled by his statement, and they ask him, 'Tell us when this will happen, and what will be the sign of your coming and of the end of the age.' As earlier discussed, they seem to equate the destruction of Jerusalem and the end of the age as one event, and Jesus answers their question without any distinction between the two.

2. An overview of warnings (24:4-14)

This section presents warnings about interpreting 'signs' of future events, particularly about the danger of deception, 'Watch out that no one deceives you'. He then specifies some areas of deception. Firstly, there will be false Christs, people claiming special significance and revelation from God. The focus of such people is invariably themselves, 'I am the Christ'. Apart from Jesus Christ himself, no messenger of God is indispensable to his message. A mark of the genuine servant of God is that he draws people to God and is able to withdraw from the scene without any loss to the impact of his message, but not so the false messenger. The false messenger draws people to himself and builds his own constituency, so that if he withdraws, his message collapses. There have always been, and will continue to be, those whose message depends on some special attribute in themselves or some special revelation they claim to have received from God, but it is those very distinctives that render them false.

Secondly, there will be false exaggeration of events: 'You will hear of wars and rumours of wars, but see to it that you are not alarmed. Such things must happen, but the end is still to come.' Some will distort the significance of great national and international events and place them in an end-time calendar to indicate the imminence of the end of the age. There are events, says Jesus, that will characterise the age before the coming of Christ but they are not evidences of his near return. There will be international conflicts, wars, rumours of wars, famines and earthquakes, persecution of believers by all nations, apostasy as many turn from the faith and betray and hate one other, false prophets will arise and deceive many, there will be an increase in wickedness, some will fall away because their love will grow cold, yet through it all the gospel will be preached to all nations. However, none of this has to do with the end of the age! When these things happen, 'see to it that you are not alarmed' (24:6), for these features will characterise the whole age prior to the end, and are not countdown markers to enable us, if we read them correctly, to have clues as to the timing of the coming of Christ! Later in the passage Jesus contradicts any idea we can work out the timing of the second coming by stating, 'the Son of Man will come at an hour when you do not expect him' (24:44). The events he has listed are the normal ingredients of the age between the first and second comings of Christ. Every century has known turmoil and conflict, earthquakes, famines, and the persecution of believers, but to attach significance to them in relation to the Lord's return is to set decoys that will deceive people.

In spite of this specific warning by Jesus there are some Christians who make their living by specialising in reading the 'signs of the times'. They delight to amaze their fellow believers by their ability to put the latest international conflict, political upheaval, famine or earthquake into some prophetic scheme and calendar that indicates the imminence of Christ's return. Jesus specifically warns us against such people, for they only deceive us! Regarding the unfolding of these events he says, 'see to it that you are not alarmed' (24:6), for they are only 'the beginning of birth pangs' (24.8). These are not evidences of the end, they are the normal features of the age.

3. Specific warnings concerning the destruction of Jerusalem (24:15-35)

There is, however, something specific which the disciples are to anticipate, described by Jesus as 'the abomination that causes desolation', spoken of by Daniel (24:15) which will precede the destruction of Jerusalem and become the cue for the people of Judea to 'flee to the mountains'. Daniel's statement where he speaks of 'the abomination that causes desolation' (see Dan. 11:31 and 12:11) was evidently pointing to the erection of an idolatrous altar in the Jerusalem temple by Antiochus Epiphanes in the second century before Christ on which he offered swine in sacrifice when he determined to replace Judaism with pagan worship. History, says Jesus, will repeat itself again in another 'abomination that causes desolation', this time to be witnessed by the disciples who will in their own lifetime see it take place. In the previous instance the temple had been liberated by the Maccabeans, but the next desecration of the temple will mark its destruction. It was in the year 70 AD that the Romans erected their standards in the temple in Jerusalem, prior to its actual destruction. This was regarded by the Jews as an act of idolatry, and is most likely the event to which Jesus is referring.

When this event takes place, then those in Judea are to flee to the mountains, anyone on the roof of his house is not to go down to rescue things from the house, no one has time to go back to the field to get his cloak. It will be a dreadful time for pregnant women and nursing mothers, for there will be distress unequalled from the beginning of the world. This graphically describes the terrible time that surrounded the destruction of Jerusalem. The end of Jerusalem and its temple began when the Roman governor of Judea, Gessius Florus, seized money from the temple in 66 AD. This provoked an uproar amongst the Jews, which in turn provoked the governor to send troops into the city, massacring 3,600 of its inhabitants. This again provoked a massive revolt by the Jews against Rome. The Emperor Nero sent a general, Vespasian, to quell the uprising, but Nero died whilst he was away and Vespasian was recalled to Rome to become the new emperor. He appointed his son Titus to fight the Jewish war, who surrounded Jerusalem with his army, cut off the city from any outside communication, and caused mass starvation. The historian Josephus tells us how the famine devoured whole families, with roads full of the dead bodies of men, women and children. Young men wandered around like shadows waiting to fall down dead. There was no mourning and few tears, for the famine dulled all natural passions. Those who were going to die looked upon those who had gone before with dry eyes and open mouths. A deep silence had gripped the city and as Josephus recorded, 'Every one of them died with their eyes fixed upon the temple'. Some turned to cannibalism and ate their own children. The horror was made worse by people flocking into the city for refuge rather than fleeing to the mountains, and in all more than one million people died. Less than ten percent survived to be taken captive and enslaved. Four years after the uprising had begun, the city and temple were destroyed.

Many had fled Jerusalem and Judea to Masada, a fortress on a hunk of rock overlooking the Dead Sea. Herod had built a virtually impregnable fortress there, but led by Zealots some Jews attacked and amazingly captured Masada, slaughtering the Roman army there. Before the Romans could retake the fortress, a mass suicide by the Jews took place to avoid defeat by Romans. These events marked the end of the Jewish state until almost nineteen hundred years later it was reborn in 1946.

Meanwhile the Christians had been themselves driven out of Jerusalem by earlier persecution from the Jews, and a few who had remained fled across the Jordan to Pella during the siege of the city. The Christian Jews were therefore not directly involved in the revolt against Rome which began in 66 AD, and this lack of patriotism marked the rejection of Christians by the Jews and a complete separation of Christianity from Judaism. Throughout the Roman world Christians were barred ever again from participation in the synagogues.

At that time, Jesus forewarned them, there will be many false alerts. There will be those who say, 'Look, here is the Christ' or 'There he is', and false Christs and false prophets will appear. Some will say Christ is out in the desert, others that he is in the inner rooms, but these will all be false. Such will be the distress of those days that 'the sun will be darkened, and the moon will not give its light; the stars will fall from the sky, and the heavenly bodies will be shaken' (24:29). This poetic language describes the desolation of those days (see Isa. 13:10; 34:4). Where then is Christ in all of this? The heightened rumours of his presence in the desert and other places indicate the expectancy of the people that he will be present with them at such a time, yet all these rumours will be false.

Then suddenly 'At that time the sign of the Son of Man will appear in the sky, and all the nations of the earth will mourn. They will see the Son of Man coming on the clouds of the sky, with power and great glory. And he will send his angels with a loud trumpet call, and they will gather his elect from the four winds, from one end of the heavens to the other' (24:30-31). This is not speaking of the second coming of Christ for which we still wait, for Jesus said, 'I tell you the truth, this generation will certainly not pass away until all these things have happened' (24:34). This was in the lifetime of the generation of these disciples. The word translated 'angels' means 'messengers' whose trumpet call may well be the preaching of the gospel, which will gather the elect from the corners of the world. It is true there may be a telescoping of far and near events into one picture, as earlier discussed, so that what is immediately true may also be subsequently true, but in the first instance this speaks of a climax surrounding the destruction of Jerusalem. A literal 'coming on the clouds' may yet take place, but this image portrays a victory of the Lord Jesus Christ in vindication and authority. R. T. France quotes G. B. Caird as saying, 'The coming of the Son of Man in the clouds of heaven was never conceived as a primitive form of space travel, but as a symbol for a mighty reversal of fortunes within history and at the national level'.[2] The destruction of Jerusalem involved a divine judgement on the people, but when things seemed at their blackest, it was time to look over the rubble and the corpses of the devastated city where all seems lost and 'the vultures will gather' (24:28), to look up and see the sign of the Son of Man, in glory and power gathering his elect from the four winds. He is not confined to the well being of Jerusalem, or the temple or Israel, but reigns supreme over it all and is still in business gathering his elect from every corner of the earth.

'Learn the lesson of the fig tree,' Jesus tells his disciples (24:32). 'As soon as its twigs get tender and its leaves come out, you know that summer is near.' These events that Jesus has been describing mark the beginning of a new era. The presence and revelation of God is not now to be found in the temple or the city of Jerusalem. These have been the leaves that announce the coming of summer, but the fruit is to be found in the era of God dwelling by his Holy Spirit in the church. Could this reference to the fig tree be related to the incident earlier in that same week when Jesus saw a fig tree by the road that had nothing except leaves. He said to it, 'May you never bear fruit again' and immediately the fig tree withered (see 21:18-19). The tree that only bore leaves has been cursed, Jerusalem has been destroyed. It is not to Israel we look any longer for the knowledge of God. A new era has opened, and above the rubble of Jerusalem (the cursed fig tree?) is the pre-eminent Christ, 'with power and great glory'.

In an earlier passage after Jesus had spoken for the first time about the church he would build, against which the gates of Hades would not overcome, he said, 'I tell you the truth, some who are standing here will not taste death before they see the Son of Man coming in his kingdom'

---

[2] R. T. France, *Matthew*, Tyndale New Testament Commentaries, p. 344.

(16:28), not referring to his second coming, for he explicitly stated it to be in the lifetime of his disciples. He was referring to Pentecost when he established his kingdom in the hearts of his people. This here too is the glory that came out of the rubble of devastated Jerusalem.

34.

The end of the age
(24:36–25:46)

The latter section of Chapter 24 continues to refer back to earlier themes in the chapter, concerning the destruction of Jerusalem, whilst at the same time projecting forward to the second coming of Christ, an event to which the three parables that follow in Chapter 25 clearly refer. If the earlier passage does telescope far and near events into one picture, there are both distinctives and similarities in the two events. The 'coming of the Son of Man' is a term used earlier in relation to events following the destruction of Jerusalem where Christ is vindicated above the rubble and chaos, but it is also used later of his return to earth.

1. The uncertainty of the timing of Christ's second coming (24:36-51)

The main distinctives between the two events are that the destruction of Jerusalem was a predictable event by those able and willing to read the signs. This was the lesson of the fig tree, 'As soon as its twigs get tender and its leaves come out, you know that summer is near.' In reading the events as they unfolded they were to 'flee to the mountains' and would have sufficient warning to do so. However, the emphasis of the section regarding the second coming of Christ is the opposite, 'No one knows about the day or hour, not even the angels in heaven, nor the Son, but only the Father' (24:36). He also says, 'Keep watch, because you do not know on what day your Lord will come' (24:42), and 'You also must be ready, because the Son of Man will come at an hour when you do not expect him' (24:44), and 'Keep watch, because you do not know the day or the hour' (25:13). This message is fairly clear: The second coming of Christ is not something we may work out and pinpoint! It is of course quite exciting to try and do that, and there is a subculture in Christendom devoted to doing so. Few will try to pinpoint a date (though some have been foolish enough to do so), but it is inevitably presented as just around the corner, with 'signs' to prove it! What we do know is that Christ is coming back. His return will be the climax of history and is the certain goal to which we are heading. What we do not know is when it will be.

The emphasis of this passage is on being prepared and ready for his coming. As in the days of Noah, said Jesus, people carried on with normal life, eating, drinking and marrying, when suddenly the flood came. There was nothing wrong with their eating, drinking and marrying, but in their preoccupation with legitimate interests they had failed to prepare themselves for the flood that was to come, despite the warnings given them by Noah. In their unpreparedness, they were swept away and lost. When the Lord comes, two men will be working in a field completely unaware of what is about to happen. One will be taken and the other left. Two women will be grinding with a hand mill, one will be taken and the other left. Like a thief who comes unexpectedly, without having made an appointment or given clues as to when he might raid, so will the coming of Christ be. We are to live as though he may come at any moment, to 'be ready' and to 'keep watch'. The servant the master trusts is the one who works in the master's absence so that when the master returns unexpectedly he finds him doing what he is supposed to be doing. But if the master returns and finds the servant eating, drinking and mistreating his fellow servants, then he will receive the deserved wrath of his master.

Jesus then illustrates the readiness he requires, in a series of three parables. The parable of the ten virgins (25:1-13), the parable of the talents (25:14-30) and the story of the separation of the sheep and the goats (25:31-46). These three parables are all to do with preparedness for the return of Christ. The stories themselves each feature an absent key figure. In the first it is the bridegroom who is yet to arrive, in the second a master who has gone away on a long journey, and in the third, the king himself is yet to return to separate the sheep from the goats. In each story, once the key figure has returned, there is a division between those who are right and those who are wrong, and for those who are wrong it is too late to make amends, and excuses are unacceptable.

2. The parable of the ten virgins (25:1-13)

This parable describes what will happen at the coming of the Son of Man, emphasising the need to be ready and to be alert. There has already been the distinction made between the 'ready' and the 'unready' (24:42ff), and now the distinction is made between the 'wise' and the 'foolish'. There are ten bridesmaids (the meaning of 'virgin' in this context is unmarried girls attending to a bride) who were awaiting the arrival of the bridegroom for his wedding. The five foolish girls did not take any oil for their lamps, the five wise did so. The bridegroom was a long time coming and they all became drowsy and fell asleep. At midnight the cry rang out, 'Here's the bridegroom! Come out to meet him.' The bridesmaids awoke and trimmed their lamps. The foolish who had no oil asked the wise for some of their oil, but there was not enough to share. The five foolish bridesmaids went hurriedly to buy oil for themselves, but while they were on their way the bridegroom arrived. The wise bridesmaids who were prepared, joined him and entered in with him to the wedding banquet, where the door was shut behind them. When the five foolish girls arrived, despite their cry for the door to be opened, they were refused entry. They were too late.

The main point of the parable is obvious and simple. We need to be ready for the arrival of the Lord Jesus Christ, for to attempt to get ready after his arrival will be too late. The bridegroom is the Lord Jesus Christ (cf. 9:15 where Jesus also describes himself as the bridegroom, on that occasion as the one who will be taken from them). The bride is not mentioned in the story, and although elsewhere the New Testament speaks of the marriage of Christ to his bride, the church (Eph. 5:25-27, Rev. 19:7), the point of the story is not taken up with the bridegroom and bride as with the condition of the ten virgins.

There is no advance warning given as to the exact time the bridegroom would arrive. This was apparently true to the marriage customs of the day. A wedding would take place when the bridegroom arrived and he would arrive at the moment of his own choosing. It could be any time over certain days or even weeks, and during that time the bridal party would have to be perpetually ready for his arrival at any time. According to William Barclay, one of the great things to do in a middle-class wedding was for the bridegroom to try and catch the bridal party napping. Sometimes he might even come in the middle of the night, as in Jesus' story, and the bridal party had a lookout who would announce, 'The bridegroom is coming', as soon as he was known to be on his way. Then the bridal party would meet him on the street.

The lesson from the foolish bridesmaids is that there are some things that cannot be left to the last minute, and there are some responsibilities that cannot be transferred to others. Certain things have to be our own! There is a time coming when getting ready will no longer be an option. It will be too late. We must be careful of pressing each point of the story beyond its intention, but frequently in Scripture oil is a symbol of the Holy Spirit. Certainly that is the relevant point to our preparedness for the coming of the Lord Jesus, for it is the indwelling of the Holy Spirit that makes us ready to meet Christ (see Rom. 8:9b). The five foolish girls were foolish solely on account of their unpreparedness to meet the bridegroom, nothing more than their lack of oil, and the five wise were wise on account of their preparedness.

The response of the bridegroom to the knocking on the door by the five girls locked outside is a decisive rejection, 'I don't know you', reminiscent of Jesus' words to those who 'say Lord, Lord', but do not 'do the will of my Father who is in heaven', whom he dismissed with the words, 'I never knew you. Away from me, you evildoers' (7:21-23). The conclusion of this parable is a solemn warning to be ready and prepared, 'Therefore keep watch, because you do not know the day or the hour.' The climax of history will take place at the return of Jesus Christ, 'at an hour when you do not expect him' (24:44).

3. The parable of the talents (25:14-30)

The next parable concerns three servants entrusted with their master's property whilst he went on a long journey. To one he gave five talents, to another two and to another one. A talent was a unit of coinage. The responsibility of the servants was to ensure the master's money did not lie idle, but was productive and profitable, something to which they would be called to account on his return. In the previous parable the virgins are represented as *waiting for the Lord*, in this one the servants are *working for the Lord*. Both are responsibilities in the light of the return of Christ.

The main features of the story are, firstly, the master entrusts different amounts to his servants; secondly, they are to bring a return on what has been entrusted to them; thirdly, the master will return on an unspecified date; and fourthly, there will be a day of reckoning. The idea of being ready is the main theme of the passage as a whole, and this is the context in which this particular parable should be understood.

The men with five and two talents went to work at once and doubled the value of their share to ten and four talents respectively. The man with one talent, for fear that he might lose what he already has, hid the money in the ground. This was not necessarily unusual as a means of securing treasures (see 13:44), but it was not the means of expanding its value. Consequently it retained the same value and gained nothing new.

There are various obvious points to this story. God gives different gifts and functions to different people. The ratio of five, two and one does not indicate a different value on the person, but a different significance to their work. There are those entrusted with greater responsibility than others, but all are to fulfil their responsibility with equal integrity. On his return, the servants were called to present to their master the fruit of their work. The man with five talents produced five more and the man with two produced two more, and the same commendation is given to both. 'Well done, good and faithful servant. You have been faithful with a few things; I will put you in charge of many things. Come and share in your master's happiness.' The man who gained five was not commended above the man who gained two. The one with the greater resources was expected to produce greater results. The principle holds true that Jesus spoke elsewhere, 'From everyone who has been given much, much will be demanded; and from the one who has been entrusted with much, much more will be asked' (Luke 12:48). We are not to compete with one another but to fulfil the mandate received from God with the resources he has given to us.

However the third man had no gain to present to his master. 'Then the man who had received the one talent came. "Master," he said, "I knew that you are a hard man, harvesting where you have not sown and gathering where you have not scattered seed. So I was afraid and went out and hid your talent in the ground. See, here is what belongs to you." His master replied, "You wicked, lazy servant!... Take the talent from him and give it to the one who has the ten talents. For everyone who has will be given more, and he will have an abundance. Whoever does not have, even what he has will be taken from him.

And throw that worthless servant outside, into the darkness, where there will be weeping and gnashing of teeth'" (25:24-30). At the root of this man's failure to extend the value of his talent was fear. He did not know the character of his master, so did not trust the motives of his master, and out of fear of the unreasonable demands he thought were being made, hid his talent to avoid the hard work and risk of using it to create more. Most failure in the Christian life has at its root a false understanding of the character and purpose of God. If that can be distorted in our thinking, then our response to him, and our conduct arising from that response, will inevitably be distorted. The man of course was wrong in his assessment of his master. He was not harvesting where he had not sown! In entrusting the talents to the three servants he was sowing, with the expectation this would produce some return. It was in fact the man himself who had that expectation, because by hiding his talent in the ground, it could do him no good itself, so the only possibility of producing profit was by harvesting seed he had not sown. He was guilty of the very thing he wrongly feared in his master.

This man is described by his master as 'wicked ... worthless ... weeping'. He was *wicked* because he was lazy. He was unwilling to busy himself in his master's interests. He is *worthless* because he produced nothing. There was no gain to his activity and pursuits. He is described as *weeping* because he was cast out into the darkness. The talent that he should have shared the benefit of (the master had said to the other two servants, 'Come and share in your masters happiness') was now given to the servant who had ten so that he could use it to gain more.

This parable is not teaching that God is a demanding capitalist. As with all parables, there is one main truth being taught, and the surrounding details must not be stretched too far. (For an example of this, see Luke 18:1-8. There the story is of a reluctant judge who eventually gives in to a woman's persistent plea, illustrating the need to 'pray and not give up'. Although the judge represents God, he is described in the story as one who 'neither feared God nor cared about men'. The focus of the story is not the judge, it is the woman, and we do not learn anything about the character of God from the story). In this story the focus is not on the master, but on the servants. It is they who have to give an account to their master, as we will each have to give an account to our Master. Paul writes, 'So then, each of us will give an account of himself to God' (Rom. 14:12), and this is the challenge of the parable.

4. The sheep and the goats (25:31-46)

This is not strictly a parable. The coming of the Son of Man is not pictured parabolically, but stated explicitly, though the passage does contain parabolic elements. The Son of Man will come with his angels, and all the nations will be gathered before him. Then will come the dividing of sheep from goats. The sheep will be invited to 'take your inheritance, the kingdom prepared for you since the creation of the world'. The goats will be told, 'Depart from me, you who are cursed, into the eternal fire prepared for the devil and his angels.' The angels are given a role in this great judgement of the people of the earth. Earlier in his parable of the weeds amongst the wheat, Jesus had said, 'The Son of Man will send out his angels, and they will weed out of his kingdom everything that causes sin and all who do evil. They will throw them into the fiery furnace, where there will be weeping and gnashing of teeth. Then the righteous will shine like the sun in the kingdom of their Father' (13:41-43).

There is a judgement day coming, and judgement will be based on works, and in particular, works towards people. Good works are not the cause of salvation but they are the inevitable consequence. When a person is in a right relationship with God they will do good works, for this is the purpose of their salvation! It is that we might be restored to the quality of life for which God originally created man. Paul makes clear, 'For it is by grace you have been saved, through faith – and this not from yourselves, it is the gift of God – not by works, so that no-one can boast' (Eph. 2:8-9). About this we need not be in doubt, but Paul's statement does not end there. He continues, 'For we are God's workmanship, created in Christ Jesus to do good works, which God prepared in advance for us to do' (Eph. 2.10). We are created 'in Christ Jesus to do good works'. If the foundation of Christian experience is faith, and the fruit of Christian experience is good works, then it is the good works that provide evidence of the faith. If there are no works, there is no faith. James leaves us in no doubt about this: 'What good is it, my brothers, if a man claims to have faith but has no deeds? Can such faith save him? ... But someone will say, "You have faith; I have deeds." Show me your faith without deeds, and I will show you my faith by what I do.... You foolish man, do you want evidence that faith without deeds is useless?... As the body without the spirit is dead, so faith without deeds is dead' (Jas. 2:14, 18, 20, 26).

Judgement Day is not going to be a theological examination! Whether we have grasped the niceties of doctrinal detail will not be the issue. The issue is whether the character of Jesus Christ is evident in the way we live and conduct ourselves, particularly in relationship to those who are in trouble and less privileged than ourselves. To the sheep on his right whom he welcomes into his kingdom he says, 'For I was hungry and you gave me something to eat, I was thirsty and you gave me something to drink, I was a stranger and you invited me in, I needed clothes and you clothed me, I was sick and you looked after me, I was in prison and you came to visit me.' They did not know it was the Lord whom they cared for, and they did not do it for reward but because the love of God constrained them.

Conversely, he said to the goats on his left, 'Depart from me, you who are cursed, into the eternal fire prepared for the devil and his angels. For I was hungry and you gave me nothing to eat, I was thirsty and you gave me nothing to drink, I was a stranger and you did not invite me in, I needed clothes and you did not clothe me, I was sick and in prison and you did not look after me.' They responded, 'Lord, when did we see you hungry or thirsty or a stranger or needing clothes or sick or in prison, and did not help you?' In effect they are saying, 'If we knew it was you we would have given to you.' Of course they would. This is the nature of pseudo spirituality. We perform it if it is for the right people! This is the hypocrisy Jesus talked about in Matthew 6, that does things to be 'seen by men'. It is not the act itself which is of value so much as being seen to perform the act by the right people. If they could have performed before God they would have done so! The Day of Judgement before the King of all the earth will expose us for what we really are. The wicked 'will go away to eternal punishment, but the righteous to eternal life'. It should be noted that punishment is described in the same terms as life, for both are 'eternal'.

These are not a series of isolated stories, but progressively develop to teach events surrounding the second coming of the Lord Jesus Christ which Jesus has been talking about to his disciples. He is a bridegroom for whom we are to be prepared. He is a master to whom we must give an account. He is a king to whose judgement we must submit. In every case there is a division between the wise and foolish, the workers and the lazy, and the sheep and the goats.

35.

The arrest, trial and crucifixion of Christ
(chs. 26–27)

The arrest and crucifixion of Jesus happened very quickly. He had arrived with his disciples in Jerusalem on Sunday, to the applause of the crowds, and it was late Thursday night when he was arrested. Through that night he was tried six times. Firstly by Annas the retired high priest, secondly before the Jewish Sanhedrin, thirdly by Pilate, who sent him to Herod, the governor of Galilee who was visiting Jerusalem at the time, then back to Pilate who washed his hands of his responsibility, and finally he was given over to the crowd for the final verdict, 'Crucify him'.

If his arrest and crucifixion seemed sudden, the resentment by the religious leaders in particular had been building for a long time. In Matthew's record it began as far back as Chapter 9, where he was accused of the serious crime of blasphemy after he said to the paralytic, 'your sins are forgiven you', a prerogative they said, which belonged to God alone. In Chapter 12 he healed a man with a shrivelled hand on the Sabbath day, and 'the Pharisees went out and plotted how they might kill Jesus' (12:14). From then on they sent various delegations to Jesus to ply him with questions in attempts to test him and trick him into incriminating himself by advocating some violation of their law. After his triumphant arrival in Jerusalem in Chapter 21, such was his provocation that the priests and elders of the people gathered in the palace of the high priest and 'plotted to arrest Jesus in some sly way and kill him' (26.4). Their intention to arrest him in some 'sly way' is evidence they knew they had no legitimate case against him, and therefore to put a sufficient case against him to warrant his death would necessarily involve resorting to deceit and trickery.

In addition to the build-up of opposition against him, ever since he had been with his disciples in Caesarea Philippi, Jesus himself had forewarned that 'he must go to Jerusalem and suffer many things at the hands of the elders, chief priests and teachers of the law and that he must be killed and on the third day raised to life' (16:21). Not only was his death fully anticipated, but the role of the 'chief priests and teachers of the law' as the means by which it would be brought about were equally clear.

The group that met at the palace of Caiaphas, the High Priest, to plot his arrest was the Sanhedrin Council, comprising seventy two Jewish leaders, the highest Jewish body allowed to exist by the Romans. This council had powers to exercise both civil and criminal jurisdiction, though it could not administer capital punishment. Only the Roman authority could do that, though in the interests of good relationships, the Roman governor normally acted in harmony with the recommendations of the Jewish Sanhedrin. The only ground on which the Sanhedrin could administer the death penalty was in violation of the sacredness of the temple (something they tried to bring against Jesus – see 26:61, and successfully did against Stephen – see Acts 7:54ff, though the stoning of Stephen has elements of mob rule rather than a proper legal death sentence).

The previous twenty four hours

The last twenty four hour period before Jesus' arrest begins in Bethany. The plot to kill him was implemented two days before the Passover (26:1-5) and has a hastiness about it as they do not want it to take place during the feast itself. It will take them a little over thirty six hours to accomplish their deed. Meanwhile Jesus is in Bethany, and is anointed by a woman with an alabaster jar of very expensive perfume which she poured on his head at the home of Simon the leper (26:6-13), something Jesus declares to be 'a beautiful thing... she did this to prepare me for my burial'. Nothing in the following events was to take Jesus by surprise. Even this act of generous worship was in anticipation of his burial.

Judas Iscariot went to the chief priests and asked what they would be willing to pay him to hand Jesus over. They gave him thirty silver coins. It is hard to understand the mind of Judas at this stage. He had given no outward evidence that he might do this. Artists usually portray Judas as looking mean and untrustworthy, but it is extremely doubtful that is true to the facts. Why would he be appointed the treasurer of the twelve if they were suspicious of his trustworthiness? When Jesus told his disciples at the Last Supper that 'one of you will betray me' (26:21) they didn't all turn and look at Judas as the obvious candidate for such a deed! He had evidently learned to cover his heart well.

The Last Supper took place at the home of a friend (26:17-30). It was there that Jesus told them about his impending betrayal. In the midst of the meal, after the departure of Judas, he took bread and wine, and passed it to the remaining disciples as a symbol of his body and the new covenant which will be inaugurated by his blood.

From there they went to the Mount of Olives where Jesus told them that not only had Judas betrayed him, but they would all fall away from him. Peter was indignant, protesting his willingness to even die with Jesus if necessary, but he would never disown him. All the others said the same about themselves!

On the side of the Mount of Olives they came to the Garden of Gethsemane. Taking Peter, James and John with him, he began to be 'sorrowful and troubled'. The awful event of the next day preoccupied him. It was not only the anguish of physical death but the much more significant and painful transaction of '... him who had no sin to be sin ...' (2 Cor. 5:21), that brought him to say, 'My soul is overwhelmed with sorrow to the point of death'. Leaving the three disciples, he went a little further and prayed three times, 'My Father, if it is possible, may this cup be taken from me. Yet not as I will, but as you will.' Jesus went willingly to the cross, but he did not waltz to the cross, he went in great anguish and sorrow. He died in the first instance for his Father, '... not as I will, but as you will'.

Whilst in the Garden, Judas came with a large crowd armed with swords and clubs, sent by the Sanhedrin Council. Judas arranged a signal with them, that the man he would kiss was the man they should arrest. He greeted Jesus, 'Greetings Rabbi', kissed him and he was arrested. Peter jumped to his defence, drew his sword and cut off the ear of the high priest's servant. Jesus rebuked him, assured him he had twelve legions of angels at his disposal should he call on them to defend him, then announced to the crowd that 'all this has taken place that the writings of the prophets might be fulfilled' (26:56). At this point, his disciples deserted him and fled.

The trial

There were various stages of the trial of Jesus which we will put together in their chronological order. Matthew's Gospel does not record them all, but for the sake of a comprehensive picture we will also refer to details given in the other three Gospels too.

1. Before Annas (John 18:12-24)

The first movement after the arrest of Jesus is not recorded by Matthew. John reports, 'Then the detachment of soldiers with its commander and the Jewish officials arrested Jesus. They bound him and brought him first to Annas, who was the father-in-law of Caiaphas, the high priest that year.' Annas had himself been high priest from the years AD 6–15,[1] so although out of office for some years at this point, is still actually referred to as high priest, at the time John the Baptist commenced his ministry (Luke 3:2) and at the time the Sanhedrin Council met in Jerusalem to discuss the fate of Peter and John following the dramatic healing of the crippled man at the temple (Acts 4:6). The Romans appointed and disposed of high priests as they considered appropriate, and although Caiaphas, son-in-law of Annas, was currently high priest, the Jews themselves regarded the office as for life, so granted Annas all the dignity and courtesies that pertain to the office. To bring Jesus before Annas seems a gesture of goodwill towards him.

Annas questioned Jesus about his disciples and about his teaching. Jesus responded by saying, 'I have spoken openly to the world. I always taught in synagogues or at the temple, where all the Jews come together. I said nothing in secret. Why question me? Ask those who heard me. Surely they know what I said.' Jesus had earlier taught, 'If I testify about myself, my testimony is not valid' (John 5:31). It was the testimony of others that would bear witness to his life and work. There was nothing secret or subversive that required some special initiation to understand, and absolutely nothing to hide. One of the officials struck Jesus in the face, 'Is this the way you answer the high priest?' he demanded. Jesus responded, 'If I said something wrong, testify as to what is wrong. But if I spoke the truth, why did you strike me?' At this, Annas sent him, still bound, to Caiaphas the current high priest.

---

[1] See *New Bible Dictionary* article, Annas. IV.

2. Before Caiaphas and the Sanhedrin Council (26:57–27:2)

Matthew's record omits the visit to Annas and takes him straight to Caiaphas and the Sanhedrin Council. The Sanhedrin was the highest Jewish court. There is some ambiguity about the composition and authority of the Sanhedrin, but it was presided over by the high priest and comprised seventy-one representatives of the elders, drawn from Jerusalem and the immediate surrounding area, including members of the Sadducees, Pharisees, Scribes as well as the lay aristocracy. A quorum was twenty three. The Sanhedrin Council was not allowed to sentence a person to death, that was the prerogative of the governor. The main business of the Sanhedrin therefore was to formulate a charge against Jesus that would have sufficient credibility to constrain Pilate to exercise that option. They know however, that their evidence is weak to non-existent, so 'were looking for false evidence against Jesus so that they could put him to death. But they did not find any, though many false witnesses came forward'. The Sanhedrin had already decided Jesus should die (see John 11:47-53), where they believed the activities of Jesus would put the Roman authorities against the whole nation, and Caiaphas had said 'It is better for you that one man die for the people than that the whole nation perish' (thereby unwittingly speaking accurately of Jesus dying 'for the people', a point John mentions later in his gospel – see John 18:14). This reasoning was likely a red herring, for on a number of other occasions they discussed his death on the grounds of their opposition to his teaching.

Despite many false ideas that were presented to help build a case against Jesus, nothing was valid until finally 'two came forward and declared, "This fellow said, 'I am able to destroy the temple of God and rebuild it in three days'".' This was a serious charge, though there was some substance to it. Jesus had earlier said, 'Destroy this temple, and I will raise it again in three days' (John 2:19), in which he was speaking of the death and resurrection of his own body. However, now that this threat could be attributed to him, the Sanhedrin Council had something they could work on. It was a charge much deeper than a threatened act of terrorism, for the temple in Jerusalem was the most holy site in Israel and to threaten it was the highest affront to God and the Jewish people (a similar charge was brought against Stephen, Acts 6:14).

Caiaphas asked Jesus to answer this charge, but he remained

silent. The high priest then said to him, 'I charge you under oath by the living God: Tell us if you are the Christ, the Son of God', to which Jesus replied, 'Yes, it is as you say. I say to all of you: In the future you will see the Son of Man sitting at the right hand of the Mighty One and coming on the clouds of heaven.' At that point the high priest tore his clothes and said, 'He has spoken blasphemy! Why do we need any more witnesses? Look, now you have heard the blasphemy', to which the Council responded, 'He is worthy of death.'

There are now two clear charges. One of threatening to destroy the temple, the other of blasphemy. By early morning, they had agreed they had sufficient grounds to ask for his sentence of death from Pilate the governor.

The interlude of Peter's denial and Judas' suicide (26:69–27:10)

While this is going on, the disciples are in disarray. Peter, despite his avowal, 'Even if I have to die with you I will never disown you' (26:35) has denied Jesus three times, firstly to a servant girl, then to another girl and finally to a group of people standing around who recognised his Galilean accent. To the latter group he 'began to call down curses on himself and he swore to them, "I don't know the man." ' Matthew dramatically writes, 'Immediately a rooster crowed.' Peter remembered that Jesus had told him, despite his promise to never leave him, he would not only leave, but disown and deny him three times before the rooster crowed to welcome the dawn of the new day, only hours away. Peter, remembering these words, 'went outside and wept bitterly'.

Meanwhile, Judas who had betrayed him earlier, seeing that Jesus had been condemned, was filled with remorse, returned the thirty pieces of silver he had been paid by the elders, went out and hanged himself. He died early on the same day Jesus was crucified. His money was used to buy a burial ground for strangers, fulfilling a prophecy of Jeremiah some six hundred years before.

3. First time before Pilate (27:2, 11-14)

Jesus is brought before Pilate for the first of two meetings. The governor asked him, 'Are you the king of the Jews?'. This is an entirely different question to any of the issues discussed by the Sanhedrin. The charges of blasphemy and a threat to the temple may have satisfied the Sanhedrin and their Jewish constituency as suitable grounds for the death sentence, but would be of little interest to the Roman governor. This was a domestic Jewish issue, not one that concerned Imperial Rome!

However, having satisfied themselves they also needed to satisfy the Roman governor, and so the charges are changed. Luke gives four specific accusations they brought to Pilate. (1) 'We have found this man subverting our nation'; (2) 'He opposes payment of taxes to Caesar'; (3) 'He claims to be Christ, a king'; and finally, (4) 'He stirs up people all over Judea' (Luke 23:1-5). All of these charges included threats against the rule of Rome in Judea.

Pilate questioned Jesus about these issues, and despite Jesus affirming that he was the King of the Jews, Pilate did not take them seriously and concluded, 'I find no basis for a charge against this man' (Luke 23:4). Pilate was a shrewd man, and had read correctly the motivation of the Sanhedrin and the true state of affairs, 'For he knew it was out of envy that they had handed Jesus over to him' (27:18).

Luke records that when told Jesus was a Galilean, and therefore not directly under the jurisdiction of the governor of Judea, Pilate sent him to Herod, king of Galilee, who happened to be in Jerusalem at the time, and whose jurisdiction he rightly came under. Pilate's weakness becomes evident for the first time here. Rather than act honourably, dismiss Jesus and reprimand the Sanhedrin, he hoped Herod would take responsibility for the case and thus release himself from a decision, which, if just would offend the Jews by releasing him, and if not, deprive an innocent man of his rights.

4. Before Herod (Luke 23:6-12)

King Herod had for a long time wanted to meet Jesus, hoping he might witness a miracle, and welcomed the opportunity to ply him with many questions, to which Jesus gave no answer. The chief priests and scribes stood by vehemently accusing him, but all to no avail. Finally, Herod and his soldiers dressed him in an elegant role, ridiculed and mocked him and sent him back to Pilate. The event brought about a reconciliation between Pilate and Herod, and that day they became friends.

5. Second time before Pilate, and the crowd demands his crucifixion (27:15-26)

On the return of the prisoner, Pilate, knowing Jesus was innocent, saw an opportunity of releasing him. It was the governor's custom at the Jewish Feast of Passover to release a prisoner, chosen by the crowd.

There were, including Jesus, four prisoners awaiting crucifixion. He decided to select two, and give the choice of the release of one of these two to the crowd. He chose the worst, Barabbas, and he chose the best, Christ.

Barabbas was 'a notorious prisoner' (27:16); he 'had committed murder' (Mark 15:7); he had taken part in insurrection in Jerusalem (Luke 23:19; John 18:40). His name, his crimes and his reputation were well known in the city. Pilate offered the release of this man to the crowd.

Alternatively they could have Jesus released. He too was well known, but not for his crimes. He was known for his kindness, his miracles and his teaching. Pilate offered the choice of the release of this man to the crowd too. During these deliberations Pilate's wife sent him the message, 'Don't have anything to do with that innocent man, for I have suffered a great deal today in a dream because of him.' This seemingly only confirmed Pilate's suspicions, but to give the responsibility of releasing Jesus to the crowd seemed an easy way out of the dilemma.

As he offered the alternatives, it was obvious to Pilate whom the crowd would choose. They would choose the release of Christ. To his amazement, when he asked, 'Which one do you want me to release to you: Barabbas, or Jesus who is called Christ?', the crowd asked for the release of Barabbas and the execution of Jesus. Pilate then questioned, 'Why? What crime has he committed?' Pilate is now acting as Jesus' advocate, defending his case to the crowd and advocating by his questions that they release Jesus. He called together the Sanhedrin and said, 'I have examined him in your presence and have found no basis for your charges against him ... he has done nothing to deserve death. Therefore I will punish him and then release him' (Luke 23:14-16). But it is to no avail. 'With one voice they cried out, "Away with this man! Release Barabbas to us."' Pilate's tactic has backfired. 'Wanting to release Jesus, Pilate appealed to them again. But they kept shouting, "Crucify him! Crucify him!"' (Luke 23:20-21). For a third time he appealed, claiming there was no fault in him but offering to punish him and then release him if that would satisfy the crowd, but to no avail.

Rather than be man enough to take responsibility for events, Pilate washed his hands of all responsibility in front of the crowd telling them, 'I am innocent of this man's blood. It is your responsibility.'

Then he released Barabbas, had Jesus flogged and handed him over to the soldiers for crucifixion.

6. Handed over to the soldiers to crucify (27:27-32)

The soldiers' treatment was barbaric. These were not Roman legionaries, but relatively local Gentile conscripts, probably recruited from surrounding areas as personal soldiers of the governor, based with him at his headquarters in Caesarea, and numbering six hundred in total. They would have no love for the Jews and would welcome the opportunity this provided for them to have a 'king of the Jews' at their mercy. They flogged him with a leather whip with pieces of bone and metal balls at various intervals that 'reduced the naked body to strips of raw flesh, and inflamed and bleeding weals'.[2] Jewish law limited the number of lashes to thirty nine, but it is not known if the Romans would adhere to this in the case of a Jewish victim. The purpose of this was to weaken the victim to a state just short of collapse or death. Some men would die as a result of the flogging, and many lost consciousness. The soldiers then stripped Jesus of his clothing and put a scarlet robe on him, they twisted together a crown of thorns and set it on his head, they spat in his face and struck him on the head again and again, mocking him as they did so, saying, 'Hail king of the Jews.'

They took off his purple robe and dressed him in his own clothes before leading him away for crucifixion. He began the journey carrying his own cross, but with the preceding treatment and the lack of any sleep the previous night, he was exhausted and weak. The weight of the cross was probably well over 300 lbs (136 kg). Roman soldiers had the right to force a non Roman to engage in any task they wanted done, and at this point they forced Simon from Cyrene to carry the cross for Jesus.

It is interesting that Mark tells us Simon was 'the father of Alexander and Rufus' (Mark 15:21), indicating these two brothers were well known to the church in Rome to whom he wrote his gospel. Paul in his own letter to the Romans says, 'Greet Rufus, chosen in the Lord, and his mother, who has been a mother to me, too' (Rom. 16:13). If this is the same Rufus, then his mother (i.e. the wife of Simon of Cyrene) had been something of a 'mother' to Paul, no doubt back

---

[2] See William Barclay, *The Gospel Of Matthew*, Vol. 2, p. 400.

in Jerusalem. Perhaps this event whereby Simon was requisitioned to carry the cross of Jesus was the means of God capturing his heart, resulting in him becoming a disciple, and his wife and sons not only becoming Christian, but actively useful in the purposes of God.

With Simon carrying the cross, they came to Golgotha, the place of a skull, outside the wall of the city, and there they crucified him.

7. The crucifixion (27:33-56)

Jesus was crucified at nine in the morning (see Mark 15:25, 'the third hour'), between two thieves, and it took him six hours to die. During the first three hours he was offered wine mixed with gall that would serve to some extent as an anaesthetic but he refused. His clothes were divided up amongst the soldiers by casting lots. Passers-by hurled insults at him, and members of the Sanhedrin made their way to the cross to mock him for his seeming impotence. The robbers at either side joined in the insults.

At mid-day, darkness came over the land for three hours, and at three o'clock in the afternoon he called out, 'My God, my God, why have you forsaken me?', and soon afterwards, uttering another cry, he bowed his head and died.

Crucifixion is a particularly terrible way to die. Invented by the Phoenicians, it was later adopted by the Romans as their means of putting to death slaves, provincials and the lowest types of criminals, though very rarely Roman citizens. The victim would die of exhaustion. Sometimes ropes, though in the case of Jesus, nails, secured the victim in place. The nails into Jesus' wrists and feet would be careful to avoid any major artery as that would speed up the process of dying and the whole point of crucifixion was its lingering, painful, slow process.

The weight of the victim's body would stretch him and in order to breathe, he would lift his body upwards by pushing up on his feet and pulling up with his arms. This would enable his lungs to expand sufficiently to inhale and then exhale. Each attempt to breathe would be painful and eventually as strength diminished the victim would die of asphyxia. He would simply be unable to breathe. A strong man could remain alive on a cross for several days, and to speed up the process the victims' legs would be broken, thus preventing them pushing up on their feet and speeding death by suffocation to a matter of minutes. There were other factors in crucifixion that contributed to death, including heart failure, excessive loss of blood through the treatment prior to the actual crucifixion, and stress-induced shock.

Jesus died after six hours. Soldiers, anxious for the victims to die so that they could be removed from the crosses before the Sabbath, came to break the legs of each of the three victims and to their surprise found Jesus already dead. Instead of breaking his legs they plunged a spear into his side, 'bringing a sudden flow of blood and water' (John 19:34).

At the moment of Jesus' death, three significant events took place, both of which are recorded exclusively by Matthew. Firstly, 'At that moment the curtain of the temple was torn in two from top to bottom'; secondly, 'The earth shook and the rocks split'; and thirdly, 'The tombs broke open and the bodies of many holy people who had died were raised to life. They came out of the tombs, and after Jesus' resurrection they went into the holy city and appeared to many people'.

The first event is of great theological significance. The curtain which divided the Most Holy Place in the temple from the Holy Place was torn from top to bottom. Only the high priest could penetrate that curtain, and only once a year on the Day of Atonement, carrying shed blood as a token of sacrifice for sin. Behind this curtain was the presence of God, hidden to the ordinary person. Now that curtain was torn apart, God had broken out. The great high priest had paid forever the just demands of a holy God. From that moment every priest has been redundant! No longer does any man act as a mediator between God and man, 'For there is one God and one mediator between God and men, the man Christ Jesus, who gave himself as a ransom for all men' (1 Tim. 2:5-6). This was the reason for his death, portrayed so dramatically by a divine act in the temple that afternoon.

The second event describes an earthquake, a physical phenomenon that accompanies the three hours of darkness 'over all the land'. The physical world responds to the death of Jesus, which has its effects on all creation, not just on the human race. There is a universality to the work of Jesus Christ on the cross that goes beyond simply the redemption of man and extends to the redemption of the whole creation. Paul stated God's purpose in Christ as 'through him to reconcile to himself all things, whether things on earth or things in heaven, by making peace through his blood, shed on the cross (Col. 1:20). Elsewhere Paul writes that 'the creation itself will be liberated from its bondage to decay and brought into the glorious freedom of the children of God' (Rom. 8:21). As a consequence we anticipate 'a new heaven and a new earth' (2 Pet. 3:13), the firstfruits of which is perhaps anticipated in this event where 'the earth shook and the rocks split'.

Thirdly, in a strange event that no other writer comments on, tombs were opened and holy people experienced a mass resurrection. It looks as though these were raised to life at the moment of Jesus' death, but did not appear until after Jesus' resurrection on the Sunday. What subsequently happened the Scripture does not record. Did they die again as Lazarus did after his resurrection? Did they rise in new resurrection bodies similar to that described by Paul when he says, 'So will it be with the resurrection of the dead. The body that is sown is perishable, it is raised imperishable' (1 Cor. 15:42) so that these people never died physically again but were transported to heaven? Was this just a temporary gesture to announce the meaning of Christ's death (similar to the tearing of the temple curtain)? Is this a symbolic statement by Matthew indicating that the death of Jesus has issued in the possibility of resurrection which we are to regard as inevitable? All these ideas, and others, have been suggested, but the Scripture itself remains silent beyond this one statement.

Certainly the physical phenomena impacted the centurion and his fellow guards who were guarding the cross of Jesus. 'When the centurion and those with him who were guarding Jesus saw the earthquake and all that had happened, they were terrified, and exclaimed, "Surely he was the Son of God!"' (27:54). They had seen him die and observed the manner in which he died, and now the physical phenomena terrified them into realising they were not dealing with a criminal but with God!

8. His burial by Joseph of Arimathea (27:57-61)

Joseph of Arimathea, a disciple of Jesus, came to Pilate to request the body for burial. Joseph was a member of the Sanhedrin Council (Luke 23:50), and is described as 'a good and upright man'. He had not consented to the decision and action of the Council that day, but his voice of objection had not been raised very loudly. Perhaps the Council meeting in Caiaphas' house late at night had been fairly secretive and, as less than a third of the council formed a quorum, they had gone ahead without Joseph's participation and perhaps that of others. In any case, if unable to help him in his life, Joseph helps him in his death. Often the body of a crucified victim was left on the cross to rot or be devoured by scavenger dogs and birds – Joseph of Arimathea gave Jesus the dignity of a tomb.

Only four people attended the funeral: Joseph himself (27:57-61), Mary Magdalene and Mary the mother of Joses (Mark 15:47), and Nicodemus, the Pharisee famous for having come to Jesus in Jerusalem by night (John 19:39). The disciples were notoriously absent, having fled at the time of his arrest (26:56). John had returned to the cross and had stood amongst those looking on, but was there at the end, witnessing the thrusting of the spear into the side of Jesus at the end, and identifying himself as 'the man who saw it' (John 19:35). But he did not concern himself with the burial. Perhaps at this point he had taken Mary the mother of Jesus to his home, having been entrusted by Jesus with her care.

9. A guard placed on his tomb (27:62-66)

The following day the chief priests and Pharisees went to Pilate and asked that the tomb be protected from those who might wish to steal the body in order to fulfil the claim made by Jesus during his life, 'After three days I will rise again'. The disciples did not anticipate a resurrection, and had these men known the disciples better they would know they did not even believe in the resurrection, even though Jesus had spoken to them many times about it. Resurrection was not part of their thinking, much less an attempt to perpetuate a fraudulent idea that one might have taken place by stealing the body. There was then no likelihood they would mount an attempt to remove the body of Jesus, or even be waiting nearby for his resurrection. However, should this happen, these men warned Pilate, 'This last deception would be worse than the first.'

Pilate consented, ensuring the tomb was first made as secure as was possible by putting a seal around the stone which was rolled in front of the entrance, and then placing a guard to defend it from any invasion that might take place.

The chapter concludes with apparent victory to the Sanhedrin. They have rid themselves of Jesus, they have silenced his disciples and they are in control of events. They have one weekend to enjoy their success!

36.

The resurrection and final commission (28:1-20)

The final chapter of Matthew's gospel reports two main events. Firstly the resurrection of Jesus from the dead and the first clumsy attempt to explain it away. Secondly, the final great commission Jesus gave his disciples when he met them on a mountain in Galilee.

1. The resurrection (28:1-15)

The previous chapter has concluded with reports of a guard on the tomb of Jesus to prevent body-snatchers from raiding the tomb in order to perpetuate a 'deception' about his resurrection. He had been buried by Joseph of Arimathea, the stone has been sealed on Pilate's orders, and a detachment of soldiers placed on guard. The latter took place on the Saturday.

At dawn on Sunday, Mary Magdalene and the other Mary arrive to look at the tomb. There was an earthquake and an angel of the Lord came from heaven, rolled back the stone and sat on it. There had been an earthquake to mark the death of Jesus as he departed this life (27:51 and 54), and an earthquake to mark his resurrection as he returned to this life.

The appearance of the angel so shocked the guards they became like dead men, and the angel announced to the two women the resurrection of Jesus, 'Do not be afraid, for I know that you are looking for Jesus, who was crucified. He is not here; he has risen, just as he said. Come and see the place where he lay.' They were then sent to 'tell his disciples: "He has risen from the dead and is going ahead of you into Galilee. There you will see him."' With a mixture of fear and joy they left to do so, when suddenly Jesus met them. Falling at his feet and clasping them they worshipped him and Jesus repeated the invitation to be sent to his disciples to meet him in Galilee.

This event is either the pinnacle of history or the greatest fraud ever perpetuated. The New Testament records the resurrection of Jesus as literal, physical fact. It is not a symbolic resurrection, it is not the teaching of Jesus that lives on, it is his literal person. Paul declares that if the resurrection is not true then all of Christianity collapses. He writes, 'And if Christ has not been raised, our preaching is useless and so is your faith ... And if Christ has not been raised, your faith is futile; you are still in your sins' (1 Cor. 15:14 and 17). Without Jesus Christ being alive, there is no gospel and there is no salvation.

However, the fact of the resurrection is not always so readily accepted. Alternative explanations for the empty tomb have been put forward. Four of the most popular are as follows:

The disciples stole the body

This was the very first explanation, put about by the Jewish chief priests and elders, for which they paid a bribe to the soldiers who were to claim they fell asleep and left the tomb unguarded. This report gained credence and Matthew's account states, 'And this story has been widely circulated among the Jews to this very day.'

This may have provided an alternative to the implications of his actual rising from the dead, but it is fatally flawed. If this were a true record of events, how would we account for the boldness of the disciples following the reports of his resurrection? On the night of his resurrection, the disciples were together 'with the doors locked for fear of the Jews' (John 20:19). They had all fled after the arrest of Jesus. The Sanhedrin were triumphant after the crucifixion of Jesus, and they inevitably feared themselves next in line. Then Jesus appeared to them in the room where they were hiding, and everything changed. They were no longer the frightened, timid group of men they had been. They were bold and courageous. The Jewish leaders themselves were baffled by this. Within a few weeks, Luke writes of the Sanhedrin, 'When they saw the courage of Peter and John and realised that they were unschooled, ordinary men, they were astonished and they took note that these men had been with Jesus' (Acts 4:13). Most of the original disciples subsequently died brutal deaths as martyrs for Christ. Peter, who had denied Jesus to a girl, then cursed and swore when he was identified as a disciple immediately following the arrest of Jesus, is not only bold in his preaching, but reliable tradition tells us he ended his days crucified upside down. James was executed by Herod in Jerusalem. Others suffered similar fates. How can we explain this, if all the time those disciples knew the body of Jesus had been removed to some other place, and they had agreed together to perpetuate a fraud. They hadn't the courage to stand for truth when Jesus was alive, let alone for a fraud after he was dead! If this was a hoax, someone, somewhere would give the game away! But they didn't – because it was true. Jesus had risen from the dead, and the disciples believed it if no one else did!

The Roman or Jewish authorities removed the body

It was rather embarrassing for the Jewish leaders to have asked the Roman authorities to provide a guard for the tomb. Wasn't there a better way to handle the threat his body might be stolen? Why not remove the body at night when no-one is around, and place it where no disciple of Jesus would be able to find it? This would be a safer and cheaper way of outwitting any attempt to simulate a resurrection!

In due course it became this very issue of the resurrection of Christ and the implications of it which rocked the city of Jerusalem. 'The priests and the captain of the temple guard and the Sadducees came up to Peter and John while they were speaking to the people. They were greatly disturbed because the apostles were teaching the people and proclaiming in Jesus the resurrection of the dead. They seized Peter and John, and because it was evening, put them in jail until the next day' (Acts 4:1-3). If they were so disturbed, there was one simple way of halting this talk about resurrection that was having such impact on the city. Produce the body of Jesus! If they could do that, the apostles' message would be destroyed immediately. If the authorities had the body hidden elsewhere they could produce it and destroy once and for all this 'myth' being perpetuated by the apostles. But they did not produce the body or make any suggestion they might do so. Clearly the authorities did not have the body of Jesus.

He was not really dead

There are various perspectives on the idea Jesus had not really died. Christian Science views it as the ultimate demonstration of mind over matter. Mary Baker Eddy, the founder of Christian Science, writes, 'Jesus' students, not sufficiently advanced fully to understand their Master's triumph, did not perform wonderful works until they saw him after his crucifixion and learned that he had not died. He presented the same body that he had before his crucifixion, and so glorified the supremacy of Mind over matter.'[1] This certainly would have been some triumph of mind over matter when you consider the awful physical brutality suffered by Jesus. Others have taken the line that when the soldiers came to the cross, and were surprised to find Jesus dead already, he actually was not dead but in a deep coma. The cool of the tomb revived him and he broke out on the third morning. One sect holds that Jesus then walked to India where he founded his true religion!

Just suppose it was true that Jesus was not dead when he was laid in the tomb, and in the ensuing thirty six hours revived sufficiently to push away the stone that had been sealed by Pilate's soldiers, had given such a fright to those guarding the tomb that they fell as dead men, and then walked out to meet Mary Magdalene and the other Mary that morning. What would we suppose their response to have been? To have fallen at his feet and worshipped him, as Matthew records, and as the other disciples later did? I think their first response would be, 'He needs a doctor urgently!' He would have lost a lot of blood, be dehydrated and in physical agony. But no one suggested a doctor! They responded in worship and recognised him for who he was.

Witnesses to his resurrection were suffering from hallucinations

Perhaps there was some mental confusion, and they thought they saw him, but in reality didn't. There was such a heightened expectancy that they became deluded. The problem is that there was no expectancy at all. There were numerous people who saw him, including 'five hundred brothers at the same time, most of whom are still living' (1 Cor. 15:6). These kind of delusions are subjective and individualistic, but here five hundred would be willing to testify to a literal seeing of Jesus, says Paul.

Apart from this, the idea that those who saw him were suffering from some mental phenomena does not address the fact of the empty tomb. The fact is, the tomb was empty. Our main interest in the death and resurrection of Christ is not primarily historical and archaeological but theological. It has to be historically true, but the implication is

---

[1] *Science and Health* by Mary Eddy Baker, pp. 45-46.

that it is a living Christ that is at the core of the Christian gospel. If he is not alive today the gospel cannot work, for it requires his living presence in the Christian to be the source of all he came to make real in human experience. It is the ultimate truth.

2. The final commission (28:16-20)

The eleven remaining disciples went to Galilee where Jesus had directed them. When they saw him, 'they worshipped him; but some doubted'. To both 'worship' and 'doubt' at the same time seems contradictory. But that is what happened. Perhaps they worshipped him in recognition of who he was, but doubted where all this was leading and whether they remained part of his programme. Perhaps his mission, which they had not understood and which had remained distorted in their thinking all the way through his ministry amongst them, was what they doubted. They may still have been expecting him as the Messiah to take the throne of David and eject the Romans from their land, yet that did not seem to be his agenda.

Whatever their doubt, Jesus commissioned them, 'All authority in heaven and on earth has been given to me. Therefore go and make disciples of all nations....' He did not wait for them to resolve their doubts. The best solution to doubt is obedience to God. Jesus earlier said, 'If anyone chooses to do God's will, he will find out whether my teaching comes from God or whether I speak on my own' (John 7:17). We become aware of the truth of Christ not only intellectually but experientially as the Holy Spirit reveals him and his ways in us. Paul speaks of how God 'was pleased to reveal his Son in me' (Gal. 1:15). It was not only a case of revealing his Son *to me*, but *in me*. God does that not so much in a classroom as in the everyday realities of life.

This final great commission has three aspects to it.

Commissioned in his power (28:18)

'All authority in heaven and on earth has been given to me...'. Some translations say, 'All power in heaven and on earth has been given to me', and both are legitimate translations of the Greek word *exousia*. Jesus used several words for power, and this one is power in the sense of authority. It is the power a policeman has by virtue of his uniform and badge. Jesus Christ has the right to give his orders and to demand obedience. The devil once offered him the kingdoms of the world and their splendour if he would bow down and worship him. Now, after his death and resurrection in which he has conquered sin and evil, all of this and more is *given* to him. He did not take authority, he received it. He has been invested with unrestricted authority by his Father.

It is with this Jesus the church is to do business. Paul writes, 'Christ is the head of the church, his body' (Eph. 5:23), and '... he is the head of the body, the church' (Col. 1:18) for the simple and inevitable reason that he alone has the right to be so. It is as the one in whom all authority in heaven and on earth is vested that he gives his commission.

Commissioned for his programme (28:19-20)

The word, 'Therefore ...' with which his commission to go into the world is prefaced, relates to his authority. There are no negotiations involved, only obedience to his instructions. Disciple making is a matter of obedience!

He does not send the disciples into the world to collect decisions, but 'to make disciples of all nations'. This involves more than encouraging people to call on God to help in times of need, but to enter into a relationship with him which will permeate every part of one's life, twenty four hours of every day, making the disciple available to the purposes of Jesus Christ and dependent on the resources of Jesus Christ in every area of their lives. Discipleship according to Jesus Christ is such that 'any of you who does not give up everything he has cannot be my disciple' (Luke 14:33). This doesn't in itself make disciples but opens the door to the developing relationship that constitutes true discipleship. Jesus said, 'If you hold to my teaching you are really my disciples' (John 8.31). The crisis of the will that precipitates full surrender to Christ, must initiate a process in the mind and heart that enables the disciple to grow in the teaching. This is the ministry the apostles were to have to the world.

But there is an important new ingredient in this commission. They are to go to 'all nations'. The previous time Jesus commissioned his disciples he placed a prohibition on them going outside of Israel, 'Do not go among the Gentiles or enter any town of the Samaritans. Go rather to the lost sheep of Israel' (10:5-6). Now the restrictions have gone, his message is for the world. He explained in the days immediately prior to his crucifixion how that the rejection of Christ by the Jews had opened the door to those outside of Israel so that on equal terms, Jew and Gentile have access to God through Jesus

Christ. It took a while for these disciples to grasp the universality of the gospel. The salvation of Gentiles and their reception into the church of Jesus Christ was not a pain-free experience for them in the early years of the church, but is the new order the gift of the Holy Spirit brought into existence.

Discipleship will involve 'baptising them in the name (singular) of the Father and of the Son and of the Holy Spirit (Trinity)'. The whole Trinity participates in salvation, yet it is our union with the one God that is demonstrated in baptism. The act of baptism is an outward public demonstration of an inward spiritual reality. Spirit baptism involves our being brought by the Holy Spirit into union with Christ, for 'We were all baptised by one Spirit into one body – whether Jews or Greeks, slave or free – and were given the one Spirit to drink' (1 Cor. 12:13). To be baptised into Christ is to be, 'baptised into his death ... buried with him through baptism into death, in order that, just as Christ was raised from the dead through the glory of the Father, we too may live a new life' (Rom. 6:3-4). Water baptism does not in itself bring a person into union with Christ in his death, burial and resurrection to new life, but it is an outward demonstration of this reality in experience. This leaves little room for 'secret disciples', for our discipleship is intended to be lived in the public domain, and borne witness to in this public way.

A further ingredient in making disciples is 'teaching them to obey everything I have commanded you'. Our task is not to teach people to *know everything he has said*, but to *obey everything he has commanded*. Beware of teaching exercises not designed to lead to obedience, for they defeat the purpose of Jesus Christ. We are not to engage in selective teaching or a selective obedience, but in 'teaching them to obey everything...'.

Commissioned with his presence (28:20)

Lastly, the disciples were commissioned with the assurance of his presence, 'And surely I am with you always, to the very end of the age.' We are not sent to work *for* God, but to be the agents whereby God may work *in us*. His presence is not as an observer of our service, but as the source and strength of our service. The disciples did not know this experientially until Pentecost. It was then that Jesus Christ took up residence within them by his Holy Spirit and the central theme of the Christian life became, 'I no longer live, but Christ lives in me.'

His presence is assured not as something spasmodic to be turned on or off, to be lost or regained, but 'to the very end of the age'. Nothing the disciples would ever face would be bigger than the resources they now had in Christ. It is this confidence that enabled these men to turn the world upside down in one generation.

Other Books of Interest
from
Christian Focus Publications

Teaching Matthew

Unlocking the Gospel of Matthew for the Expositor

David Jackman and William Philip

Matthew's Gospel is a substantial book - its large sections on teaching and theological reflection seeming to predominate over the 'action' of the story. However, precisely because there are such rich seams of theology, and so much teaching from Jesus himself, it is a wonderful treasure-trove.

It also excels as a way of explaining the message of the New Testament gospel so as to open up a sense of its continuity with the whole Old Testament, and the fulfilment of God's covenant promises in Jesus Christ.

Though principally aimed at preachers who are preparing expository sermons, Teaching Matthew will help Bible teachers in a variety of settings as well as those simply reading Matthew for themselves.

Each chapter ends with a brief conclusion to help crystallise your thinking.

David Jackman is the President of the Proclamation Trust and Director of the Cornhill Training Course, London, England, whose aims are the effective communication of the gospel, especially through preaching. Previously he was the minister of Above Bar Church, Southampton.

William Philip is Minister of St George's Tron Church, Glasgow, Scotland. Previously he directed the general ministry of the Proclamation Trust and before that worked as a doctor specialising in Cardiology.

ISBN 1-85792-877-6

Mark

Good News from Jerusalem

Geoffrey Grogan

'Written in simple, non-technical language. . . . the reader will be amply rewarded by the author's explanation of the text and its application to modern life.'
Michael Bentley

Mark's Gospel is a book for today's people. It is vivid, graphic and appeals powerfully to the eye of the imagination.

This is an age of new interest in the supernatural, with so many possibilities of deception. In Mark we find Jesus, the true God and perfect Man, working the supernatural works of God.

This is an age when we are bombarded by harrowing pictures of suffering and we ask "Why?" In Mark we find God's great Suffering Servant, showing us that God cares.

This is the age of change when everything moves faster, the age of tearing down yesterday and rebuilding in a new image. In Mark we find God's way of breaking down the greatest wall of all, built by our rebellion against Him.

This is still an age in which people are still fascinated by Jesus. Who was this Man? Indeed, if, as Mark believed, he really did rise from the dead, we should re-phrase the question, Who IS this Man? Who does he claim to be?

Mark's dynamic book brings to us all this, and much more.

Geoffrey Grogan lectured at London Bible College and was principal of Glasgow Bible College for over two decades. His international reputation as a Bible teacher resulted in him being awarded an honorary doctorate from the Open University for his outstanding contribution to theological education.

ISBN 1-85792-905-5

Romans
The Revelation of God's Righteousness
Paul Barnett

'Paul Barnett's refreshing commentary on the Letter to the Romans is marked by warmth, clarity, careful exegesis of the text, and a fine grasp of the historical circumstances surrounding this letter. Throughout his exposition Dr Barnett sensitively applies the apostle's profound, yet much-needed, message to our own context. I warmly commend this clear exposition of the apostle Paul's gospel.'

Peter O'Brien, Moore College, Sydney

'The deft hand of a scholar preacher is everywhere evident in the neat organization, precision, lucid explanative and warmth of this most helpful work.'

R. Kent Hughes, College Church in Wheaton

'Paul Barnett combines a thorough going exegesis which is sane and helpful, as well as lucid and well argued, with a pastor's heart and a good eye for application. This is a brilliant commentary on a key book, which I warmly and wholeheartedly recommend. Every preacher and lay reader should have it and read it!'

Wallace Benn, Bishop of Lewes.

Romans is all about the revelation of God's righteousness in freely offering salvation to all people through faith. Written about AD 56 or 7 in Corinth whilst he was on his way to Jerusalem, Romans historically fits into the book of Acts near the end of Paul's third missionary journey.

Paul Barnett is retired Bishop of North Sydney, Visiting Fellow in History at Macquarie University, Senior Fellow in the Ancient History Documentary Research Centre, Macquarie University, Teaching Fellow at Regent College, Vancouver and Faculty Member Moore Theological College Sydney. He was also Head of Robert Menzies College, Macquarie University.

ISBN 1-85792-727-3

Judges

Such a Great Salvation

Dale Ralph Davis

'an excellent... crisp, lively... exposition on Judges'
Bibliotheca Sacra

'the most practical expository work that this reviewer has ever encountered'
Southwestern Journal of Theology

'Dr. Davis has a great sense of fun. He must often have his class or his congregation in stitches!'
Christian Arena

The Church has a problem with Judges; it is so earthy, puzzling, primitive and violent – so much so that the Church can barely stomach it. To many it falls under the category of 'embarrassing scripture'. Such an attitude is, of course, wrong - so Ralph Davis here makes Judges digestible by analysing the major literary and theological themes discovered in each section. He provides a 'theocentric' exposition that rings with practical relevance.

Dale Ralph Davis is Pastor of Woodlands Presbyterian Church, Hattiesburg, Mississippi. Previously he was Professor of Old Testament at Reformed Theological Seminary, Jackson, Mississippi. He has also authored commentaries on Joshua, 1st Samuel, 2nd Samuel and 1st Kings

ISBN 1-85792-578-6

Christian Focus Publications
publishes books for all ages

Our mission statement –

STAYING FAITHFUL
In dependence upon God we seek to help make His infallible Word, the Bible, relevant. Our aim is to ensure that the Lord Jesus Christ is presented as the only hope to obtain forgiveness of sin, live a useful life and look forward to heaven with Him.

REACHING OUT
Christ's last command requires us to reach out to our world with His gospel. We seek to help fulfill that by publishing books that point people towards Jesus and help them develop a Christ-like maturity. We aim to equip all levels of readers for life, work, ministry and mission.

Books in our adult range are published in three imprints.
Christian Focus contains popular works including biographies, commentaries, basic doctrine and Christian living. Our children's books are also published in this imprint.
Mentor focuses on books written at a level suitable for Bible College and seminary students, pastors, and other serious readers. The imprint includes commentaries, doctrinal studies, examination of current issues and church history.
Christian Heritage contains classic writings from the past.

Christian Focus Publications, Ltd
Geanies House, Fearn, Tain,
Ross-shire, IV20 1TW, Scotland, United Kingdom
info@christianfocus.com

For details of our titles visit us on our website
www.christianfocus.com